Collected Bodhi Leaves Publications

Volume II

Numbers 31 to 60

BPS Pariyatti Editions

BPS Pariyatti Editions
An imprint of Pariyatti Publishing
www.pariyatti.org

Published with the consent of the original publisher.

First BPS Pariyatti Edition, 2017
ISBN: 978-1-68172-515-4 (hardback)
ISBN: 978-1-68172-331-0 (paperback)
ISBN: 978-1-68172-079-1 (PDF)
ISBN: 978-1-68172-077-7 (ePub)
ISBN: 978-1-68172-078-4 (Mobi)
LCCN: 2017910765

Typeset in Palatino Pali

Triple bodhi leaf cover image used with permission from Keith Carver Photography: www.keithcarverphotography.com

KEY TO ABBREVIATIONS

A	Aṅguttara Nikāya	Paṭis	Paṭisambhidamagga
Ap	Apadāna	Peṭ	Peṭakopadesa
Bv	Buddhavaṃsa	S	Saṃyutta Nikāya
Cp	Cariyāpiṭaka	Sn	Suttanipāta
D	Dīgha Nikāya	Th	Theragātha
Dhp	Dhammapada	Thī	Therigātha
Dhs	Dhammasaṅgaṇī	Ud	Udāna
It	Itivuttaka	Vibh	Vibhaṅga
Ja	Jātaka verses and commentary	Vin	Vinaya-piṭaka
Khp	Khuddakapāṭha	Vism	Visuddhimagga
M	Majjhima Nikāya	Vism-mhṭ	Visuddhimagga Sub-commentary
Mil	Milindapañha	Vv	Vimānavatthu
Nett	Nettipakaraṇa		
Nidd	Niddesa		

The above is the abbreviation scheme of the Pali Text Society (PTS) as given in the *Dictionary of Pali* by Margaret Cone.

The commentaries, *aṭṭhakathā*, are abbreviated by using a hyphen and an "a" ("-a") following the abbreviation of the text, e.g., *Dīgha Nikāya Aṭṭhakathā* = D-a. Likewise the sub-commentaries are abbreviated by a "ṭ" ("-ṭ") following the abbreviation of the text.

The sutta reference abbreviation system for the four Nikāyas, as is used in Bhikkhu Bodhi's translations is:

AN	Aṅguttara Nikāya	DN	Dīgha Nikāya
MN	Majjhima Nikāya	SN	Saṃyutta Nikāya
J	Jātaka story		
Mv	Mahāvagga (Vinaya Piṭaka)		
Cv	Cullavagga (Vinaya Piṭaka)		
SVibh	Suttavibhaṅga (Vinaya Piṭaka)		

Contents

Meditation—First Steps to Control of the Senses

P. M. Rao

Bodhi Leaves No. 31

First published: 1966

Meditation—First Steps to Control of the Senses

Every year when the thrice-sacred day of Vesak comes around, we temporarily withdraw our minds from worldly affairs and begin to think devoutly of the Blessed One. We chiefly think of him as the Lord of Compassion and dwell gratefully on the hundreds of rebirths he endured for the sake of suffering humanity, and when trying to picture him before our mind's eye, we think of him as the Lord of Meditation, sitting cross-legged, serene, passionless, majestic—and thus is born a New Year's resolution: that we should take meditation practice seriously this year.

Not many of us, however, can get a *kammaṭṭhānācariya* (a meditation master) to guide us and so we take up a form of meditation that we think we can practise safely without a guide, namely, the *brahma vihāra* (the divine abodes or sublime states). We take ourselves to a lonely spot, sit in a comfortable posture, and proceed to radiate towards the four quarters thoughts of goodwill, compassion, communal joy and equanimity as described in the suttas. Just when we are feeling satisfied that a good beginning has been made, however, an odd thing happens. We had hoped to have sound sleep that night and pleasant dreams; but the sleep was disturbed and the dreams meaningless and deeply charged with emotion. The next day is even worse; we find ourselves feeling peevish and catch ourselves losing our tempers at the least provocation. So, naturally, our enthusiasm wanes a bit, but we continue the practice half-heartedly for a couple of days more and seeing no improvement, finally give it up. Some people, who are less discreet than ourselves, may take up *kasiṇa* exercises, with unfortunate results.

What then could have gone wrong in these cases? The error, I think, lay in not fully grasping the purpose of meditation. We think of it in terms of physical exercises undertaken to develop the muscles. We think *brahma vihāra* is like the simple invigorating exercises with which we start a course in physical training. Similarly, we compare *kasiṇa* exercises to exercises with dumb-bells and hope that the initial strain caused by wrestling with the mind will wear off through regular practice. But mental strain is cumulative and when taken beyond the safe point may lead even to complete mental derangement. The futility of struggling with the mind is graphically described in the scriptures thus:

"So, Aggivessana, I set my teeth, and pressing tongue to palate by an effort of will, I strove to hold down, to force down my mind and so to control it. And as I struggled, Aggivessana, with the effort, the sweat burst forth from my arm pits ....

"Thus, Aggivessana, was my energy strenuous and unyielding, mindfulness was thus indeed established undisturbed, but my body was perturbed, it was not calmed thereby, because I was overpowered by the stress of my struggling ...." (MN 36)

It may appear to some that the reason for failure in the *kasiṇa* exercises is understandable but not of the *brahma vihāra* since there was no apparent struggle involved. But here is an analysis of our first attempt: for the first minute or so we were really able to radiate thoughts of goodwill with ease, but some time later we were perturbed to find that our mind had shifted to other thoughts; we then clenched our jaws and balled our fists with determination to concentrate and strangely enough the mind shot off at a tangent in half a minute this time, though it took us much longer to realise it. Then we felt our calves getting benumbed and we changed our posture while trying to maintain our thoughts of goodwill. In the meantime a fly settled on our nose and started doing callisthenics. While trying to ignore it we were sure an insect was creeping up our spine. By the time we had settled both we had an urge to have a peep at the watch and were aghast to find we had spent twenty minutes, out of which hardly two minutes had been spent on actual concentration. We struggled on for ten minutes more and rose thankfully hoping to do better next time, and feeling that, anyway, the first step in "meditation" had been taken. But we could not escape the consequences of the half-hour struggle.

Before we take up meditation therefore, the necessary preconditions must be fulfilled: "What advantage is gained by training in meditation? The thoughts are trained. And what advantage is gained by training the thoughts? Passion is abandoned" (A II 3.

10). Thus, the ultimate purpose of meditation is nothing short of complete passionlessness. Surely then, this cannot be attained by a mere half-hour's seclusion every day when the rest of the time is spent in complete lack of restraint. Meditation is not a magic formula that can miraculously transform us from ordinary sense-enjoyment-loving beings into masters of passionlessness. We might ponder on the fact that concentration is the last step in the Noble Eightfold Path. We should therefore take our whole way of life in hand and turn to meditation as a help in its transformation. To begin with, we should not take the *sīlas* for granted. We should constantly ask ourselves: "Have I injured anyone? Have I thought lustful thoughts? Have I spoken or thought ill of others? Have I been chattering uselessly?" and so on. We should decide to lead consecrated lives. Whenever on a full-moon day we observe *ashtānga-sīla* (Pali: *aṭṭhaṅgika sīla*, the Eight Precepts) we feel this sense of consecration. But we should try to maintain this feeling of consecration every minute of our waking hours. It might help us to think that there are certain earth-bound devas who constantly watch our every thought, word and deed.

While thus rigorously observing the *sīlas*, the transformation of our way of life can be hastened by development of awareness of our every thought, word and deed. It is good practice to watch ourselves as we would watch others. This practice gradually weakens verbal thinking, that is, our normal habit of keeping up that incessant, silent commentary on everything we perceive. It is difficult to maintain a continuous flow of such commentary while one is busy watching oneself in a detached way. A warning, however, is necessary. In the beginning, this awareness should be practised only for a few minutes at a time and the mind should not be unduly strained. The whole practice can be made highly enjoyable by watching one's person as a whole in relation to the environment and not concentrating on the breathing alone, or on the movements of the hands alone or on those of the feet alone. When the mind is thus allowed to rove over the whole person, enjoyment can be derived out of this practice. The mind, in its normal functioning, alternately flits outward for a few seconds towards objects of sense and then inwards for a few seconds to maintain verbal thinking. The practice of self-awareness, however, gradually makes our perceptions more acute while at the same time attenuating verbal thinking. It is as if a man who had been gradually becoming myopic but had not realised that his vision was blurred were to wear spectacles of the correct power and he suddenly sees the world in sharp focus in all its glory of riotous colour and light and shade.

Care should be taken however, to make it an enjoyable practice. Whenever there is a feeling of perturbation or of a taut sensation in the head, the practice must be discontinued for some time. Success in this practice depends entirely on the knowledge that we are reversing our normal values. We normally feel free when the mind runs uncontrolled after sense-objects and we feel fettered when our thoughts are controlled. We must realise that it is no true freedom when thoughts think themselves but it is real freedom when we think them. Every little mastery we gain on our thoughts should therefore bring us pleasure. When we have reached that stage where we derive actual pleasure out of this practice we shall have created the preconditions for the practice of concentration. For there is no concentration without calming of the body and mind, and there is no calming of the body and mind without a feeling of joy permeating the whole body and mind.

The above important truth has been well illustrated in the *Ānāpāna-saṃyutta* (SN 54.9). The Lord, after describing in many ways the advantages of contemplation of loathsomeness, goes into retreat for fifteen days. On return from retreat, however, the Lord finds that the monks had become so disgusted with life that half of them had committed suicide. The Lord, therefore, called the monks together and warned them against the practice of concentration without preliminary calming of the body and mind, and for this recommended the practice of *anāpānasati*—but the operative sentences in this practice are: "Calming this body-compound I breathe in and breathe out. Feeling rapture I breathe in and breathe out. Feeling joy I breathe in and breathe out."

Concentration practice at all times must be undertaken under able guidance, but even simple exercises to be harmless and fruitful must be undertaken only after a determined effort to lead a consecrated life, a life of purity and joyous self-awareness in which concentration exercises shall take their rightful place. This is the least we can do to show our eternal gratitude to the Compassionate One.

Control of the Senses

When the Bodhisatta had failed to attain the goal by means of the formless concentration attainments and the extreme austerities and penances, he said to himself: "I recall how, when my father the Sakyan was at work, I sat in the cool shade of a rose-apple tree and aloof from the pleasures of the senses, aloof from unwholesome states of mind, I entered upon and abode in the first jhāna which has thought conception and discursive thinking, is born of aloofness and has rapture and happiness. Could this, I wonder, be the way to wisdom?" And on this occasion came to the Bodhisatta the consciousness that follows truth: "Yes. This is the way to wisdom." (MN 36) And after developing the four jhānas one after another the highest wisdom was attained.

And we, who have been following the noble quest with bated breath, wonder whether we too could follow the method of the jhānas on the way to Nibbāna. But the only descriptions we find of the jhānas in the Sutta Piṭaka are in a set of recurring formulae similar to the one given above on the first jhāna and we have to turn to tradition for the actual practice. But the formula for the first jhāna has certain interesting and intriguing expressions—the chief of them, which concerns us here, being the set of phrases "aloof from pleasures of the senses" and "aloof from unwholesome states of mind."

What does "aloofness" signify in the above context? It conjures up in our minds the picture of a man standing safe on a rocky promontory while the waves in all their fury dash vainly against the rocks. To some extent, in our work-a-day world in the midst of sense-objects, we can imagine this aloofness to consist in turning the eyes away from a beautiful object or turning a deaf ear to a catchy tune. But how does one remain aloof amidst a flood of thoughts while sitting in seclusion far from the distractions of the sense-objects of the world? We can think of various things to do when unwholesome thoughts arise. We can, as described in the *Vitakkasaṇṭhāna Sutta*,[1] suppress them or ignore them, or replace them with wholesome thoughts, or we might ponder over their

1 Translated in Wheel No. 21, *The Removal of Distracting Thoughts.* jhāna is but an example of such an approach necessarily modified according to the needs of the occasion.

evil consequences, or try to remove the causes that gave rise to them. But we cannot imagine what it is to be aloof from them. A deeper study of the suttas, however, shows us that the word "aloofness" refers to a powerful psychological method for overcoming unwholesome propensities. The Blessed One had evolved a general approach for the mastery of some of the problems that arise in the way of the aspirant for Nibbāna, and the attainment of aloofness in the first

This method cannot be better understood than by studying its application to the closely allied subject of control of the senses. But before any method can be really successful, however, we must start with the purification of our attitudes towards the world in general and to sense control in particular. We must eschew all dogmas because dogmas are the shackles that hinder all spiritual progress. Suppose one believes that there is a destiny that shapes all our ends and at the same time recognizes the need to struggle to control our senses (a not uncommon combination of views in this world). Let us also suppose that he encounters a particularly attractive object of desire, and it would be the line of least resistance for him to surrender to the desire saying, "I was destined to do it." Again one may have a theory that the attainment of a jhānic state is a sign of spiritual perfection—in this case one would naturally put more emphasis on the methods leading to the jhānic state, looking upon control of senses as just an adjunct to the attainment of the state. On the other hand, one may go to the other extreme and think that leading the good life and control of the senses are ends in themselves. The right attitude in these matters is to consider every attainment as but a step to a higher one, the final aim being nothing short of unconditioned Nibbāna.

This apparent digression was found necessary as it is easy to be dogmatic about what are and what are not the right methods to use for the control of the senses. Ideas based on a naive interpretation of the First Sermon have resulted in the view that all austerities are to be condemned. But we have only to refer to the Bodhisatta's reply to Namuci (Māra) on the banks of the Nerañjara when the latter tried to dissuade him from pursuing a life of severe austerity:

"While dries the blood, my bile and phlegm dry up;
While wastes the flesh, mind more serene becomes.

Steadier awareness, wisdom, mind-intent.
While thus I live, enduring utmost pain,
Mind seeks no pleasures. See a being cleansed."
(Sutta Nipāta v. 434; from *Woven Cadences*, by E. M. Hare)

What the Blessed One condemned was a theory of "Purification by Austerities" unrelated to the actual effects of austerities on one's unwholesome propensities. So, in an individual case, if austerities like seclusion, fasting, sleeping on hard beds or a rough life in general help in controlling the senses, they may certainly be practised. If, on the other hand, they merely sour the disposition and make one irritable, it would be better not to practise them, or to practise them with less severity. What is meant to be emphasized here, is that though we are about to discuss a powerful but purely psychological method for control of the senses, a psycho-physical approach, if found helpful, should not be ignored.

The control of the senses, in order to be effectively mastered, must find a definite place in a psychologically sound scheme for the attainment of Nibbāna. It is in fact so placed in schemes described at several places in the discourses. The monk who undertakes the discipline first fulfils the rules of the order. They are of the nature of "don'ts" which inculcate in him good moral habits. The accent here is on the negative aspects of self-control namely, the restraining from doing evil things. There is no emphasis yet on the positive aspects which must deal essentially with the mind. The next step is the development of contentment—contentment with the meagre requirements of a bhikkhu's life; this step is for bringing his mental life into harmony with a life of physical restraints. Once this basis has been laid, we come to mental culture proper with the control of the senses. Here is how the oft-repeated formula runs:

"In perceiving a form with the eye, a sound with the ear, an odour with the nose, a taste with the tongue, an impression with the body, an object with the mind, he dwells neither on the whole nor its attributes. And he tries to ward off that which, by being unguarded in his senses, might give rise to evil and unwholesome states, to greed and sorrow; he watches over his senses, keeps his senses under control."

At first sight one might be inclined to think that the method is a trivial one—that of simply trying to ignore unwholesome thoughts as and when they arise. We can understand the full implications of the method if we consider an example from everyday life. Suppose one had to cross a busy street at a place where there is no pedestrian crossing. What does one do? One looks to the left and to the right at the traffic from both sides; one judges the speeds at which the various vehicles are running and cautiously walks across the street, sometimes walking slowly to allow a fast vehicle to run past, sometimes walking fast to go ahead before a slower vehicle has time to come up; one proceeds thus warily and alertly till one reaches the safety of the sidewalk on the other side.

Now let us analyse the various factors involved in this process. In looking to the left and to the right, alertness is involved; in looking at the various vehicles and judging their speeds, analysis is involved. In the cautious walk across the street and in the regulation of one's speed, both alertness and judgement based on the initial analysis are involved. But these two factors do not describe the whole process. To find out what extra factor is involved, we have merely to visualize under what conditions disaster might occur. While looking at an oncoming car, one's attention might be arrested by its beauty or by the fact that its occupants are known to one. To the extent one pays more attention to one vehicle, one naturally pays less attention to others, and the result is sure disaster. One can be successful only when one's attention dwells on a vehicle just long enough to judge its speed and position and no more. If, on the other hand, one pays less attention than necessary, disaster is sure to follow.

If the above analysis has been carefully followed it should be easy to understand the factors involved in the method for developing control over the senses. The words "In perceiving a form with the eye … an object with the mind" refer to the preliminary act by which the mind is in fact allowed to dwell for the necessary length of time on the thing perceived—this is in contradiction to the view of those who might think that the proper thing to do is to turn a blind eye or a deaf ear to things, because to ignore things is to court disaster as surely as it is to ignore the traffic in a busy street. Once this preliminary act is over, it is as dangerous to allow the mind to dwell on the whole of an object or its attributes as it is to pay attention to the occupants of a car or its beauty when it is speeding towards one in the middle of a busy street. The factor of analysis is referred to in the words, "And he tries to ward off that which by being unguarded in his senses might give rise to evil and unwholesome states"—that is, he knows beforehand, through analysis, what evil and unwholesome states of mind might arise if one foolishly allows the mind to dwell too long on the objects of perception. This contradicts the view of those who believe that objects of thought should not be analysed or judged. The factor of alertness is referred to in the words "He watches over his senses."

If, as explained above, ignoring of thoughts is to be considered dangerous, one may raise the objection that this contradicts the teaching of the Blessed One in the *Vitakkasaṇṭhāna Sutta*, where ignoring of thoughts is one of the methods advocated. The answer is that while the *Vitakkasaṇṭhāna Sutta* refers to a mind already overcome by unwholesome thoughts, the method for control over the senses is for a mind that is on guard against the arising of unwholesome thoughts. We may compare the former to the case of a man who is in the hands of the enemy and therefore has to use every possible method to escape, and the latter to the case of a man who carries a weapon in his hand, at sight of which the enemy slinks from sight. Or we may compare the former to medicine taken when one is ill while the latter can be compared to a protective inoculation. Indeed, control over the senses is for the development of spiritual strength as against mere morality.

To come to the actual practice of control over the senses, it must once again be emphasized that it is not advisable to undertake the practice of any part of the Teaching in isolation, unrelated to the rest of the Noble Eightfold Path. Therefore, before any further steps are taken, one must ensure that one has made some progress in *sīla* or moral habits as represented by the five precepts for laymen and *Pātimokkha* (the code of discipline) for monks, the guiding principles in their practice being *hiri* (shame) and *ottappa* (fear of the consequences of one's actions). The next step is to analyse one's own character. Though characters in general can be classified into three types, namely, those in which lust predominates, those in which hatred predominates, and those in which delusion predominates, so far as our contacts with society are concerned, it is the first two that are most important. A careful analysis can tell which of the two tendencies is predominant in us. If we are of the type that constantly looks out for pleasant things and are easily pleased when we get them, if even plain or ugly objects excite lustful thoughts in us, we have lust predominant in our character. If, on the other hand, we are hard to please and are inclined to find fault with even the good and the innocent, we can be sure that hatred is our dominant characteristic. Once we are aware what our dominant traits are, we know what to look out for in our day-to-day intercourse with society. The Aṅguttara Nikāya (IV 54 f) describes for us, for example, how a person with a predominantly lustful character might behave:

"He associates with women, permitting them to massage his body, or bathe his body or he sits around playing, laughing or joking with them, or he looks deep into a woman's eyes." These activities may be classed under "allowing the mind to dwell on the whole of object."

"Next, he constantly keeps his ear open to listen to feminine sounds coming from over the wall or from the next compound, sounds such as feminine laughter, women talking, women singing or women weeping; or he sits remembering his last experiences with women—how he used to laugh with them, speak with them, play with them; or he watches greedily other people enjoying themselves." These activities may be classed under "allowing the mind to dwell on the attributes of an object."

It should be possible to make up a similar list of activities indulged in by one in whom hatred predominates. He detests certain individuals and seeks opportunities to quarrel with them. He cannot bear to listen to anything good spoken about them, takes an uncharitable view of even their charitable acts—such might be the results of allowing the mind to dwell on the personalities of the hated ones.

He might be easily irritated by little things, is cantankerous, and a fault-finder, enjoys lecturing even to his friends and loved ones ostensibly "for their own good" but really because he knows it will hurt them. He might even say kind things about a wicked person hoping thereby to irritate good people—such might be the result of dwelling on attributes that tend to trigger his aggressive inclinations.

By not allowing one's mind to dwell on lust-provoking or hatred-provoking things, by refraining from activities such as those described above, one will be able to watch with joy the growth of spiritual strength within oneself, a visible growth from strength to strength each day demonstrating in actual experience why the Dhamma is called *ehi-passiko*—"Come and see."

The Threefold Division of the Noble Eightfold Path

Piyadassi Thera

Bodhi Leaves No. 32

First published: 1967

The Threefold Division of the Noble Eightfold Path

Reprinted from *The Buddha's Ancient Path*

While lying on his deathbed, addressing the disciples the Buddha said: "The Doctrine and the Discipline (*dhamma-vinaya*) which I have set forth and laid down for you, let them, after I am gone, be your teacher."

From this it is quite clear that the Buddha's way of life, his religious system, comprises the doctrine and the discipline. Discipline implies moral excellence, the taming of the tongue and the bodily actions, the code of conduct taught in Buddhism. This is generally known as *sīla*, virtue or moral training. The doctrine deals with man's mental training, taming of the mind. It is meditation or the development of mental concentration, *samādhi*, and wisdom, *paññā*. These three, virtue, concentration and wisdom, are the cardinal teachings which when carefully and fully cultivated raise man from lower to higher levels of mental life; lead him from darkness to light, from passion to dispassion, from turmoil to tranquillity.

These three are not isolated reactions, but integral parts of the Path. This idea is crystallized in the clear admonition of the Enlightened Ones of all ages—"Cease from all evil; cultivate the good; cleanse your own mind." [2]

These oft-quoted but ever fresh words convey briefly the message of the Master indicating the path to purification and deliverance. The path, however, is generally referred to as the Noble Eightfold Path (*ariyo aṭṭhaṅgiko maggo*). Though some prefer to call this the Ariyan Eightfold Path, it may be noted that the term *ariyan* does

2 *Sabba pāpassa akaraṇaṃ—kusalassa upasampada, sacittapariyodapanam-etam buddhanasāsanaṃ*. Dhammapada v. 183.

not stand here for any race, caste, class or clan. It simply means noble or excellent.

The Eightfold Path is arranged in three groups: virtue, concentration and wisdom (*sīla, samādhi and paññā*).[3] This Path is unique to Buddhism and distinguishes it from every other religion and philosophy.

The eight factors of the Path are:[4]

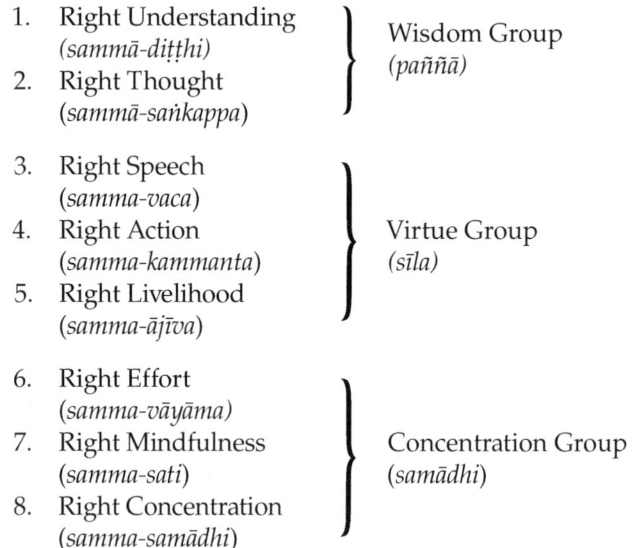

1. Right Understanding (*sammā-diṭṭhi*)
2. Right Thought (*sammā-saṅkappa*)

Wisdom Group (*paññā*)

3. Right Speech (*samma-vaca*)
4. Right Action (*samma-kammanta*)
5. Right Livelihood (*samma-ājīva*)

Virtue Group (*sīla*)

6. Right Effort (*samma-vāyāma*)
7. Right Mindfulness (*samma-sati*)
8. Right Concentration (*samma-samādhi*)

Concentration Group (*samādhi*)

Referring to this Path, in his First Discourse,[5] the Buddha called it the Middle Path (*majjhima paṭipadā*), because it avoids two extremes: indulgence in sensual pleasures which is low, worldly and leads to harm, is one extreme; self-torture in the form of severe asceticism which is painful, low and leads to harm is the other.

3 MN 44

4 Ibid.

5 Known as Setting in Motion the Wheel of Truth (*Dhamma-cakkappavattana*), SN 56:11; Vin I 10.

Living in the palace amidst song and dance, luxury and pleasure, the Bodhisatta[6] knew by experience that sense pleasures do not lead mankind to true happiness and deliverance. Six years of rigorous mortification, which he, as an ascetic, so zealously practised in search of purification and final deliverance, brought him no reward. It was a vain and useless effort. Avoiding these two extremes he followed a path of moral and mental training and through self-experience discovered the Middle Path consisting of the three groups.

In this essay a brief account of the three groups and how they aim at promoting and perfecting a path that consists of eight factors will be discussed.

It must always be borne in mind that the term 'path' is only a figurative expression. Though conventionally we talk of treading a path, in the ultimate sense the eight steps signify eight mental factors. They are interdependent and interrelated, and at the highest level they function simultaneously; they are not followed and practised one after the other in numerical order. Even on the lower level each and every factor should be tinged with some degree of right understanding; for it is the key-note of Buddhism.

Let us first hear these words of the Buddha:

"O monks, it is through not understanding, not penetrating four things (*dhamma*) that we have run so long, wandered on so long in this round of existence both you and I, And what four? Virtue, concentration, wisdom and deliverance. But when these four things, O monks are understood and penetrated, rooted out is the craving for existence, destroyed is that which leads to renewed becoming, and there is no more coming to be."[7]

Further says the Master:

"Concentration (meditation), O monks, supported by virtue brings much fruit, brings much advantage. The mind supported

6 Skt. *Bodhisattva*, one who adheres to or is bent on (*satta*) the ideal of enlightenment or knowledge of the Four Noble Truths (bodhi). It is specially applied to an aspirant for full enlightenment (*sammā-sambodhi*).
7 DN 16.

by wisdom is wholly and entirely freed from the intoxication of sense desires, from becoming, and ignorance." [8]

These sayings of the Buddha explain the function and the purpose of cultivating virtue, meditation and wisdom. Deliverance means living experience of the cessation of the three root causes of evil, greed, hatred and delusion or ignorance (*lobha, dosa, moha*), that assail the human mind. These root causes are eliminated through training in virtue, meditation and wisdom.

Thus it is clear that the Buddha's teaching aims at the highest purification, perfect mental health, free from all tainted impulses.

Now this deliverance from mental taints, this freedom from ill, lies absolutely and entirely in a man's own hands, in those of no one else, human or divine. Not even a Supreme Buddha can redeem a man from the fetters of existence except by showing him the path.

The path is: virtue, concentration and wisdom, which are referred to in the discourses as the threefold training (*tividha sikkha*) and none of them is an end in itself; each is a means to an end. One cannot function independently of the others. As in the case of a tripod which falls to the ground if a single leg gives way, so here one cannot function without the support of the others. These three go together supporting each other. Virtue or regulated behaviour strengthens meditation and meditation in turn promotes wisdom. Wisdom helps one to get rid of the clouded view of things—to see life as it really is—that is to see life and all things pertaining to life as arising and passing away.

It is now quite clear that in the interplay of doctrine and discipline (*dhamma-vinaya*) or knowledge and conduct (*vijjā-caraṇa*) the two constitute a single process of growth. "As hand washes hand, and foot washes foot, so does conduct purify wisdom and wisdom conduct."[9] This fact may be borne in mind by students of Buddhism, as there is a tendency, especially in academic circles, to regard the teachings of the Buddha as mere speculation, as a mere doctrine of metaphysics without practical value or importance.

8 Ibid.

9 DN 4.

The Buddhist way of life, however, is an intense process of cleansing one's speech, action and thought. It is self-development and self-purification. The emphasis is on practical results and not mere philosophical speculation, logical abstraction or even mere cogitation.

In strong language did the Buddha warn his followers against mere book-learning thus:

"Though he recites the sacred texts a lot but acts not accordingly, that heedless man is like a cowherd counting others' cattle (not obtaining the products of the cow). He shares not the fruits of the tranquil man.

"Though he recites only a little of the sacred texts but acts in accordance with the teaching, abandoning lust, hate and delusion, possessed of right understanding, his mind is entirely released and clinging to nothing here or hereafter. He shares the fruits of the tranquil man." [10]

These are clear indications that the Buddhist way of life, the Buddhist method of grasping the highest truth, awakening from ignorance to full knowledge, does not depend on mere academic intellectual development, but on a practical teaching that leads the follower to enlightenment and final deliverance.

The Buddha was more concerned with beings than with inanimate nature. His sole object was to unravel the mystery of existence, to solve the problems of becoming. This he did by comprehending in all their fullness the Four Noble Truths, the eternal verities of life.

This knowledge of the Truths he tried to impart to those who sought it, and never forced it upon others. He never compelled or persuaded people to follow him, for compulsion and coercion were foreign to his method of teaching. He did not encourage his disciples to believe him blindly, but wished them to investigate his teaching which invited the seeker to 'come and see' (*ehipassika*). It is seeing and understanding, and not blind believing, that the Master approved.

---

10 Dhammapada vv.19, 20.

To understand the world within, one must develop the inner faculties, one's mind. The Buddha says: "Mind your mind."[11] "The wise tame themselves."[12]

Today there is ceaseless work going on in all directions to improve the world. Scientists are pursuing their methods and experiments with undiminished vigour and determination. Modern discoveries and methods of communication and contact have produced startling results. All these improvements, though they have their advantages and rewards, are entirely material and external.

Within this conflux of mind and body of man, however, there are unexplored marvels to occupy men of science for many many years.

Really, the world, which the scientists are trying to improve, is, according to the ideas of Buddhism, subject to so much change at all points on its circumference and radii, that it is not capable of being made sorrowfree.

Our life is so dark with ageing, so smothered with death, so bound with change, and these qualities are so inherent in it—even as greenness is to grass, and bitterness to quinine—that not all the magic and witchery of science can ever transform it. The immortal splendour of an eternal sunlight awaits only those who can use the light of understanding and the culture of conduct to illuminate and guard their path through life's tunnel of darkness and dismay.

The people of the world today mark the changing nature of life. Although they see it, they do not keep it in mind and act with dispassionate discernment. Though change again and again speaks to them and makes them unhappy, they pursue their mad career of whirling round the wheel of existence and are twisted and torn between the spokes of agony.

After all, a scientist or a plain man, if he has not understood the importance of conduct, the urgency for wholesome endeavour, the necessity to apply knowledge to life, is, so far as the doctrine of the Buddha is concerned, an immature person, who has yet to

11 DN 16.

12 Dhammapada v. 80.

negotiate many more hurdles before he wins the race of life and the immortal prize of Nibbāna.

For an understanding of the world within, science may not be of much help to us. Ultimate truth cannot be found in science. To the scientist, knowledge is something that ties him more and more to this sentient existence. That knowledge, therefore, is not saving knowledge. To one who views the world and all it holds in its proper perspective, the primary concern of life is not mere speculation or vain voyaging into the imaginary regions of high fantasy, but the gaining of true happiness and freedom from ill or unsatisfactoriness (*dukkha*). To him true knowledge depends on the central question: Is this learning, according to actuality? Can it be of use to us in the conquest of mental peace and tranquillity, of real happiness?

To understand the world within we need the guidance, the instruction of a competent and genuine seer whose clarity of vision and depth of insight penetrate into the deepest recesses of life and cognize the true nature that underlies all appearance. He, indeed, is the true philosopher, the true scientist who has grasped the meaning of change in the fullest sense and has transmuted this understanding into a realization of the deepest truths fathomable by man—the truths of the three signs or characteristics (*ti-lakkhaṇa*): impermanence, unsatisfactoriness, non-self (*anicca, dukkha, anattā*).[13]

No more can he be confused by the terrible or swept off his feet by the glamour of things ephemeral. No more is it possible for him to have a clouded view of phenomena; for he has transcended all capacity for error through the perfect immunity which insight alone can give.

The Buddha is such a seer, and his path to deliverance is open to all who have eyes to see and minds to understand. It is different from other paths to salvation, for the Buddha teaches that each individual, whether layman or monk, is solely responsible for his own liberation.

---

13 The true nature of the five aggregates, or mind and body, is grasped and seen in the light of these characteristics. Such seeing is known as insight (*vipassanāñāṇa*).

Mankind is caught in a tangle, inner as well as outer, and the Buddha's infallible remedy, in brief, is this: "The prudent man full of effort, established well in virtue, develops concentration and wisdom and succeeds in solving the tangle."[14]

The Buddha's foremost admonition to his sixty immediate arahant disciples was that the Dhamma should be promulgated for the welfare and happiness of many, out of compassion for the world.[15] The whole dispensation of the Master is permeated with that salient quality of universal loving compassion.

Sīla or virtue, the initial stage of the Path, is based on this loving compassion. Why should one refrain from harming and robbing other people? Is it not because of love for self and others? Why should one succour the poor, the needy and those in distress? Is it not out of compassion for those others?

To abstain from evil and do good is the function of *sīla*,[16] the code of conduct taught in Buddhism. This function is never void of loving compassion. *Sīla* embraces within it qualities of the heart, such as love, modesty, tolerance, pity, charity and happiness at the success of others, and so forth. *Samādhi* and *paññā*, or concentration and wisdom, are concerned with the discipline of the mind.

As stated above, three factors of the Eightfold Path (Nos: 3, 4 and 5) form the Buddhist code of conduct (*sīla*). They are: Right Speech, Right Action and Right Livelihood.

Right Speech is to abstain (a) from falsehood and always speak the truth; (b) from tale-bearing which brings about discord and disharmony, and to speak words that are conducive to concord and harmony; (c) from harsh and abusive speech, and instead to speak kind and refined words; and (d) from idle chatter, vain talk or gossip and instead to speak words which are meaningful and blameless.

Right Action is abstention from (a) killing, (b) stealing, and (c) illicit sexual indulgence, and cultivating compassion, taking only things that are given, and living pure and chaste.

---

14 S I 13/SN 1:23.

15 Vinaya Mahāragga.

16 Vism: Sīlaniddesa.

Right Livelihood is abandoning wrong ways of living which bring harm and suffering to others: trafficking (a) in arms and lethal weapons, (b) in animals for slaughter, (c) in human beings (i.e. dealing in slaves which was prevalent during the time of the Buddha), (d) in intoxicating drinks and (e) poisons; and living by a profession which is blameless and free from harm to oneself and others.

From this outline of Buddhist ethics, it is clear that the code of conduct set forth by the Buddha is no mere negative prohibition but an affirmation of doing good—a career paved with good intentions for the welfare and happiness of all mankind. These moral principles aim at making society secure by promoting unity, harmony and right relations among people.

This code of conduct (*sīla*) is the first stepping stone of the Buddhist way of life. It is the basis for mental development. One who is intent on meditation or concentration of mind must develop a love of virtue; for it is virtue that nourishes mental life and makes it steady and calm.

The next stage in the Path to Deliverance is mental culture, concentration (*samādhi*) which includes three other factors of the Eightfold Path: they are Right Effort, Right Mindfulness and Right Concentration (Nos. 6, 7 and 8).

Right Effort is the persevering endeavour (a) to prevent the arising of evil and unwholesome thoughts that have not yet arisen in a man's mind, (b) to discard such evil thoughts already arisen, (c) to produce and develop wholesome thoughts not yet arisen, and (d) to promote and maintain the good thoughts already present.

The function of this sixth factor, therefore, is to be vigilant and check all unhealthy thoughts, and to cultivate, promote and maintain wholesome and pure thoughts arising in a man's mind.

The prudent man who masters his speech and his physical actions through *sīla* (virtue) now makes every endeavour to scrutinize his thoughts, his mental factors, and to avoid distracting thoughts.

Right Mindfulness is the application or arousing of attention in regard to the (a) activities of the body (*kāyānupassanā*), (b) feelings or sensations (*vedanānupassanā*), (c) the activities of the mind (*cittānupassanā*), and (d) mental objects (*dhammānupassanā*).

As these factors of the Path are interdependent and co-operating, Right Mindfulness aids Right Effort and together they can check the arising of unwholesome thoughts already entertained. The man vigilant in regard to his actions, verbal, physical and mental, avoids all that is detrimental to his (spiritual) progress. Such a one cannot be mentally indolent and supine. The well-known discourse on the Foundations of Mindfulness (*Satipaṭṭhāna Sutta*)[17] deals comprehensively with this fourfold Mindfulness.

Right Concentration is the intensified steadiness of the mind comparable to the unflickering flame of a lamp in a windless place. It is concentration that fixes the mind right and causes it to be unmoved and undisturbed. The correct practice of *samādhi* (concentration or mental discipline) maintains the mind and the mental properties in a state of balance. Many are the mental impediments that confront a yogi, a meditator, but with the support of Right Effort and Right Mindfulness the fully concentrated mind is capable of dispelling the impediments, the passions that disturb man. The perfectly concentrated mind is not distracted by sense objects, for it sees things as they really are, in their proper perspective.

Thus mastering the mind, and not allowing the mind to master him, the yogi cultivates true wisdom (*paññā*) which consists of the first two factors and the final stage of the Path, namely, Right Understanding and Right Thought.

Right Thought includes thoughts of renunciation (*nekkhamma-saṅkappa*), good will (*avyāpāda-saṅkappa*) and of compassion or non-harm (*avihiṃsa-saṅkappa*). These thoughts are to be cultivated and extended towards all living beings irrespective of race, caste, clan or creed. As they embrace all that breathes there are no compromising limitations. The radiation of such ennobling thoughts is not possible for one who is egocentric and selfish.

A man may be intelligent, erudite and learned, but if he lacks right thoughts, he is, according to the teaching of the Buddha, a

17 See Wheel No. 19.

fool (*bala*), not a man of understanding and insight. If we view things with dispassionate discernment, we will understand that selfish desire, hatred and violence cannot go together with true wisdom. Right Understanding or true wisdom is always permeated with right thoughts and never bereft of them.

Right Understanding, in the ultimate sense, is to understand life as it really is. For this, one needs a clear comprehension of the Four Noble Truths, namely: the Truth of (a) *dukkha*, suffering or unsatisfactoriness, (b) the arising of *dukkha*, (c) the cessation of *dukkha* and (d) the Path leading to the cessation of *dukkha*.

Right Understanding, or penetrative wisdom, is the result of continued and steady practice of meditation or careful cultivation of the mind. To one endowed with Right Understanding it is impossible to have a clouded view of phenomena, for he is immune from all impurities and has attained the unshakable deliverance of the mind (*akuppa cetovimutti*).

The careful reader will now be able to understand how the three groups, virtue, concentration and wisdom, function together for one common end: deliverance of the mind (*ceto-vimutti*), and how through genuine cultivation of man's mind, and through control of actions, both physical and verbal, purity is attained. It is through self-exertion and self-development that the aspirant secures freedom, and not through praying to and petitioning an external agency. This indeed is the Dhamma discovered by the Buddha, made use of by him for full enlightenment and revealed to the others:

"Virtue, and concentration, wisdom, supreme freedom, these things the Illustrious Gotama realized. Thus fully understanding them the Buddha, Ender of Ill, the Teacher, the Seeing One utterly calmed, taught the Dhamma to the monks." [18]

In spite of the scientific knowledge that is steadily growing, the people of the world are restless and racked with fear and discontent. They are intoxicated with the desire to gain fame, wealth, power and to satisfy the senses. To this troubled world still seething with hate, distrust, selfish desire and violence, most timely

18 A II 2; A IV 106; D II 123.

is the Buddha's message of love and understanding, the Noble Eightfold Path, referring to which the Buddha says:

> "This is the path itself,
> For none other leads To purity of vision:
> If you follow it and so confuse
> King Māra, all suffering will end.
> Since I have learned how to remove
> The thorns,[19] I have revealed the path.
> You yourselves should (always) strive,
> Tathāgatas only teach.
> Those who walk in meditation [20]
> Free themselves from Māra's bondage." [21]

— §§§ —

19 Dhammapada vv. 274, 276.

20 Thorns of passionate desire and so forth.

21 Both concentrative calm (*samatha*) and insight (*vipassanā*).

Extinction Without Remainder and The Fruit of Meditation

Buddhadāsa Bhikkhu

Bodhi Leaves No. 33

First published: 1967

Extinction Without Remainder[22]

'Extinction without remainder' is approached in two ways. In one method, one should habitually maintain the 'extinction without remainder' of the attachment expressed as 'This is I' and 'This is mine.' In the other method, when the body is about to break up one should let go of everything, including body, life and mind. Let them be extinguished for the last time, and do not allow any fuel whatsoever for another birth to be left or desired. One should therefore use the first method as the regular daily practice. When the body is about to break up, or in an accident when one does not die on the spot but has some full and clear consciousness left for a time, one should use the latter method. If one dies suddenly and is extinguished with the consciousness of one who has practised according to the first then the result is similar; that is, one does not wish to the reborn.

The first method should be practised regularly either before bedtime or fresh from getting up, or whenever one has the spare time to purify the mind. One should compose the mind until it becomes steady by counting the breaths, or by whatever method suits one best. This should be done for a time, and then one should investigate various things in order not to be attached to them or to cling to the view that they are one's own. There should be no exception whatsoever. One should see that they are only dependent factors circulating in the wheel of life. If one is attached to anything, one is bound to suffer immediately. Circulation in the wheel of life is a direct suffering. Every time one is born, one suffers. However one is born, it is suffering. As whatever one is born, it is suffering according to the type of birth. For instance, if one is born as a son, one suffers as a son. If one is born a rich man, one suffers as a rich man. If one is born as a poor man, one suffers as a poor man. If one is born as a good man, one suffers as a good man. If one is born as a bad man, one

22 Translated from the Thai by Prieb Bunnage.

suffers as a bad man. If one is born as a fortunate man, one suffers as a fortunate man. If one is born as an unfortunate man, one suffers as an unfortunate man. Therefore, nothing is better than not to be born as anyone: that is extinction without remainder. When we speak of 'birth' it means not only birth from a mother's womb, but also the birth of the mind; that is, of the idea 'I am such' which arises from time to time—for instance, I am a son; I am a poor man, or a rich man; I am a good-looking person, or I am an ugly person; I am a fortunate person, or an unfortunate person; and so on. These are what we call grasping thoughts of 'I am such' and 'Mine is such.' This 'I and mine' is called grasping. It is born from the womb of its mother, which is ignorance. It is born thousands of times each day, and whenever it is born, suffering is unavoidable. Whenever the eye sees forms, or the ears hear sounds, or the nose smells, or the tongue tastes, or the body touches through the skin, or the mind thinks of past events and makes them into a complete story, the word 'I' will be born immediately if one does not keep the senses under control. And as soon as the 'I' arises, suffering must also occur. Therefore one must be careful never to let the 'I' poke its head out from its mother's womb. When the eye sees forms, or the ears hear sounds, and so on, one should have the wisdom to know what to do with them, or one should remain unperturbed. The act of seeing or hearing is quite all right, provided that one never allows the 'I' to be constructed out of desire or feeling connected with the object which one sees or hears. If this is done, we can say that the 'I' is not born. That is, it has no existence. When it is not born it does not die, and so there is no suffering. This is what I mean by saying that to be born does not only mean physical birth direct from the mother's womb. It also means the birth of the idea of 'I' from its own mother's womb—ignorance.

Here, extinction without remainder means not allowing the 'I' to arise. Since it has ignorance as its mother, one should kill its mother with knowledge, or with the wisdom that there is nothing worth being attached to.

On the other hand, the thought of 'I' may arise when one is not mindful. If one tends to be unmindful very often, it can be cured by being ashamed or afraid. One is ashamed that one has given way to ignorance, which is the chief characteristic of undeveloped minds, and is unworthy of those who aspire to true knowledge. By being afraid I mean that there is nothing more dangerous than the birth of a thought dominated by ignorance. It opens the way to craving, and these two are the double gates of hell and all states of suffering. In this way, uncorrected ignorance leads to ruin. When there is often shame and fear of this kind, mindfulness will gradually get better until one becomes a person who follows the road to extinction without remainder perpetually.

Every day, before bedtime and on getting up, one ought to keep an account of this business of cultivating the way towards extinction without remainder, for one should know the income and expenditure all the time. This is done by taking a survey of one's thoughts and actions. It is more beneficial than prayers and should be practised as an adjunct to one's regular meditation, either before or after it.

This business of extinction without remainder is not connected with gazing at an object, or seeing colours or visions with closed eyes, or seeing strange miracles, or sacred beings. It is concerned with intelligent wisdom or direct clear awareness. If one really has perfect mindfulness, it can produce bodily and mental lightness; an indescribable bodily and mental ease. But one must never think of this, because to do so would make it a source of new grasping. If that happens it will never be extinguished, but will remain forever. That is, it will be born endlessly and will be the cause of even worse worry than before.

Those who are not successful in practising insight are those who want to grasp happiness, and they aim at Nibbāna according to their own way of grasping. The 'I' always arises in the view of Nibbāna which each person grasps. It will never be extinguished in that way.

Therefore, if one wants something to contemplate, one must contemplate that there is nothing to cling to, even such a thing as Nibbāna. *Sabbe dhammā nālaṃ abhinivesāya*: all things should not be grasped at.

To summarize, one must have a clear understanding of non-attachment constantly, every day and night, awake or asleep. One should maintain intelligent wisdom all the time. Never let the grasping by way of 'I' or 'This is mine' occur. Even if one happens to die during one's sleep, one still has the possibility of not being born again. This is called 'existence in extinction without remainder'—in other words the state of non-self, having only Dhamma in a mind which is void of self. Then it can be said that 'self' is not born and there is only 'extinction without remainder.' If one becomes unmindful of this fact one way or another, one should be willing to start again. Do not be discouraged or get tired of this mental exercise, as we do with our physical exercise all the time. Let the body and mind receive the correct training together. Whenever one practises, with every in-breathing and out-breathing one should maintain wisdom. Then mistakes will never arise.

The second method of practice is done when one is about to die. I should say that it is a very easy practice, like jumping down steps when one is already falling down them. It would be difficult only if one dare not jump when one is falling down the steps. This would be painful, because one would fall down in a hopeless manner. After all, this body cannot continue any longer. The mind or "the owner of the house" should therefore jump down too. At that time, one should have the wisdom to see clearly that nothing is worth grasping, hoping for, existing for, or being born again for. Let it end. Let the curtain drop on the last scene, because whatever one touches, or in whatever form of being one is born, it is all suffering. If one can practise this, the mind will lose its hope, and when the hope is destroyed there will be nothing to cling to. The mind will then be extinguished with the body, leaving no fuel behind for another birth. By 'fuel,' I mean 'hope' or 'desire,' or clinging to something in particular.

Suppose, for instance, that one is injured by a fierce animal coming from behind, or one is run over by a car, or is crushed by a falling building, or is suddenly murdered, and so on. Should there be any consciousness left, even for a second, one should, at that moment, direct one's mind towards extinction without remainder or clarify this idea in the mind in the way that one is used to practising every day and night. Then allow the mind to be blown out. This is enough for 'jumping down the steps' towards extinction without remainder. When the mind is blown out without having any time to become conscious, one should regard the practice of the awareness of extinction without remainder, which is contemplated on and aimed at perpetually, as the basis of extinction. It is still extinction without remainder.

If one suffers from great pains or torturing illness, one should stick out one's mind to receive this great pain and make a mental remark: "The more painful it is, the sooner extinction without reminder will come. Thanks to the pain!" When this is done, the joy in the Dhamma will curb all pains. They will not appear, or at most will be very slight. Thereby we shall be restored to our normal sanity, and then we can laugh at the pain itself.

Suppose that one suffers from an illness such as paralysis and one is to die of that disease. One should hold that one's self has ended when the illness numbs the body. The body that is left with winking eyes has no meaning. This is because one's mind has been inclined to extinction without remainder before one was taken ill, or when one still had perfect control of the body. Therefore when that control is lost it should be the end of it all. Although the life is not yet ended, there is nothing to be called 'This is I' or 'This is mine.' Therefore, when one's body is still in a good condition one should complete the extinction without remainder with the help of intelligent wisdom. It will remain effective until the time of the illness, even in the case of paralysis as mentioned before. There will be no failure nor any possibility of being defeated by any pain whatsoever, since one has destroyed the 'I' completely with the body still in sound condition.

To summarize all methods of practice, one must understand extinction without remainder in two categories; namely, one must have a mind really filled with wisdom, clearly understanding that there is nothing to hold on to, or to grasp. In this mind completely void of clinging and attachment there is no 'I' or 'This is mine.' There is only Dhamma, the absolute deliverance which is nominally called 'The Three Gems' or 'The Path of Deliverance,' or whatever it is which is the sublime hope of those who cling. But we shall not attach ourselves to these things. This is extinction without remainder, or Nibbāna. In its full sense *'Ni'* means without a remainder and *'bāna'* means going, or blowing out. Nibbāna therefore means going without any remainder. It has the characteristics of a meaning, a practice, and a blessing as described above.

Work all work with Void-Mind,
Give the fruits to the Void.
Eat from the storage of Void.
Die well from the first day.

Dhamma, blessings and Loving-kindness to all beings

— §§§ —

The Fruit of Meditation[23]

The second fruit of meditation is that the mind is fully prepared to have penetrating insight into all the phenomena, for practising meditation is like sharpening a knife for cutting cleanly, or like polishing a glass so as to see clearly. A well-trained mind is amenable like a tame monkey or elephant. It is active, strong and unwavering under the impulse of passion, anger, hate, envy and the like. Such a mind cannot be overpowered by these defilements. When these evil forces try to stimulate the mind, there arises a sense of humour and one laughs at them, and so they cannot distract the mind which is well trained.

When your mind is endowed with these two fruits of meditation, namely the immediate profit and the penetrating insight, you can see the world through inward sight. Henceforth nothing in the world can prick you through your sense organs. Nothing can lead your eye, nose, ear, tongue or body into temptation. Your mind will be free from all kinds of temptations and attachments. All worldly objects or allurements will appear to be something humorous. You can laugh them off. You will feel as if the world as a whole is reduced to a handful of something and is completely in your grip, for it cannot delude your mind while you see it inwardly in its real nature. If you can establish your mind in this state and do not lose your inward sight, no matter in what posture or place you may be, it must be regarded as a very great attainment of stability. But as you are not yet very skilful, for your introversion or intuition is newly grown and undeveloped, it may easily fade away. So you must guard it with all your efforts. As the Scriptures say: Just

23 From *Towards Buddha-Dhamma*, translated by Nāgasena Bhikkhu.

as a chief queen takes care of the child in her womb who will one day be a Wheel-Turning Monarch (a world Emperor ruling by righteousness), lest she should have a miscarriage, so one should guard diligently one's newly-grown insight until it is stable. For its sake you should willingly give up income and rights in much the same way as when we are ready to sacrifice everything upon contracting a fatal disease. To this end, you must live in an environment which is suitable for meditation and avoid disagreeable persons and places in the same way as a sick person avoids taking things which disagree with him.

Now you should also know that the practice of controlling the mind in this manner does not make you abnormal or disagreeable to society, or make you walk, stand or sleep in unusual or strange ways. Also, you are not supposed to sit meditating all the time or everywhere you go, for after you have gained mastery over meditation, the taste of it becomes one with your mind. Although you have done or practised meditation for the first time, your mind is bathed in the pleasing taste of it for a considerable time until, for want of heedfulness on your part, it fades away. Defilements such as passion, delusion, anger, hatred and jealousy can hardly pollute you. If you are a politician you can debate carefully, patiently and convincingly. If you are a missionary you can laugh off the strongest opposition and mockery of non-believers. Whatever may be your occupation or profession, you can do it successfully and you will be self-sufficient. You may go to any place or associate with anybody, and you will be able to maintain mindfully the state of equilibrium, or what has now become a normality for you. All that has been said will suffice to show how the mind well trained through the practice of meditation is useful both from the material as well as the spiritual point of view.

So, to conclude this brief account of meditation, we have seen that mind control results in happiness and immediate profit or *diṭṭhadhammikattha* and makes you able to attain still higher states. To see things in their real nature or to attain Buddha-dhamma calls for one-pointedness of mind. The stronger the one-pointedness of mind you have, the easier and more rapidly you can attain Buddha-dhamma. In case you fail to attain the Dhamma now, you will manage to attain it before long if you make it your way of living and are determined to practise it all years and months until the end of your days.

There is another important way that should be taken into consideration for attaining Buddha-dhamma. That is to serve others. It means to render help to others by teaching or showing the way to Buddha-dhamma itself. When you have trained your mind to the extent that you can keep a check on your emotions, you are able to teach or guide others in proportion to the experience that you derived therefrom. The Buddha disapproved of teaching what one cannot put into practice by oneself. But he encouraged the teaching of that which one can really practise. The Buddha himself served humanity in this respect. Teaching others is beneficial, for one teaches oneself as well regarding the attainment of Buddha-dhamma, in the cultivation of benevolence or friendly feeling, and moreover the intellect is developed. Also, one should know that this is the line of conduct that the Buddha set forth as an ideal way of conduct. Therefore I exhort you, out of your compassion, to help others towards their emancipation, by guiding them to the extent you have emancipated yourself. The friendly feeling that you cultivate through guiding others is very beneficial for the concentration and culture of mind. This is so because when you are cross-questioned you have to investigate and think over the issue carefully and deeply. You have to understand the matter thoroughly before you can reply. So in this way, by helping others you help to elevate yourself. We find in the *Vimuttāyatana Sutta* (AN 5:26/A III that some people attained the summum bonum while trying to explain to others that very matter, i.e., regarding the summum bonum itself. This is because some individuals have a strange kind of mentality in that they can better and more easily think and feel delighted when they teach or advise others. In the case of such people, new ideas flash into the mind and phrases leap to the mouth simultaneously and they, out of their deep understanding, feel very much exhilarated all the time. So it is clear that to try to think in order to guide others when asked is not only to enlighten others but to enlighten oneself at the same time. Thus it is something desirable and to be practised; and it is clear that the line of conduct explained above constitutes a salient feature, and that to serve others is very beneficial for the attainment of Buddha-dhamma.

In conclusion, may I repeat that the way to attain Buddha-dhamma is to harbour no feeling of attachment to anything, no matter whether sense-objects, views or one's own assumed (supposed) 'self.' All troubles arise from attachment, which has ignorance as its mother. The feeling of attachment is an instinct which is common to all creatures who can think, and the more one thinks (outwardly), the stronger the attachment will be. The power of thinking makes one able to enjoy the different kinds of tastes of sense-objects more and more. And the more one clings on to the taste, the stronger the bond of attachment becomes.

What I mean is that man should use his faculty of thinking for higher values; that is to say, he should try to be free from self-deception in proportion to the products of his brain. So let the production of your mind be your servant rather than being your master. Let it be helpful rather than destructive to your wellbeing. It should not delude you. Man must be better than the animal by using his power of thinking in a proper and constructive way. His knowledge should not bring about his own ruin. He should possess decisive knowledge with regard to good and bad, right and wrong. To do away with attachment is to gain that wisdom which drives away ignorance. When a man has no attachment or attraction, the very forms, sounds, etc, do not delude him, for they lay bare to his insight their real nature. Man can then handle them in the right way; that is, they can no longer exercise an influence on him in terms of passion, grievance and the like. On the contrary, they become helpful and instructive and promote his quietude or healthy state of mind and body. The moment you dismiss the feeling of attachment from your mind, you realize the Buddha-dhamma radiating in you. You discover or rediscover what the Great Buddha discovered and taught. Every one of us should attain it, for it marks the standard of perfection in manhood. This is the end of the holy life. This is the realistic ideal, or aim of life. You must strive for it, for you can raise yourself above the world and worldly phenomena, and can control them thereby. You can be free from or above all the problems of life.

Indeed, no problems of life can touch you and you become superior to all worldly things. There is no state of your being, whether monk or nun, layman or laywoman, male, female, young or old, which can be a hindrance to you, and there is no form, sound, odour, taste or tangible thing in this world or in any other world—truly, there is absolutely nothing whatsoever which can in the least disturb your majestic quietude. Indeed, the only thing left is an immovable and unmoved state where there is no birth, old age, suffering or death. This state is the very perfection of the values of life which everybody who earnestly follows the Great Buddha, the Enlightened One, the Perfect One, hopes for and sets his heart on.

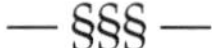

Protection Through Satipaṭṭhāna

Nyanaponika Thera

BODHI LEAVES NO. 34

First published: 1967

PROTECTION THROUGH SATIPAṬṬHĀNA

Once the Buddha told his monks the following story (Satipaṭṭhāna Saṃyutta, SN 47:19):

"There was once a pair of jugglers who performed their acrobatic feats on a bamboo pole. One day the master said to his apprentice: 'Now get on my shoulders and climb up the bamboo pole.' When the apprentice had done so, the master said: 'Now protect me well and I shall protect you! By protecting and watching each other in that way, we shall be able to show our skill, make a good profit and safely get down from the bamboo pole.' But the apprentice said: 'Not so, master! You, O master, should protect yourself, and I too shall protect myself. Thus self-protected and self-guarded we shall safely do our feats.'

"This is the right way," said the Blessed One and spoke further as follows:

"It is just as the apprentice said: 'I shall protect myself'—in that way the foundations of mindfulness (*satipaṭṭhāna*) should be practised. 'I shall protect others'—in that way the foundations of mindfulness should be practised. Protecting oneself, one protects others; protecting others, one protects oneself.

"And how does one, in protecting oneself, protect others? By the repeated and frequent practice of meditation (*asevanāya bhāvanāya bahulīkammāya*).

"And how does one, in protecting others, protect oneself? By patience and forbearance, by a non-violent and harmless life, by loving kindness and compassion."

This sutta belongs to the considerable number of important and eminently practical teachings of the Buddha which are still hidden like buried treasure, unknown and unused. Yet this text has an important message for us, and the fact that it is stamped with the royal seal of satipaṭṭhāna gives it an additional claim to our attention.

Individual and Society

The sutta deals with the relations between ourselves and our fellow beings, between individual and society. It sums up in a succinct way the Buddhist attitude to the problems of individual and social ethics, of egoism and altruism. The gist of it is contained in those two concise sentences:

"Protecting oneself, one protects others" (*Attānaṃ rakkhanto paraṃ rakkhati*), and

"Protecting others, one protects oneself" (*Paraṃ rakkhanto attānaṃ rakkhati*).

These two sentences are supplementary and should not be taken or quoted separately. Nowadays, when social service is so greatly stressed, people may be tempted to support their ideas by quoting only the second sentence. But any such one-sided quotation would misrepresent the Buddha's standpoint. It has to be remembered that in our story the Buddha expressly approved the words of the apprentice, that one has first to watch carefully one's own steps if one wishes to protect others from harm. He who himself is sunk in the mud cannot help others out of it. In that sense, self-protection forms the indispensable basis for the protection and help given to others. But self-protection is not selfish protection. It is self-control, ethical and spiritual self-development.

There are some great truths which are so comprehensive and profound that they seem to have an ever-expanding range of significance that grows with one's own range of understanding and practising them. Such truths are applicable on various levels of understanding, and are valid in various contexts of our life. After reaching the first or second level, one will be surprised that again and again new vistas open themselves to our understanding, illumined by that same truth. This also holds for the great twin truths of our text which we shall consider now in some detail.

"Protecting oneself, one protects others"—the truth of this statement begins at a very simple and practical level. This first material level of the truth is so self-evident that we need say no more than a few words about it. It is obvious that the protection of our own health will go far in protecting the health of others in our environment, especially where contagious diseases are concerned. Caution and circumspection in all our doings and movements will protect others from the harm that may come to them through our carelessness and negligence. By careful driving, abstention from alcohol, self-restraint in situations that might lead to violence—in all these and many other ways we shall protect others by protecting ourselves.

The Ethical Level

We come now to the ethical level of that truth. Moral self-protection will safeguard others, individuals and society, against our own unrestrained passions and selfish impulses. If we permit the "three roots" of evil—greed, hate and delusion—to take a firm hold in our hearts, then their outgrowths will spread far and wide like a jungle creeper, suffocating much healthy and noble growth all around. But if we protect ourselves against these three roots, our fellow beings too will be safe. They will be safe from our reckless greed for possessions and power, from our unrestrained lust and sensuality, from our envy and jealousy; safe from the disruptive consequences of our hate and enmity which may be destructive or even murderous; safe from the outbursts of our anger and from the resulting atmosphere of antagonism and conflict which may make life unbearable for them.

The harmful effects our greed and hate have upon others are not limited to the times when they become passive objects or victims of our hate, or when their possessions become the object of our greed. Both greed and hate have an infectious power which vastly multiplies their evil effects. If we ourselves think of nothing else than to crave and to grasp, to acquire and possess, to hold and to cling, then we may rouse or strengthen these possessive instincts in others. Our bad conduct may become the standard of behaviour for those around us—for our children, our friends, our colleagues. Our own conduct may induce others to join us in the common satisfaction of rapacious desires; or we may arouse in them feelings of resentment and competitiveness. If we are full of sensuality, we may also kindle the fire of lust in them. Our own hate may provoke them to hate and vengeance. We may also ally ourselves with others or instigate them to common acts of hate and enmity. Greed and hate are, indeed, like contagious diseases. If we protect ourselves against these evil infections, we shall to some extent at least also protect others.

Protection Through Wisdom

As to the third root of evil, delusion or ignorance, we know very well how much harm may be done to others through the stupidity, thoughtlessness, prejudices, illusions and delusions of a single person.

Without wisdom and knowledge, attempts to protect oneself and others will usually fail. One will see the danger only when it is too late; one will not make provision for the future; one will not know the right and effective means of protection and help. Therefore, self-protection through wisdom and knowledge is of the greatest importance. By acquiring true wisdom and knowledge, we shall protect others from the harmful consequences of our own ignorance, prejudices, infectious fanaticism and delusions. History shows us that great and destructive mass delusions have often been kindled by a single individual or a small number of people. Self-protection through wisdom and knowledge will protect others from the pernicious effect of such influences.

We have briefly indicated how our own private life may have a strong impact on the lives of others. If we leave unresolved the actual or potential sources of social evil within ourselves, our external social activity will be either futile or markedly incomplete. Therefore, if we are moved by a spirit of social responsibility, we must not shirk the hard task of moral and spiritual self-development. Preoccupation with social activities must not be made an excuse or escape from the first duty, to tidy up one's own house first.

On the other hand, he who earnestly devotes himself to moral self-improvement and spiritual self-development will be a strong and active force for good in the world, even if he does not engage in any external social service. His silent example alone will give help and encouragement to many, by showing that the ideals of a selfless and harmless life can actually be lived and are not only topics of sermons.

The Meditative Level

We proceed now to the next higher level in the interpretation of our text. It is expressed in the following words of the sutta: "And how does one, by protecting oneself, protect others? By the repeated and frequent practice of meditation." Moral self-protection will lack stability as long as it remains a rigid discipline enforced after a struggle of motives and against conflicting habits of thought and behaviour. Passionate desires and egotistic tendencies may grow in intensity if one tries to silence them by sheer force of will. Even if one temporarily succeeds in suppressing passionate or egotistic impulses, the unresolved inner conflict will impede one's moral and spiritual progress and warp one's character. Furthermore, inner disharmony caused by an enforced suppression of impulses will seek an outlet in external behaviour. It may make the individual irritable, resentful, domineering and aggressive towards others. Thus harm may come to oneself as well as to others by a wrong method of self-protection. Only when moral self-protection has become a *spontaneous* function, when it comes as naturally as the protective closing of the eyelid against dust—only then will our moral stature provide real protection and safety for ourselves and others. This naturalness of moral conduct does not come to us as a gift from heaven. It has to be acquired by repeated practice and cultivation. Therefore our sutta says that it is by repeated practice that self-protection becomes strong enough to protect others too.

But if that repeated practice of the good takes place only on the practical, emotional and intellectual levels, its roots will not be firm and deep enough. Such repeated practice must also extend to the level of meditative cultivation. By meditation, the practical, emotional and intellectual motives of moral and spiritual self-protection will become our personal property which cannot easily be lost again. Therefore our sutta speaks here of *bhāvanā*, the meditative development of the mind in its widest sense. This is the highest form of protection which our world can bestow. He who has developed his mind by meditation lives in peace with himself and the world. From him no harm or violence will issue. The peace and purity which he radiates will have an inspiring, uplifting power and will be a blessing to the world. He will be a positive factor in society, even if he lives in seclusion and silence. When understanding for, and recognition of, the social value of a meditative life ceases in a nation, it will be one of the first symptoms of spiritual deterioration.

Protection of Others

We have now to consider the second part of the Buddha's utterance, a necessary complement to the first: "Protecting others, one protects oneself. And how? By patience and forbearance, by a non-violent and harmless life, by loving-kindness and compassion (*khantiyā avihiṃsāya mettatāya anuddayatāya*)."

He whose relation to his fellow-beings is governed by these principles will protect himself better than he could with physical strength or with any mighty weapon. He who is patient and forbearing will avoid conflicts and quarrels, and will make friends of those for whom he has shown a patient understanding. He who does not resort to force or coercion will, under normal conditions, rarely become an object of violence himself as he provokes no violence from others. And if he should encounter violence, he will bring it to an early end as he will not perpetuate hostility through vengeance. He who has love and compassion for all beings, and is free of enmity, will conquer the ill-will of others and disarm the violent and brutal. A compassionate heart is the refuge of the whole world.

We shall now better understand how those two complementary sentences of our text harmonize. Self-protection is the indispensable basis. But true self-protection is possible only if it does not conflict with the protection of others; for one who seeks self-protection at the expense of others will defile as well as endanger himself. On the other hand, protection of others must not conflict with the four principles of patience, non-violence, loving-kindness and compassion; it also must not interfere with their free spiritual development as it does in the case of various totalitarian doctrines. Thus in the Buddhist conception of self-protection all selfishness is excluded, and in the protection of others violence and interference have no place.

Self-protection and protection of others correspond to the great twin virtues of Buddhism, wisdom and compassion. Right self-protection is the expression of wisdom, right protection of others the expression of compassion. Wisdom and compassion, being the primary elements of Bodhi or Enlightenment, have found their highest perfection in the Fully Enlightened One, the Buddha. The insistence on their harmonious development is a characteristic feature of the entire Dhamma. We meet them in the four sublime states (*brahmavihāra*), where equanimity corresponds to wisdom and self-protection, while loving-kindness, compassion and sympathetic joy correspond to compassion and the protection of others.

These two great principles of self-protection and protection of others are of equal importance to both individual and social ethics and bring the ends of both into harmony. Their beneficial impact, however, does not stop at the ethical level, but leads the individual upwards to the highest realization of the Dhamma, while at the same time providing a firm foundation for the welfare of society.

It is the writer's belief that the understanding of those two great principles of self-protection and protection of others, as manifesting the twin virtues of wisdom and compassion, is of vital importance to Buddhist education, for young and old alike. They are the cornerstones of character building and deserve a central place in the present world-wide endeavour for a Buddhist revival.

"I shall protect others"—thus should we establish our mindfulness, and guided by it devote ourselves to the practice of meditation, for the sake of our own liberation.

"I shall protect others"—thus should we establish our mindfulness, and guided by it regulate our conduct by patience, harmlessness, loving-kindness and compassion, for the welfare and happiness of many.

The Four Cankers (*Āsavā*)

T. H. Perera

Bodhi Leaves No. 35

First published: 1967

The Four Cankers (Āsavā)

"They who have given up passion, enmity,
And ignorance, the arahants poison-purged, [24]
I honour and revere, O Mātali."

Saṃyutta Nikāya, Sakka Saṃyutta, 11:19

Honour to that Exalted One, Arahant, Buddha Supreme! Lord Buddha, as recorded in the *Mahā Saccaka Sutta*, Majjhima, No. 36, realised in the last watch of the night: "These are the cankers ... This the arising of the cankers ... This is the ceasing of the cankers

... This the Path leading to the cessation of the cankers." Thus cognizing, thus perceiving, my mind was delivered from the canker of sensual craving; from the canker of craving for existence; from the canker of ignorance. Being delivered, I knew: "Delivered am I," and I realised: "Rebirth is ended, fulfilled is the holy life (*brahmacariya*), done what was to be done; there is none other life beyond this."

This Sutta lists three cankers (*āsavā*), namely: canker of

1. Sensual craving (*kāmāsavā*)
2. Craving for existence (*bhavāsavā*)
3. Ignorance (*avijjāsavā*)

Here, in craving for existence is also included the canker of false views (*diṭṭhāsavā*). "Being delivered" means the knowledge of gaining the Path (*maggañāṇa-lābha*), and "delivered" means the awareness of its fruition (*phala-ñāṇa*). This fact leads to two distinct divisions of aryan disciples, the *sekha* and the *asekha*. The former includes all those disciples who have gained, through being trained in morality (*sīla*), concentration (*samādhi*) and wisdom (*paññā*), the following Paths (*magga*) and fruitions (*phala*) of Sainthood, namely, Stream-Winner (*sotāpanna*), Once-Returner

---

24 It means the cankers (*āsavā*). This figure of speech means an arahant who is thoroughly cleansed of the poisonous mix or ooze. The word *Āsavā* can also mean an intoxicant drug.

(*sakadāgāmi*), Never-Returner (*anāgāmi*) and the Perfect One (*arahant*) who has gained Path knowledge (*magga-ñāṇa*) only—in all, seven individuals. The term *asekha* includes all those disciples who have completed the aryan training by gaining the fruition-knowledge (*phala-ñāṇa*) of a Perfect One. These are the eight individuals (or four pairs of aryan disciples) whom the Buddha speaks of in the *Ratana Sutta*:

> "Those eight individuals, praised by the virtuous, constitute four pairs. They, the worthy of offerings, the disciples of the Sugata,[25] gifts given to these yield abundant fruit. Verily, in the Sangha is this precious jewel. By this truth may there be happiness!"

None of us can ever hope to cut across the turbulent waters of the cosmic ocean of births and deaths, unless and until we have attained the status of these eight noble individuals along with Nibbāna, often spoken of as the nine transcendental Dhammas (*nava lokuttara dhamma*). In the *Mahā Maṅgala Sutta* gratitude (*kataññutā*) is mentioned (among other things) as one of the highest blessings. Lord Buddha stands pre-eminent among all beings on whom we should bestow our reverential gratitude. The highest form of gratitude that we could confer upon him is to objectify Nibbāna by treading the Noble Eightfold Path. Arahantship is the crowning glory of the Noble Path. It should be noted here that arahantship or deliverance from suffering is synonymous with Nibbāna,[26] and arahantship is attained by the total destruction of the cankers *(āsavas)*. I make this assertion on very good authority. At verse 93 of the Dhammapada, the Blessed One says:

> *Yassāsavā parikkhīṇā—āhāre ca anissito*
> *Suññato animitto ca—vimokkho yassa gocaro*
> *Ākāse' va sakuntānaṃ—padaṃ tassa durannayaṃ.*

---

25 The Buddha.

26 Note by Nārada Thera: Nibbāna is deliverance from suffering (*vimokkha*). It is called void because it is void of lust, hatred and ignorance, not because it is nothingness or annihilation. Nibbāna is a positive supramundane state which cannot be expressed in mundane word. It is signless because it is free from the signs of lust etc. Arahants experience Nibbānic bliss while alive. It is not correct to say that arahants exist after death, for Nibbāna is neither eternalism nor nihilism. In Nibbāna nothing is eternalised, nor is anything, except passions, annihilated. Arahants experience Nibbānic bliss by attaining to the fruit of arahantship in this life itself.

"He whose cankers are destroyed, he who is not attached to food, he who has deliverance, which is void and signless, as his object—his path, like that of birds in the air, cannot be traced."[27]

For the benefit of most of us who are worldlings[28] intent on putting an end to this sorrow-laden process of being born, ageing and dying, I shall deal with the four types of cankers which we must, sooner or later, destroy to arrest the process of becoming (*bhava*). The four types of cankers are:

1. Canker of sensuality (*kāmāsavā)*
2. Canker of existence *(bhavāsavā)*
3. Canker of false views *(diṭṭhāsavā)*
4. Canker of ignorance *(avijjāsavā).*

The Meaning of Canker

In simple language it is a malignant defilement of the mind that arrests its spiritual progress towards complete liberation. With respect to the spheres of existence *(bhūmi)*, it extends up to the highest Brahma realm, the sphere of neither-perception-nor-non-perception (*n'eva saññā-nāsaññāyatana)*, and with respect to the mind-flux *(santati)* it prevails right up to maturity-knowledge *(gotrabhū-ñāṇa)*. It oozes out, like water oozing out from tiny holes in a pot of water, through the unlocked doors of the six senses. In the manner of a man, who under the influence of liquor, loses his normal sense and commits various offences against society, even so under the influence of this poisonous drug (SN 1:23/S I 13), man loses all sense of shame and fear, and acts in a manner detrimental to his own welfare as well as the welfare of others. In short, it lengthens saṃsāric existence with all the suffering inherent in it. The destruction of the cankers has to be done by one's own efforts. Lord Buddha has shown the way to do it. Mere belief in a supernatural being and the false sense of security and salvation in that belief will never help; nor will matted hair or a tiger's skin dress. The Blessed One very pithily puts it at verse 394 of the Dhammapada:

27 Trs. by the Venerable Nārada Mahā Thera.

28 Those who are neither *sekhas* nor *asekhas*, i.e. those who have neither entered the Path nor attained to the fruition of arahantship (*arahat-phalaṭṭha*).

Kiṃ te jaṭāhi dummedha?
Kiṃ te ajinasāṭiyā?
Abbhantaraṃ te gahanaṃ
Bāhiraṃ parimajjasi?

"What avails thee of thy matted hair, O fool? What of the dress of tiger's skin? Within thee is full of defilements, why cleanest thou the outside?"

1. Canker of Sensuality *(kāmāsavā)*

This means the desire for sensual pleasures. Sensuality is twofold: the desire to enjoy the delightful and pleasurable things found in the sentient sphere of existence, and the objects that induce sensual enjoyment, namely: the desire for sights, the desire for sounds, the desire for smell, the desire for taste and the desire for tangibles. Beings intoxicated with the enjoyment of these sense objects lose all sense of proportion and behave like lunatics, and chase after these sense objects to enjoy them *ad libitum*. Insatiate are their desires, now here, now there, seeking after more pleasures in pastures new. At the moment of death, their minds, stupefied with sense-desires, provide these sense-indulgers with a new mind-form in one of the four planes of woeful existence. While living on this plane, bereft of fear and shame, they feel no compunction whatsoever in transgressing the five precepts of non-killing, non-stealing, sexual purity, truthfulness and total abstinence from intoxicants.

The cause of sensuality is wrong thinking on an object that is sensually pleasant and agreeable. This object can be sensuality itself, or that which gives rise to sensuality. Wrong thinking on this sensuality-object is to take the impermanent as permanent; the ugly as beautiful; pain as pleasure; no-soul as soul. Sensuality is wiped out by right thinking, that is to consider the object as unwholesome and inauspicious. In the words of the Blessed One: "the condition for keeping out new sensuality and for casting out old sensuality is abundant right reflection on the sensuously inauspicious or unpromising object." This is the task assigned to the jhānas (*vivicceva kāmehi*, detached from sense-desire). "Wherefore," says the Blessed One, "develop the jhānas (absorptions), O bhikkhus, and be not heedless! Do not direct your mind to sense-desires that you may not for your heedlessness have to swallow the iron ball in hell, and that you may not cry out when burning: 'this is pain'." (Dhammapada v. 371).

2. Canker of Existence (*bhavāsavā*)

This is the desire for continued or eternal existence (*bhava-taṇhā*) either in the form-world or formless-world (*rūpārūpaloka*). This is the so-called eternity belief of the theists who hold the belief in an eternal soul. In contradistinction to the eternity belief is the belief in self-annihilation (*vibhava* or *uccheda-diṭṭhi*), in which the soul is annihilated at death, and as a result there is no life after death. This is the doctrine maintained by the materialists. Lord Buddha rejected both these beliefs and taught the Middle Way, based on the natural law of cause and effect, or kamma, action-reaction. It must be clearly understood that kamma is the volitional act and its result or reaction (*vipāka*) follows the act. The principle involved is good begets good; bad or evil begets bad or evil.

Hence it is kamma that results in birth either in the form-world (*rūpa-loka*) or in the formless-world. A person who is dissatisfied with sense-desires, a really refined and holy person develops his mind (*bhāvanā*) to gain concentration (*samatha* or the *jhānas*). So long as he abides in the jhāna, he will experience a subtle and exhilarating sense of relief gained by total detachment from sense-desires. At death if he happens to be abiding in one of the four form-world jhānas, his dying consciousness will lead to birth in a form-world consonant with the jhāna he was abiding in at the moment of death. There is also the individual who finds no delight in form-world existence, for he is convinced that suffering is due to this body of flesh and blood. Accordingly he objectifies a higher spiritual value and content. Based on the fourth form-world jhāna, he develops his mind to gain the formless-world spheres. At the moment of death, while still abiding in one of the four formless-world jhānas, he will be born in a formless-realm in keeping with the jhāna of his dying consciousness. This is the highest form of existence, where no trace of matter exists but only the mind. In both spheres of existence—form and formless—one may enjoy several *kalpas* of life, yet the fact remains, that one is liable to be born again in the sentient spheres and may also suffer in the states of woe. Therefore, intoxicated with the drug of eternal existence man is confined within the limits of saṃsāra to continue the process of being born and dying. It is for this reason it is called a canker.

The Buddha-dhamma does not at all value either type of existence. It goes beyond the cosmos, beyond conditioned existence. While accepting the *jhānas* as a *sine qua non* for further development of mind, it has bestowed upon man the priceless pearl, insight-wisdom *(vipassanā-ñāṇa).* In fact, *vipassanā* is a sole monopoly of Buddha-dhamma. Wherefore, says the Blessed One at the Saṃyutta Nikāya (Devatā Saṃyutta, SN 1:23/S I 13):

"They that have lust and hate and nescience[29] spurned,
The arahants, immune from deadly drugs.[30]
For them the tangle[31] all unravelled lies,
Where mind and body wholly cease to be,
And earthly sense and sense celestial;—
Here is the tangle riven utterly."

3. Canker of False View *(diþþhāsavā)*

The *Brahmajāla Sutta* or the Discourse on the Supreme Net (DN 1) gives us a list of 62 beliefs (*diṭṭhi)* current in the time of the Buddha. These beliefs are compared to a net in which beings are caught and made to run hither and thither and from which no escape is possible. Such is the fate of all mortals who are infected with the canker of false beliefs. There is, in this Sutta, a very interesting and illuminating passage which speaks of the beginning of theistic beliefs. Here, a person at the end of his jhānic existence in the world of Brahmā, is born on this earth. He leaves home for the homeless life and practises asceticism. At the height of a jhānic experience, he beholds the Brahmā world from where he came, but, mind you, *he does not see beyond.* In a moment of ecstatic emotion, he rushes to the conclusion that, at the beginning, heaven and earth and everything in it was the work of God, the Omnipotent, the Omniscient, the All-Seeing, the Lord of All, the Creator, the most High and Almighty Father of beings that are and are to be. This illustrates how various theistic beliefs have arisen, and also

29 *Rāga, dosa, moha,* the extinction of which is Nibbāna.

30 The *āsavā*: sensuality, lust for continued life, false views and ignorance.

31 Craving (*taṇhā*); it is compared to the interwoven foliage of ferns and bamboos. Craving entwines one from within and without.

explains the various inconsistencies and contradictions in regard to God and the creation, in regard to his nature and intentions and in regard to man's position in relation to God. All these divergent views are due to the fact that one attempts to expatiate on his limited experience in order to build up a concept of universality—the fallacy of part for the whole. This is the bane of conceptual ideas, which necessitates periodical revisions to harmonise and accommodate them in the light of the scientific knowledge. Truth is truth; it is indivisible and cannot change. Lord Buddha speaks of himself as the *Tathāgata*. One of the interpretations of this multi-meaning word is: he practised what he preached and preached what he practised *(yathāvādī tathākārī yathākārī tathāvādī).*

There is an attempt made by men of goodwill and understanding to harmonise and blend and bind together the truths in all faiths. It is a praiseworthy attempt in so far as it tends to arrest the growing malaise of irreligion, of religious fanaticism, of religious discrimination and the insidious attempt to proselytize the "heathen" to the true faith. But partial truths will never help anyone to gain total emancipation from suffering. No wonder that I heard, the other day, a distinguished Christian prelate, remarking that he believed in *kamma* and the Noble Eightfold Path as the solution to man's ills, but he advised his audience "to infuse the spirit of God" into its working! This "spirit of God," this Soul, this Ego, this Divine Spark, this Eternal Entity forms the central core of all theistic faiths. It is chiefly because of this belief that Lord Buddha calls the third impediment to sainthood the canker of false beliefs, upon which clings the eternity belief *(sassata diṭṭhi)* and the belief in annihilation *(uccheda-diṭṭhi).* In the Māra Saṃyutta, of the Saṃyutta Nikāya at SN 4:16/S I 250, the Blessed One says:

"The body's shape,[32] all that we feel,[33] perceive,[34]
And know by sense,[35] and whatso will hath planned[36]—
This congeries—whoso doth know it well;
That's is not I, that is not Mine—he thus

32 Form *(rūpa).*

33 Feelings *(vedanā).*

34 Perceptions *(saññā).*

35 Consciousness (*viññāṇa*).

36 Mental formations (*saṅkhārā*). These are the five aggregates (*khandhas*) or "congeries" that make up the psychophysical combination called a "being."

Breaks from its charm. Him thus dispassionate,
The self at peace, all fetters left behind,
Him, though they hunting seek in every sphere
Of life, the hosts of Māra ne'er will find."[37]

Of all these *diṭṭhis* the most vicious, the most pernicious and the most inimical to spiritual progress is moral nihilism (*natthika-vāda*). One holder of this retrograde doctrine was a prince called Pāyāsi (DN 23) who propounded the following: 1. There is no life after death, i.e. no rebirth, 2. All beings are born through parents alone, there is no other source of birth, 3. There is no result *(vipāka)* of good or evil acts, in other words kamma is a myth. Then there is another form of *diṭṭhi* known as confirmed or absolute scepticism *(niyata-micchādiṭṭhi)* which is the denial of all that is good, noble and pure in life—the heresy *par excellence.*

4. Canker of Ignorance (*avijjāsavā*)

The Dhammapada at verses 242 and 243 illustrates very eloquently the taint of ignorance:

"Misconduct is the taint of a woman.
Stinginess is the taint of a donor.
Taints, indeed, are all evil things
both in this world and in the next.
A worse taint than these is ignorance, the greatest taint.
Abandoning this taint, be taintless, O bhikkhus."

(Transl. Nārada Thera)

The conspicuous characteristic of a taint is to corrupt or to infect or to eat into an object, be it physical or mental. In this sense the canker of ignorance eats into man's moral fibre and debilitates his mind to such an extent as to make him consider evil as good; the unpleasant as pleasant; the impermanent as permanent; the unreal as real; soullessness as the soul and so forth, and thereby he succumbs to acts of cruelty, killing, stealing, sexual misconduct, lying etc, which, at death, condition a woeful existence in one of the four hells.

Deep and sober thinking on the quotation above, particularly verse 243 will convince you that the entirety of the Buddha-dhamma is

37 He has attained Nibbāna.

devoted to the task of eliminating ignorance (*avijjā*) or darkness and enthroning knowledge (*vijjā*) or light. You will agree with me that you and I have been and are being chained to the wheel of life (*saṃsāra*) "in a long running-on and faring-on both for me and for you" because of ignorance or darkness; until that glorious awakening when we, in the full glow of knowledge or light, shall penetrate the Four Noble Truths: this is suffering; this is the origin of suffering; this is the cessation of suffering; this is the Path leading to the cessation of suffering, and thus put an end for ever to this sorrow-fraught process of being born, decaying and dying (*saṃsāra-dukkha*). Then and only then shall we make our final bow, our final farewell to saṃsāric existence or becoming.

It is not my intention here to dilate on the causal nexus (*paṭicca-samuppāda*) or the wheel of life, in which ignorance (*avijjā*) is a basic condition for the coming into being of this mind-form flux. It is also by the total eradication of ignorance that the mind-form flux ceases to flow. I take it that every genuine Buddhist, who is interested in putting an end to this mind-form flux with its inherent suffering, has made it a daily routine practice to meditate on the causal nexus along with its twelve dependent conditions, for "who sees uprising by way of cause sees Dhamma, who sees Dhamma sees uprising by way of cause" (*yo paṭiccasamuppādaṃ passati so dhammaṃ passati, yo dhammaṃ passati so paṭiccasamuppādaṃ passati*).

Ignorance (*avijjā*) and delusion (*moha*) are taken as synonyms. To my mind, it appears that there is a subtle distinction between the two. The Pali word *avijjā* literally means not-knowing and *moha* literally means delusion. The former is the inability to know or see things as they really are, while the latter clouds an object and obscures mental vision. It is a mental state *(cetasika)* and is the parent of greed *(lobha)* and ill-will *(dosa)*. In the Saṃyutta Nikāya, Nibbāna is defined as the extinction of greed, ill-will and delusion (*rāgakkhayo dosakkhayo mohakkhayo idaṃ vuccati Nibbānaṃ*). Wisdom is the very opposite of ignorance. It is wisdom (transcendental wisdom) that eliminates ignorance and leads to the realisation of the Four Noble Truths. In the *Dhammacakkappavattana Sutta* (Vinaya Mahāvagga and Saṃyutta Nikāya), Lord Buddha concludes his inaugural address to the five bhikkhus of Isipatana with these words pregnant with the joy of deliverance: "and there arose in me the knowledge (*ñāṇa*) and insight (*dassana*)—unshakable is the deliverance of mind, this is my last birth, and now there is no existence again." It is crystal clear that these two attainments, "knowledge and insight" dispelled ignorance (*avijjā*). Here ignorance stands as a mighty impediment all through saṃsāra, obstructing spiritual progress on the one hand, and on the other hand generating fuel for fresh rebirth and storing it in the accumulator of volitional activities (*saṅkhāras*). Of course, all these four cankers taken as mental states (*cetasikas*) come under *lobha, dosa* and *moha*. Of these cankers *(āsavā)*, the canker of sensuality is eradicated at the stage of *anāgāmi;* the canker of false views is eradicated at the stage of *sotāpanna*, while the cankers of existence and ignorance are eradicated at the stage of arahanthood.

Nibbāna can be attained only through the total eradication of these four cankers by extra-sensory wisdom which stands as the apex of the Buddha's Noble Eightfold Path in its triple division of morality (*sīla*), concentration (*samādhi*) and wisdom (*paññā*). Let us step into the "chariot" and take the "straight road" that will bring us to "Nibbāna's presence." I shall conclude this essay with an appropriate quotation from the Devatā Saṃyutta of the Saṃyutta Nikāya (SN 1:46/S I 33):

> 'Straight' is the name that Road is called, and 'Free
> From Fear' the Quarter whither thou art bound.
> Thy Chariot[38] is the 'Silent Runner' named,[39]
> With Wheels of Righteous Effort[40] fitted well.
> Conscience the Leaning Board[41]; the Drapery[42]
> Is Heedfulness; the Driver is the Law,
> I say, and Right Views, they that run before.[43]
> And be it woman, be it man for whom,
> Such chariot doth wait, by that same car,
> Into Nibbāna's presence shall they come.

— §§§ —

---

38 The Noble Eightfold Path.

39 Literally the Uncreaking, unlike a chariot where the axle fits badly into naves, or which squeaks when mounted. Comy.

40 The Dhamma-cakka, says the Ven. Buddhaghosa.

41 Lest the warriors fall out. Comy. Conscience is consciousness.

42 Such as a lion's skin etc. Comy.

43 To prepare the way.

Renunciation

T. Prince

Bodhi Leaves No. 36

First published: 1968

Renunciation

I

The idea of renunciation has never been a particularly attractive one for most people, even when its importance as an ideal has been admitted. For much of the Western world today, however, renunciation seems not so much unpalatable as unfamiliar, and indeed all but incomprehensible. This was not always so, of course. The people of the Middle Ages were well acquainted with the traditional Christian conception of this world as something which presents many snares for the soul, and is of little importance when compared with the eternal life to come. That this conception has ceased to be as influential as it once was, is the result of a number of complex historical processes, but as far as present-day attitudes are concerned, the factor of the greatest and most immediate importance would probably be the rapid development of science and technology in the nineteenth and twentieth century.

Science has, I think, influenced people's attitudes towards the world in three ways. Firstly, it appears to have confirmed by its achievements the ancient Greek philosophers' faith in the ability of human reason to fathom all the mysteries of the universe. Secondly, these impressive achievements have led people to feel the physical world, which has up till now been the province of scientific investigation, is the only world worth investigating, and even the only "real" world. And thirdly, by providing, through the technology which it has made possible, an abundance of good things for our enjoyment, science has encouraged a preoccupation with the objects and pleasures of the senses, and a corresponding indifference to those things which are presumed to lie outside the range of the senses.

If, then, this world we perceive is the only reality, and the senses and the reason are the only valid means of knowledge, it follows that renunciation of the world is pointless, and that aspiration to a reality which transcends the reason and the senses is bound to be futile.

There have always been many people who would agree with this, and materialist philosophers were not lacking even in the Buddha's day. But I think it would be true to say that ideas of this nature have never been so widely accepted as they are in Western and Western-influenced countries today. Even religious thought has been affected, and a number of progressive Christian theologians are trying to adapt their doctrines to the spirit of the age by glossing over the element of renunciation in Jesus' teaching and Christian tradition, and stressing, after the Jewish fashion, involvement in the world rather than detachment from it. A similar tendency can be observed elsewhere: in many of the "new religions" of modern Japan, for example, or in the writings of Indian thinkers like Radhakrishnan and Sri Aurobindo.

In light of all this, Buddhism must be considered somewhat unfashionable. Some critics have accused (and still accuse) it of being pessimistic, nihilistic and life-denying. Of course, Buddhism is not pessimistic. In fact, it is the most optimistic of religions, for it teaches that man can perfect himself here and now, and free himself by his own efforts from all suffering and unhappiness. Nor is it nihilistic. As the Buddha has often pointed out, he taught only the annihilation of suffering and ignorance. And if Buddhism is life-denying, it is only because it is death-defying, for life and death are inseparable. Nevertheless, these critics have sensed an important truth about the Dhamma; that it is essentially a teaching of renunciation. In one sense, Buddhism is more "this-worldly" than any other religion, since it takes as its starting point, not some remote and transcendental being or act, but the world as it is experienced by ordinary living beings. In another sense, however, it is more "other-worldly" than most, for according to the Buddha, the world as we know it has three fundamental characteristics: it contains nothing that is permanent; it is, for that reason, essentially unsatisfactory to those who see it as it really is, and are not led astray by superficial appearances; and finally, it contains nothing worth consideration as "me" or "mine," nothing that is in any way unchanging or substantial. These three characteristics are the basis of the Buddha's Teaching, and the second of them, known as "ill" or "suffering," is the theme of the Four Truths which the Buddha expounded in his first sermon.

There is nothing ambiguous about this. The Buddha was well aware that much pleasure and happiness is to be found in the world as it is ordinarily experienced, but he insisted that these pleasures were transient and therefore relative and limited, and that true happiness is only to be found by renouncing what is worldly, transient, relative and limited, and seeking instead what is transcendental, unchanging, absolute and unlimited. This absolute state (if one can describe it so) is what is called Nibbāna. It can be defined, if at all, only in negative terms, for what is completely transcendental is necessarily indescribable. It is certainly not a God creating and sustaining the world, nor is it a Godhead which is the source or substance of the world. In fact, although it can be attained by those still living in the world, it really has no connection with the world whatever, and for that reason its nature cannot be conveyed by means of such an earthbound thing as language, although the poetic (i.e., non-literal) use of language may certainly be able to suggest something of its quality, as in the following famous passage: "There is, monks, a realm where there is neither earth, nor water, nor fire, nor wind… neither this world nor the next, neither sun nor moon. There, monks, I say there is neither coming, nor going, nor remaining; neither deceasing nor being born. Without foundation is it, without continuity, without support: this is the end of suffering" *(*Udāna*)*.

II

Buddhism, then, is a teaching of renunciation. It remains to see what is renounced and why. The Buddha said: "What I teach is just ill (or suffering) and its cessation." What is renounced, then, is ill, suffering, unsatisfactoriness. But what is unsatisfactoriness? Here is the Buddha's answer: "Birth is ill; old age and decay are ill; death is ill; sorrow, lamentation, pain, grief and despair are ill; not to get what one wants is ill. In short, the five groups that are the object of clinging are ill." These "five groups," taken together, constitute the totality of what we call a "being," and what that being feels to be its "self." They may be translated as follows: form or matter, feeling, perception or ideation, motivation or mental activities, and consciousness. It is oneself, then, that is the source of suffering, and it is self that must be renounced if one would be free from suffering. This is a truth which is recognized by most religions, but only in Buddhism is it fully understood. The feeling of "self," the deep-rooted sense of "I-ness," involves the desire for the continued existence of self. It generates, in other words, greed and attachment, both for the self and also for those things which enhance the existence of the self and make it feel secure, such things as sense-pleasures, possessions, kinship with others, and so on. It also generates hatred for or aversion from what is anti-self, that is, from those things which threaten the continued existence or the happiness of the self by attacking it (or whatever it identifies itself with) or by frustrating it in any way. Thus the self can never be really happy, for it is continually agitated by desires and fears which bind it tightly to the world, and cause the "ill" for which the Buddha has prescribed the cure.

It will be seen from this brief analysis that the self and the world are interdependent, our emotional responses to the world strengthening our sense of self, and our sense of self causing the illusory appearance of a permanent and substantial world with objective qualities of desirability and undesirability. Therefore, renunciation of the world and the renunciation of the self are but two aspects of the same thing, and what we see as the world may, on deeper analysis, be found present within ourselves. So the Buddha said: "In this very body, six feet in length, with its sense-impressions, its thoughts and ideas… are the world, the origin of the world, the cessation of the world, and the Way that leads to the cessation of the world" (AN).

III

In the practice of renunciation, three stages may be distinguished. First of all, there is outward renunciation, as when a man or woman leaves the household life to become a monk or a nun. Outward renunciation has no intrinsic value, and may theoretically be dispensed with, but there is no doubt that it makes true renunciation very much easier. True renunciation is a matter of the heart and mind rather than the body. It is renunciation of the world of desires and aversions within, rather than of the world of "objects" without. Finally, there is the ultimate renunciation, which is the renunciation of one's "self" in its entirety, and the consequent destruction of all ill.

To illustrate the traditional Buddhist method of renunciation, I should like to examine a stereotype passage which occurs, with slight variations, at a number of places in the Pali Canon. It describes the ideal life of the monk, beginning with his first hearing of the Dhamma and concluding with his attainment of Nibbāna. It starts as follows:

"Suppose that a Perfect One *(Tathāgata)* arises in the world, an Accomplished One *(Arahant)*, fully Awakened, complete in knowledge and conduct, knower of the worlds, sublime (literally "well-gone"), incomparable, trainer of those to-be-tamed, teacher of gods and men, Awakened (Buddha), blest (*Bhagavant*). Having thoroughly understood, by his own supernormal insight, this world with its gods, its Māra (the personification of death), its Brahmā (the most exalted of the gods), its ascetics and brahmins, its gods and men, he declares his knowledge. He preaches the Truth (*Dhamma*), good in its beginning, good in its development, good in its consummation. He makes known the holy life in all its fullness and purity.

"A householder, or a householder's son, or one born into some good family, hears that Dhamma. Having heard it, he comes to feel faith in the Perfect One. Possessed of this faith, he reflects thus: 'The household life is cramped. It is a path choked with dust. To leave it is to come out into the open air. It is not easy for one who lives at home to lead the holy life in all its perfect fullness and purity, bright as mother-of-pearl. Surely I should now shave off my hair and beard, go forth into the homeless life.' In course of time, he gives up his possessions, be they many or few, and his circle of kinsmen, be it small or large, shaves off his hair and beard, puts on the yellow robe, and, leaving his home, goes forth into the homeless life."

So far, this is outward renunciation. Now the new monk must turn his attention to the world within. The first step is to free his mind from the domination by unwholesome emotions and sense-desires, and to this end he begins to discipline himself by strict observance of morality. The text continues: "So he lives the homeless life, observing self-restraint according to the rules of the Order, possessed of good conduct, seeing danger in the slightest offence, accepting and training himself in the precepts." There follows a detailed account of over forty things which the monk must shun.

The first seven are of basic importance, for they are the most general in character. They are also worth looking at because they stress the positive qualities of mind which the monk should be developing at this time, thereby helping to dispel the impression, which a series of prohibitions tends to give, that observance of the moralities is something dry and negative. In fact, just as one only renounces saṃsāra in order to obtain Nibbāna, so the sole purpose of renouncing bad or unwholesome qualities is to allow good or wholesome ones to take their place. The wording of these first seven precepts makes this quite clear:

"Here, the monk, having abandoned the taking of life, continues to abstain therefrom. Having once used stick and sword, now feeling shame, he is kind and compassionate to all living things… Having abandoned the taking of what is not given, he continues to abstain therefrom. Taking only what is given, he waits for the gift. Committing no theft, he lives as one who become pure… Having abandoned unchasity, he is chaste and keeps aloof, abstaining from coition, from the practice of the village-folk… Having abandoned false speech he continues to abstain therefrom, and is a speaker of truth. Pledged to truth, he is reliable and trustworthy, never lying to the world… Having abandoned slander, he continues to abstain therefrom. What he hears here, he does not repeat elsewhere in order to raise a quarrel against the people here. What he hears elsewhere, he does not repeat here in order to raise a quarrel against the people there. Thus he reconciles those who are divided, and encourages those who are friends. Harmony is his pleasure, his delight and joy, and he speaks words that creates harmony… Having abandoned harsh speech, he continues to abstain therefrom. Whatever words are gentle, pleasing to the ear, affectionate, touching the heart, polite, pleasant and agreeable to the people—such are the words he speaks… Having abandoned trivial chatter, he continues to abstain therefrom. His words are timely, in accordance with the truth, meaningful, concerning the Dhamma and the Discipline and the Order. He speaks words that are worth treasuring. They are uttered at the right time, are accompanied by reasons, are well-defined, and profitable."

These are the first seven moral observances. The rest concern other things to be avoided, such as harming vegetation, and various activities connected with mealtimes, personal adornments, entertainments, games, trading, and so on. The section on morality concludes as follows:

"Then the monk, being thus complete in morality, sees no reason for fear on any side, as far as self-restraint in his conduct is concerned. Just as a ruler, duly anointed, whose enemies have been crushed, sees no reason for fear on any side, as far as enemies are concerned; so the monk, thus being complete in morality, sees no reason for fear on any side, as far as self-restraint in his conduct is concerned. And, possessed of this noble group of moralities, he experiences unalloyed happiness within himself."

So far, the monk has progressed through two stages of renunciation. First, he has publicly renounced the world and left the household life. Then, by strict self-discipline, he has ensured that no moral lapse on his part will cause him to become entangled once again in the life that he has left behind, and his success in this self-discipline has given him a confidence and a happiness that he never had before. Thus, he has made his initial, outward renunciation secure. Now he is free to turn his attention to renunciation of the other, inner world, of the psychophysical life which is his "self." He begins by endeavouring to become detached from the activities of his senses, and of his mind and body, by the practice of mindfulness. He will now observe the things which impinge on his senses, watching to see that he does not react to them in an unwholesome or "unskilful" manner. Thus morality becomes mind-control. Then, when sense-impressions are no longer capable of agitating his mind unduly, he learns to become aware of his bodily actions as he performs them, contemplating his body disinterestedly, as though it were somebody else's:

"How is the monk guarded as to the doors of his senses? [The senses are considered metaphorically as so many doors through which impressions enter the mind.] Having perceived a form with his eye, he does not fasten on its general appearance, or on its secondary characteristics. [In other words, he does not allow himself to become fascinated by it, or by any aspect of it, or to feel that it is "mine." He simply watches with equanimity as phenomena come and go.] As long as he lived with his faculty of sight unrestrained, he fell prey to craving and unhappiness, to evil and unskilled states of mind. So he undertakes restraint, watching over his faculty of sight and restraining it. (And similarly with the other faculties: hearing, smelling, tasting, touching, and cognizing things with the mind.) The monk, possessed of this noble restraint of the faculties, experiences unalloyed happiness within himself. And how is the monk mindful and aware? The monk, in going forth or returning, is clearly aware of his action. So also when looking ahead or looking around, when bending his arm in or stretching it out, when wearing his robe or carrying his alms bowl, when eating, drinking, chewing or tasting, when defecating or urinating, when walking, standing, sitting, sleeping, waking, speaking or keeping silent; in all this he is clearly aware of what he is doing. Thus is the monk mindful and aware."

The monk has now shaken off most of his worldly desires, and has gained a considerable degree of detachment from himself. As a consequence, he is perfectly content with his lot and with his few necessary possessions: "He is contented with the robes that protect his body and the alms food that protects his belly… Just as a bird carries its wings with it wherever it flies, so the monk is contented with the robes that protect his body and the alms food that protects his belly, and he has only them with him wherever he goes. Thus he is content."

Now, having surrendered attachment both to the world and to his own body, the monk can concentrate all his efforts on the true source of ill, which is his mind. Sitting in a quiet spot, he strives to cleanse his mind of what are known as the "five hindrances." The text describes the process as follows:

"Having given up covetousness for the world, he remains with his heart (or mind) free from and cleansed of covetousness. Having given up ill will and hatred, he remains with his heart free from ill will and hatred. Friendly and compassionate to all living things, he remains free of them. Conscious of light, mindful and fully aware, he cleanses his heart of sloth and torpor. Having given up restlessness and worry, he remains free of them. Inwardly calm, he cleanses his heart of restlessness and worry. Having given up doubt, he remains having passed beyond doubt. No longer uncertain of what is skilful (or wholesome), he cleanses his mind of doubt."

Having brought about a subsidence of the five hindrances, he is filled with an exhilarating sense of freedom. The Buddha compares his feelings of relief and happiness to those of a man who has just discharged a debt, or recovered from a painful illness, or been freed from prison, or released from slavery, or who has safely crossed a dangerous wilderness. This subsidence of the five hindrances, and the ensuing calmness and happiness of the body and mind, make it possible for the monk to attain what is called the first "absorption." This is the first of a series of levels of consciousness which can be achieved by the successful practice of intense concentration of the mind—a process which is often called, rather vaguely, "meditation." The attainment of these absorptions not only produces a blissfulness that is far beyond the range of worldly pleasures, it is also (and this is more important to the Buddhist) makes the mind an instrument of knowledge that can transcend the limitations of the senses.

After attaining the first absorption, the monk passes on to the second, third and fourth, shedding successively thought conception, the exhilarating and blissful sensations that arise in him, and finally all feelings of happiness and unhappiness, pleasure and displeasure. He is now in a state of pure mindfulness and equanimity, and his mind—which has become "composed, purified, spotless, undefiled, pliant, workable, firm and imperturbable"—is capable of that direct and penetrating insight into the true nature of existence which brings deliverance. Now he has left the world a long way behind, but he must turn his mind back to it, if he would complete the process of renunciation; for the final deliverance comes, not from looking away from the world or the self, but from seeing through them. So he scrutinizes his self, his body and his mind, noting that "this is my body, possessed of form, composed of the four elements, springing from father and mother, built up by solid and liquid food; a thing impermanent by nature, fragile, perishable, and subject to total destruction. And this is my consciousness, bound up with and dependent on it."

At this point he is said to be able to acquire certain supernormal powers if he wishes, including the ability to recall his own innumerable past lives, and the direct awareness of the death and rebirth of other beings in accordance with their past actions.

His final deliverance, his ultimate renunciation, comes now with the destruction of what are known as the *āsavas* (Pali) or *asravas* (Sanskrit), a word which defies translation. Literally, it means a flowing in or a flowing out. These "cankers" (as they may be called for convenience) epitomize the forces which bring about continued existence or "becoming," and their destruction involves complete and perfect understanding of the conditioned and unsatisfactory nature of becoming, as it is summed up in the Four Truths. "It is as if," the Buddha says, "there were a pool of water in the mountains, limpid, clear and still, and a man were to stand on the bank and see with his eyes the various shells, the gravel and pebbles, and the shoals of fish moving about or at rest." So the monk, "with his mind composed, purified, cleansed, spotless, undefiled, pliant, workable, firm, and imperturbable, directs his mind to the destruction of the cankers. He knows as it really is: 'This is ill, this is the origin of ill, this is the cessation of ill, and this is the Way that leads to cessation… These are the cankers, this is their origin, this is their cessation, and this is the Way that leads to their cessation.' Knowing and seeing thus his heart is freed from the cankers of sense-desires, the canker of becoming (that is, the desire for continued existence), and the canker of ignorance. Free, he knows that he is free, and he understands: 'Exhausted is birth, the holy life is fulfilled, what was to be done has been done, there will be no more of the present state.'"

With this final and certain insight, renunciation of both self and world becomes complete, and the monk, now an *arahant,* has attained the deathless state, Nibbāna.

IV

Having considered the theory and practice of renunciation as it is set forth in the Pali texts, I should like to conclude by examining some possible misconceptions concerning the nature of renunciation in general and Buddhist renunciation in particular.

First of all, one may note that the text quoted in the previous section deals with the life of a monk. This is true of the great majority of the discourses in the Pali Canon, and some people have concluded that Buddhism teaches a path of total renunciation which can only be followed by monks and nuns. To show that this is a misunderstanding, one need only point to the many instructions on political, social, moral and religious matters which the Buddha addressed to lay people. One might also mention the many lay men and women throughout Buddhist history who have successfully followed the Buddha's Teaching even to the threshold of Nibbāna. And finally, there is the fact that, although a discourse may be addressed to monks, it is not necessarily intended for them exclusively. So the Commentary to the *Greater Discourse on Mindfulness* (DN 22), for example, says: "The monk is given here as an example of those dedicated to the practice of the Teaching... Whoever undertakes that practice... is here included under the term 'monk.'"

Nevertheless, while the Buddha never neglected his lay followers, it cannot be denied that he gave more attention to his monks and nuns. It is as if, he says, there were a farmer with three fields; one good, one middling, and one poor. He would sow the good one first, then the middling one, and he may or may not sow the poor one. These three fields the Buddha likens respectively to his monks and nuns, his lay followers, and "recluses, brahmins, and wanderers of other sects." Just as the farmer sows his crop in the fields, so the Buddha teaches Dhamma to all impartially, even to the last of the three groups, for "if they were to understand even a single sentence, that would be a blessing and a happiness for them for a long time" (SN). It is clear, however, that, as the farmer will expect a greater yield from the first field so the Buddha expected his teachings to bear more fruit amongst his monks and nuns then among the laity. The reason is that the Dhamma, as has been said, aims at an inner renunciation, and the outward renunciation of the monastic life consequently provides the best conditions for its practice. To perfect oneself in morality, mindfulness and concentration is no easy task, and monks and nuns are not hampered in their pursuit of it by having to worry about earning a living, about money, property, family, and all the daily noise and bustle that distracted the householder's life even in ancient India, and no doubt do so still more in our modern urban civilization. In short, although the path of renunciation is theoretically open to all, whoever and wherever they are, yet success in following it can be greatly affected by one's outward circumstance, and a layman will have to overcome many more obstacles than a monk.

What, then, of the weaker vessels among the laity who may not have the opportunity, the ability, or even the desire to renounce the world? It would be a mistake here to imagine that the Buddhist is called upon to make an immediate, once-and-for-all choice between saṃsāra and Nibbāna, renouncing the world in the same spirit as the candidate for Christian baptism renounces Satan and all his works. For a start, there is no need for the Buddhist to hurry unless he truly desires to do so. An infinity of deaths and births stretches before him, and he has plenty of time in which to prepare himself for renunciation if he is not yet ready for it—provided, of course, that he continues to lead a morally blameless life, thus ensuring that he will continue to be born in more or less favorable circumstances in future.

Again, there is no sharp distinction in Buddhism between the saved and the damned. There are many degrees of spiritual development, and, as a skilled teacher should, the Buddha always adapted his message to the needs and capacities of his audience. To those who were aware of the hollowness of worldly things he taught the path of final deliverance, while to those who were still in love with the world he simply pointed out the way to lead a good life, one which would bring as much benefit as possible, and as little harm or suffering, for themselves and others. He never demanded more from anybody than they were capable of at any given time, saying that, just as the great ocean deepens gradually as one goes further out from shore, and does not plunge down abruptly, so "in this Dhamma and Discipline the training is gradual, the practice is gradual, the progress is gradual. There is no abrupt attainment of the ultimate knowledge (i.e., the liberating insight of him who has won Nibbāna)" (*Udāna*).

So there is no need for anybody to try and plunge into deep water before he has first learned to swim in the shallows. Such a procedure would in fact be very dangerous, as the Dhammapada warns (verse 311): "As a blade of grass will cut the hand when wrongly grasped, so the ascetic life will drag one down to hell if wrongly taken up." And the disciple need not lack for means of self-improvement even at the beginning of the path. Devotional practices, living as blameless a life as possible by observing the precepts, trying to be kind to others and speak and think kindly of them, study of and reflection on the Dhamma, degree of self-knowledge through mindfulness, and some practice of meditation perhaps; all of these things, among others, are within the reach of the most worldly-minded, and will have a good result. One does not have to be a saint, or even a monk or nun, to attempt them. Patience and persistence are all that is necessary to ensure progress. Here one might recall the words of the Dhammapada: "Do not underrate goodness, thinking 'it will not come to me.' By falling drops of water a water jug is filled, and a wise man will be full of goodness, even though he accumulates it bit by bit"(v. 122). And again: "Let the wise man gradually remove the impurities from himself, as the smith from silver, bit by bit and from moment to moment"(v. 239).

A second misconception is that renunciation is a gloomy and depressing business. A biographer of the Christian mystic St. John of the Cross says that on a first reading of his work: "Few persons, however spiritually minded, will fail to find it repellent. It strikes a deadly chill, not only into the unhealthy heat of sense-affection, but into the glowing warmth of what one had hoped and believed to be pure love of God. It calls on one to go out from God-given light into a black and unknown darkness." I think that, God aside, many people are repelled in a similar way when they first encounter the Buddha's Teaching of renunciation, which may be one reason for the recurrent charges of nihilism and pessimism. The reason for this reaction is not far to seek, and the clue lies in the words "unknown darkness."

For most people, the pleasures of the senses (and in Buddhism, one must remember, this can include the pleasures of the mind) are the only pleasures, the only source of happiness that they know. Naturally, they do not take kindly to the suggestion that they give these up for some far-off and indescribable goal. But it is only ignorance that makes the goal appear dark. The darkness is, as it were, only the objective counterpart of a subjective blindness, and, in fact, as those who have had experience of this forbidding "darkness" repeatedly assert, the successful abandoning of sense-pleasures brings a happiness far greater than anything that they had known hitherto.

It is not difficult to see why this should be so, when one considers the way in which sense-pleasures come about. A sense-pleasure arises from the gratification of a desire, in the following way. First of all, a desire arises and creates a kind of tension in the mind of the being which feels the desire. Since this tension is felt as unpleasant, the being is then impelled to get rid of it by gratifying the desire. When the desired object is obtained, the desire is gratified, and the tension in the mind is relaxed. From the relaxation of the tension flows a sense of satisfaction and fulfillment, a greater or lesser degree of happiness or pleasure. Now, as long as existence continues (for the continuity of existence itself is, in the Buddhist view, contingent upon the desire for it), desires of one kind and another will be continually arising, at every moment, and agitating the mind. This means that the relaxation of tension, and hence the pleasure of happiness, which comes from their gratification can never be anything but temporary and incomplete.

If, then, happiness comes, not from desire itself (which in fact causes pain), but from its subsiding, it follows that the renunciation of sense-desires, so far from making one miserable, really opens up the only path to true and lasting happiness. And when the goal has been attained, becoming has ceased, and the mind is no longer troubled by the arising of any kind of desire. The result must be a state of calm and imperturbable happiness that ordinary beings, still enmeshed in worldly desires, can scarcely comprehend. Even the temporary quiescence of the mind in deep "meditation" is said to create a sense of bliss that far surpasses anything in ordinary experience, and in this way to give a foretaste of the unutterable peace of Nibbāna. It is important to bear all this in mind, otherwise it might be easy to imagine that Buddhism is "pessimistic" and that Buddhists seek to renounce the world out of hatred for it. But there is no more un-Buddhist emotion than hatred, whether for the world or anything else, and to attempt renunciation for that reason would not be only futile but deadly. The correct motive for renunciation is rather that given in the Dhammapada (v. 290): "If by surrendering a slight happiness one may realize a great happiness, the wise man should give up the slight happiness, considering the greater one."

Another error would be to suppose that Buddhists, like followers of some other religions, think that one should renounce the world because it is corrupt, or evil, or ugly; but no Buddhist has ever held such a view. It is not that worldly happiness and beauty are non-existent, or sinful, or even worthless. It is just that they are flawed by their transience and their liability to change into suffering and ugliness. The Buddhist ideal is to feel neither attachment in the case of happiness and beauty, nor revulsion in the case of suffering and ugliness, but simply to observe things as they really are, with equanimity and perfect freedom of mind.

A different kind of mistake is to think that renunciation is impossibly difficult, only to be achieved, if at all, by a superhuman effort of will and forcible suppression of natural desires. Of course, to sever the ties that bind one to the world is rarely an easy or a pleasant task, and strict self-discipline and persistent effort are necessary until the goal has been attained. Nevertheless, renunciation should never be forced. The man who has to force himself to renounce the world only shows that he is not yet ready to do so, and he must learn to be more patient, for otherwise he will only strengthen his bonds instead of loosening them. We did not have to compel ourselves to abandon the games and toys of our childhood; we simply outgrew them. So should it be with one who renounces worldly pleasures and preoccupations. Even though he may not yet be entirely free from nostalgia for these things of his spiritual childhood, he is beginning to outgrow them, and he no longer truly desires them. For him, renunciation, while it may be difficult, is not a forbidding and distasteful task. It is, on the contrary, the only way to genuine and lasting happiness. True renunciation does not involve "driving Nature out with a pitchfork": it is simply a question of learning to let go.

Finally, I would like to consider the objection that renunciation is a flight from the world's problems, a selfish escapism. I think that enough has already been said to show that renunciation is by no means an easy way out of anything. On the contrary, it requires a considerable effort of self-discipline. Again, the aim of renunciation is to overcome the ills of the world, to understand and destroy the suffering that is at the root of the world's problems, and not run away from it. As for the charge of selfishness and lack of concern for the welfare of others, it could be answered in a number of ways. First, one might point out that, in the Buddha's words, "it is not possible for one who is himself sunk in a mire to pull out another who is in the same situation. But it is possible for one who is not sunk in a mire to pull out another who is"(MN 8). In other words, no one can give effective help to others unless he has first helped himself. Nobody can solve for others problems that he has not yet solved for himself, and that is why self-development must precede altruistic activity.

Secondly, one might reply that not only is deliberate selfishness impossible for a true follower of the Buddha, for he will be aiming at the destruction of "self," but also, as was seen above, kindness and compassion towards all living things are enjoined on the monk as an indispensable part of the path. After he has succeeded in his aim, and attained final deliverance, he will continue to live only for the sakes of others, in order to pull them "out of the mire." The Buddha himself set the example in this, and when his first sixty monks had realized Nibbāna, he sent them out singly to preach with those words: "Go your way, monks, for the benefit of the many, for the happiness of the many, out of compassion for the world, for the welfare, the benefit, the happiness of gods and men" *(Vinaya Mahāvagga)*.

Finally, it should be remembered that compassion for the world and detachment from the world are not incompatible. On the contrary, they are inseparable, for compassion is purest only where it is totally disinterested. It is easy to see that if I help another from some ulterior motive, such as expectation of a reward, my compassion, if compassion is present in me at all, will be tainted by self-interest. What is perhaps not so obvious is that if I am in any way concerned about my action or its results, if I *care* about the person I am helping, my motives are still touched with selfishness, for I am identifying myself (my "self") with my action or with the other person. Furthermore, since a sense of self is an indication that ignorance has not been completely eliminated, it shows that I am not yet "out of the mire," and my help will, for that reason, be less effective than the help of someone who is completely disinterested. Thus one arrives at the paradoxical conclusion that perfect compassion can arise, and perfect help can be given, only where there is perfect detachment, and that those who have totally renounced the world are precisely the people who can be of most benefit to it. The clearest illumination of this is the life of the Buddha himself. He began by renouncing the world, and finally transcended it. And yet, despite the fact that he had nothing whatever to gain from it, he spent the remainder of his long life, after his Awakening, tramping on the roads of north-eastern India in order to help "beings" which he knew full well had no substantial existence. There is no doubt that he did this out of the purest compassion, for being totally disinterested in the matter, he could have had no other motive; and to the extent of the help that he was able to give, twenty-five centuries of Buddhist history bear eloquent witness.

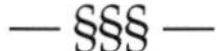

The Preparatory Path

John D. Ireland

Bodhi Leaves No. 37

First published: 1968

The Preparatory Path

Merit and Meditation

Buddhism is essentially practical, and what is rather loosely called "meditation" is its key practice. Meditation largely replaces the ritual of other religions and completely replaces prayer. Indeed, Buddhism lays the greatest emphasis on *bhāvanā*, meditation, or more correctly, the development of the mind and what may be termed its spiritual faculties.

An aspect of this practicality is the systematic way the Buddhist Path is presented. Throughout its long history, beginning with the actual teaching of the Buddha and continuing in the literature that has built up around it down the centuries, the spiritual path has been carefully mapped out, step by step. However, for us today it may (mistakenly) appear to be unnecessarily complex, and there is therefore the temptation of seeking for a short cut and missing out steps that in our ignorance we may regard as nonessential. An example of this is inattention to the rules of moral conduct (*sīla*) laid down by the Buddha and not cultivating the social virtues of generosity, patience, kindliness, helpfulness towards others and similar duties. However, these things are essential as they obviate purely selfish motives and lay the foundations for effectively progressing towards the final goal of our spiritual career.

The practice of moral and other 'good' acts within our social environment produces what is called 'merit' (*puñña*). The Buddha's teaching regarding this has certainly been subject to abuse, as when people think of it as a kind of heavenly bank account where good deeds can be stored for the later reward of the good results due. But this is actually a travesty of its true meaning and demonstrates a misunderstanding of the Buddhist theory of moral causation (*kamma*).

The realisation of the goal, Enlightenment, does not happen by chance nor is it even the inevitable result of practising certain meditation exercises to develop calm (*samatha*) and insight

(*vipassanā*). These are certainly some of the conditions that lead to the realisation of the Unconditioned or Nibbāna, but are by no means all of them. There are many factors involved and it is only when all these conditions have accumulated and ripened that that experience will take place. This state of 'ripeness' or 'spiritual maturity' also needs an accumulation of merits or *puñña*, not only from this life but going back through many lives, so we are told. This is often mentioned in the discourses of the Buddha, where certain individuals came to him and immediately gained realisation, whereas others did not or, rather, could not, due either to the presence or absence of sufficient merit from the past.

The practice of meritorious acts, such as self-discipline and self-sacrifice, have one important thing in common; that is attenuation of 'self,' the absence of self-centred motivation. This is the key to the whole Buddhist path, for the chief characteristic of one who has reached its consummation is his complete lack of self-reference, emotional or instinctive. He has fully realised and acts from the standpoint of *anattā*—non-self.

A characteristic of one who has sufficient *puñña* and 'self-attenuation' is the ease with which he can place his faith in the teacher, the Buddha, and put aside doubt or reservations arising from self-clinging and act and think spontaneously and wholeheartedly, thus quickly realising any instruction given. It is the unwholesome emotions of greed, hate and delusion arising from demerit (*pāpa*—deeds that are the very opposite of meritorious) that cloud the intellect and give rise to conflict and doubt. And it is these that are the main stumbling-blocks to spiritual advancement.

Going for Refuge

It is generally understood that, among the preliminaries to the practice of the Buddhist path, what is known as 'going for refuge' is one of the most important. It is intended here to go into this in some detail and to set forth something of what is meant and implied by 'going for refuge.' The importance of the refuges cannot be overstressed and whatever other things should be cultivated will be found to be included by implication within this process of refuge taking.

The three refuges are: Buddha, Dhamma and Sangha. The basic meaning of these is that Gotama, who lived about 2500 years ago, was a Buddha or Enlightened One, the doctrine he taught was the Dhamma and the community of disciples that gathered around him was the Sangha. But as they stand, these are not really sufficient to be understood as the Triple Refuge and so we must delve a little deeper to discover how these three can be of importance for us here and now.

Although Gotama the Buddha is no longer with us, the principle or capability within ourselves to realise Enlightenment is, and it is this that constitutes the Buddha as Refuge. The Dhamma is the path leading to that Enlightenment, and the Sangha as refuge is the community of those who have attained the state of Ariya.[44]

Now, to begin with, in what way are these three to be understood as refuges? A refuge is a shelter or protection from danger and distress, that is, these three refuges are one's resort to avoid the suffering of wandering in the round of birth and death, *saṃsāra*. To set out in search of a refuge we must first realise the nature of this mental and physical world we are living in, we must understand something of at least the first of the Four Noble Truths, the Truth of Suffering (*dukkha*). Those who are quite happy and contented with life, who do not feel the deep stirrings of dissatisfaction, of 'uneasiness' (a literal meaning of *dukkha*), will naturally see no need to seek a refuge. But for those who do, there is only one course open to them—to work towards the liberation that is Nibbāna, the final refuge from *dukkha*.

Although we may refer to Nibbāna as the ultimate refuge, in practice going for refuge is completed at a certain stage of our spiritual progress when we reach certainty and assurance within ourselves

---

44 *Ariya-puggala*: noble personality. The formal description of this Sangha includes the phrase: *cattārī purisa yugāni aṭṭha-purisa puggalā esa Bhagavato sāvaka saṅgho*: "The four types of individuals, embracing eight classes of (noble) personality . . . " This signifies those who have attained the state of Stream winner, Once-returner, Non-returner or Arahant, either at the stage of Path (*magga*) or Fruit (*phala*) These eight comprise the Ariya Sangha as (distinguished from the Puthujjana Sangha (*puthujjana*: all those, either of the Sangha or the laity, who are still bound by all the ten fetters (*saṃyojana*))—Editor.

as to the final realisation of the goal and the path we should follow to realise it; this is technically called `entering the stream' (*sotāpatti*). The practice of the Noble Eightfold Path gradually culminates in the correct practice of *samādhi–vipassanā*. Samādhi here means a calm, even, balanced and integrated state of mind, a mind that is whole (*ekodi*), that is, a mind that functions at all levels, intellectually, emotionally and volitionally, as a unity, with the sole purpose of working towards final liberation. Such a mind is well equipped 'to see things as they really are' and act without conflict within itself according to this 'clear seeing,' or *vipassanā*.

The completion of going for refuge is characterized by a deep and unshakeable faith and a certainty of knowledge in the three refuges as being the highest and only secure refuge it is possible to conceive of—but from which beings have strayed, through delusion and attachment to the illusory things of this world.

To return from these rarefied heights to more practical considerations, how does one actually begin this process of going for refuge?

At the outset there should be the understanding that this is a serious step to take; something that is not undertaken lightly, for it is a step that may well alter the whole course of one's life. Therefore it should be a deliberate and conscious act, decided upon only after careful thought. The traditional method of going for refuge is to approach a bhikkhu respectfully and ask him for the refuges; it is usual to ask three times and one then repeats the formula three times after him—this is to impress upon one the seriousness of the step one is taking. With the refuges one also takes upon oneself the responsibility of cultivating the moral precepts, either the five or the eight precepts for laymen.

Besides repeating the refuge formula, one goes for refuge, according to the commentary on the Majjhima Nikāya, in four ways:[45]

1. by paying homage;
2. by the acceptance of discipleship;
3. by acceptance of the guiding ideal; and
4. by self-surrender.

---

45 The following list of four is abstracted from *The Threefold Refuge* by Nyanaponika Thera (Buddhist Publication Society, 1965)

1. Paying homage means having a reverential attitude and respect for the Buddha, Dhamma and Sangha. It includes such acts as placing one's hands together, bowing down and prostrating oneself before the Buddha and his representatives (the *bhikkhu-saṅgha*) and the performance of worship and devotion (*pūja*). Also, listening attentively and with a humble attitude to expositions of the Teaching and so forth.

2. Acceptance of discipleship means one accepts the Buddha, Dhamma and Sangha as one's teacher, wishing to learn from them.

3. Acceptance of the guiding ideal is the accepting of the Buddha, Dhamma and Sangha as one's only true guide, ideal and refuge. And one does not seek for guidance outside of them, that is to say, one does not look to any other religion to help one nor place any reliance upon superstitions, luck, charms, etc.

4. Finally, there is self-surrender. One surrenders oneself completely—one's hopes, ambitions, even life itself—to the Buddha, Dhamma and Sangha. One turns away from worldly things and devotes oneself to the task of treading the path leading to Enlightenment and freedom.

It may be noted that another aspect of going for refuge, and perhaps this is what makes it so important, is that it corrects any one-sided tendencies and deficiencies of character, helps bring the mind to spiritual maturity, and gives confidence and fearlessness. It thus makes one fit to tread the difficult path to Enlightenment and lessens the likelihood of going astray or stopping halfway, which is very probable without this security or faith as foundation and the certainty of knowledge that accompanies it.

The Preparatory Path

In the previous section there was set forth something of the theoretical and practical aspects of 'going for refuge' as the basic requisite of faith in the Buddha's Teaching, and as being the most important preparatory task for gaining entry into it. The Ch'an (Zen) master Hui Hai says in his treatise:

"You ought first to discover whether a man is sincere in his faith and qualified to practise it without backsliding before you expound it to him…."[46]

The 'it' refers to the profounder instructions for gaining realisation in the Ch'an school. However this idea of sincerity of faith is true of any school or Buddhist tradition and is something quite fundamental. A similar idea is expressed in one of the most ancient texts of Buddhism, the Sutta Nipāta, where the Buddha says to the Brahmin Dhotaka,

"I cannot free anyone in the world who still has doubt." (Sn 1064)

However, faith does not usually stand alone but is incorporated with other factors in several of the traditional 'lists' of which there are a large number in Buddhist literature. It is the first of the five spiritual faculties (*indriya*), for example, and in this scheme faith is balanced and harmonized with wisdom. For without wisdom, faith would become mere blind belief, and without faith, wisdom would just be intellectual sophistry.

The other three factors in the list of faculties are *samādhi,* which gives depth; energy, which activates; and mindfulness, that controls and balances the development of the other four.

Besides cultivating the five spiritual faculties there is another more general list found in a discourse from the Udāna, the *Meghiya Sutta* (Ud 4.1). In this discourse there are found five things that, in the words of the discourse, "mature a mind immature for release," that is, they prepare and lead the mind to the spiritual maturity necessary for correctly treading the path that leads to final Enlightenment. It is this spiritual maturity that qualifies one to practise the Dhamma 'without backsliding' or going astray and it is this that distinguishes the 'wise man' (*paṇḍita*) from the 'fool' (*bāla;* 'the immature one').

Summarized, the five things (*dhammā*) are:

1. the spiritual friend,
2. moral discipline,

46 *The Zen Teaching of Hui Hai,* pp. 77–78 translated by John Blofeld (Rider and Co. 1962).

3. conversation centred around the practice,
4. strenuous effort, and
5. wisdom.

It is perhaps the first, the spiritual friend (*kalyāṇa-mitta*), that is the real basis, for it is from him that all good and necessary qualities cultivated by one ultimately stem. It is from the spiritual friend that one learns the Dhamma, both by precept and example, and the unequalled Friend of all beings is the Buddha himself who, by handing down his Teaching to us, exemplifies, through the wisdom and compassion contained in it and in his life, the quintessence of what a spiritual friend should be. Lower down the scale, the spiritual friend is the ordinary human teacher who introduces us to the Dhamma and its practice. Inspired by his example, one goes for refuge, cultivates the moral precepts and makes a beginning in unfolding one's spiritual potentialities.

In the discourse to Meghiya it is specifically mentioned that the moral precepts laid down by the Buddha are to be followed scrupulously and that one should 'see danger' in the slightest deviation from them. This is not to say one should rigidly adhere only to the 'letter of the law' at the expense of its spirit, for one without the other is both harmful and useless. The proper cultivation of the moral precepts produces a clear conscience or 'non-remorse' (*avippaṭisāra*), which is an essential step in clearing the way to further advancement. Remorse, worry and regret over acts committed and omitted is a great obstacle, especially for the practice of meditation, and it is by keeping a strict moral discipline that one can move forward, unhindered by self-reproach.

The discourse mentioned above also lists the kinds of talk helpful in producing spiritual maturity: that is, talk on moral discipline, meditation practice and so forth, and by implication the non-indulgence in frivolous, idle chatter and worldly topics of conversation. For this one needs to associate with like-minded friends and to avoid those not in sympathy with one's spiritual aspirations. It should be obvious that without perseverance and effort nothing worthwhile, even in worldly matters, can be achieved and this is even more true in the most difficult task of all—to realise Enlightenment. And to proceed correctly in all that has been indicated so far needs, above all, wisdom. For this preparatory stage, it is not necessary to take into consideration the higher reaches of wisdom as a transcendent state that views reality face to face, but in its down-to-earth aspect, more akin to ordinary common sense; the ability to discriminate right from wrong, to accept wisely what is useful and helpful and reject what is useless and harmful in one's spiritual career. One needs wisdom to be able to see things objectively and judge the best course to take, to assess oneself with all one's faults rightly and to develop a clear view of one's ultimate goal and the obstacles that must be surmounted to realise it. Of course it is inevitable that we will all make mistakes at some time or another, but it is just these and the ability to learn from them that help the faculty of wisdom to grow—one's own direct experience.

When this preliminary work has been done there should come a time when one's practice of the path becomes easy and natural and the obstacles less. In the Saṃyutta Nikāya SN 35:241, the Buddha uses the simile of the log of wood floating on the Ganges—that, if unobstructed, will inevitably reach the ocean. So will we, skilfully guided by the spiritual friend and our own understanding and wisdom, eventually reach the ocean of Nibbāna.

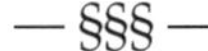

The Advantages of Merit

A sermon given at Wat Bovoranives, Bangkok

Bhikkhu Khantipālo

Bodhi Leaves No. 38

First published: 1968

THE ADVANTAGES OF MERIT

"So when a woman or a man, shall have with gifts or virtuousness;
Or with refraining or constraint, a store of merit well laid by;
In shrines or in the Sangha's (gifts), or in a person or in guests;
Or in a mother or a father, even in an elder brother;
This treasure-store is well laid by, a follower unlosable;
By renouncing things that pass, that merit (gained), he passes on;
This store can satisfy indeed, every desire of god or man;
No matter what they wish to have: All that is got by merit's grace;
And every human excellence, any delight in godly worlds;
Even Nirvana's excellence: All that is got by merit's grace.
So great indeed are its rewards, simply, this merit's excellence;
For that the steadfast and the wise, commend a store of merit made."

From the *Treasure Store Discourse*
(*Nidhikaṇḍa Sutta*, Khuddhakapāṭha 8,
revised trs. of Ven. Nyanamoli Thera)

The subject of this discourse, meritorious action and its benefits, is of vital importance to the Buddhist Way of training. "Merit," which is the English equivalent of the Pali word *puññā*, is defined by ancient scholars as: "that which purifies and cleanses the mind." The mind if permitted to take its own course will, because of the blemishes contained in it, drag one into all sorts of troubles and unwholesome situations. There is really no need to be ruled by the unskilful or evil tendencies in one's own mind, nor is there any good reason why one should make life unpleasant for other people. What then are these evil, unskilful tendencies? Greed is an evil, unskilful tendency dragging one to desire and covet, to accumulation and hoarding, to a sense of exclusive possessiveness expressed in the thought, "This is mine," even to lies and theft, rape and murder. Merit purifies the mind of greed. Hatred is an evil unskilful tendency dragging one to dislike and abhorrence, to anger, even fury, to develop the sense of "I do not want," "I will not have"—even to harsh words, quarrels, fighting, murder, wars and wholesale destruction. Merit purifies the mind of hatred. Delusion is an evil unskilful tendency dragging one to become enmeshed in greed and hatred, and making these two reactions seem right, true and worthy courses. The dulling fog of delusion spreads through the mind preventing learning, understanding and wisdom from arising. It encourages the spirit of "I don't know" and underlies the feeling of "I don't want to know." It is responsible for doubts and indecisiveness taking all sharp awareness away from the mind. Merit helps to purify the mind of delusion.

We see from this that the range of merit is wide indeed and that to be a meritorious person is very valuable since it is not until the very end of the Way that one is able, having cast away demerit already, also to cast away meritorious action. Demerit may be defined as the possession of resultant fruits from evil unskilful actions, themselves rooted in the abovementioned roots of unskill: greed, hatred and delusion, whether these are expressed by way of the door of body, the door of speech or the door of mind. It leads one into entanglement with the world and to the accumulation of sufferings. Merit, on the other hand, is derived from all those intentional actions whether of body, speech or mind, which are rooted in absence of greed, absence of hatred and absence of delusion—which can also be called wisdom. It leads one towards freedom from the bondage of desire and suffering.

Merit, or that which purifies, cleanses the mind of evil while strengthening what is beneficial and skilful. How is this done? If one takes the mind just as it comes and so allows all or even most desires to affect speech and bodily actions, then the roots of unskill—greed, hatred and delusion—grow apace and can strangle all beneficial and skilful qualities. When, however, one consciously decides to make an effort at disciplining the mind, or one makes an effort to perform actions of speech and body which are skilful, then the roots of desire are pruned and the roots of unskill are checked in their growth. This effort that one makes is at the same time the strengthening of the skilful roots and of merit. Merit is always connected with what is skilful and beneficial, either to oneself or else to other beings. Thus, merit can be looked upon as those actions which improve the quality of the mind. They tend to raise the level on which the mind usually runs, refining and purifying it of grosser elements.

It is the making of the merit that ensures that a Buddhist leads a balanced and harmonious life. It is not sufficient just to read about Buddhism and so have a theoretical knowledge of it (as in the opposite way it is insufficient to blindly follow tradition without a knowledge of what it really means), valuable though such an outline knowledge may be. A man who never gets further than the books remains at best a good scholar, while the sincere Buddhist finds many helpful things for practice in his life. Lord Buddha has always encouraged the laypeople, not only bhikkhus, to practise the Dhamma. To a layman, this sometimes sounds too difficult. They may think on hearing the word "practice": "Oh, I should become a bhikkhu and live in the forest." But practice of Dhamma is not only for bhikkhus, since there are many things of Dhamma to do in everyday life. Generosity and giving are Dhamma. Moral conduct and keeping the Precepts pure are Dhamma. Mind development or meditation is Dhamma; respect and reverence are Dhamma. Help and service to others are Dhamma. Giving away one's merits is Dhamma; rejoicing in others' merits is Dhamma; preaching the Dhamma is an act of Dhamma. Straightening out one's views is Dhamma. All these aspects of Dhamma are also ways of making merit. They comprise the Ten Ways of Making Merit so frequently taught in Buddhist countries as a guide for the layman's practice of Dhamma.[47]

These are compared in the Treasure Store Discourse, from which some verses have been quoted above, to a hoard of wealth. Unlike worldly acquisitions so easily lost or destroyed, merit is said to be "a follower unlosable," one from life to life, and the benefits of these merits cannot be lost though eventually they may be exhausted unless further merit is made, or until one aims beyond merit. Treasure is usually hoarded with the motive of selfishness. With what motive is merit made? Also, does one have to wait to reap the fruits of merit in the future, or even in a future life? These two questions can be answered together by saying that the basic fruit of merit—which is happiness—can be experienced here-and-now, while other fruits may be reaped in the future. Happiness naturally follows the man who purifies his mind and rejoices in doing what is skilful.

47 *Dasa-puñña-kiriya-vatthu*; see list at the end of this essay.

Another fruit of merit is opportunity and the ability to make use of opportunities. As the saying goes: "Merit opens doors everywhere." The meritorious man finds his way unobstructed. Whatever work he takes up, he is able to bring to a successful conclusion. When he wishes to undertake this or that venture, he finds that the necessary doors have opened to permit him to go ahead. Of course, a meritorious man may also misuse his chances in this life as when a man born into a wealthy family, his birth there being due to merit, then pursues wealth further by false and evil ways, or simply is just lazy and neglectful. Then there are those who, although they have the opportunities for a good education, only waste their chances, and so on.

The motive in merit-making though often primarily concerned with the well-being of one's self, actually has great advantages for others. Giving benefits the receivers. Moral conduct benefits all beings with whom one comes into contact. Mind-development eventually benefits great numbers of people who come to be influenced by those who have but little greed, hatred and delusion. Reverence ensures harmony in any society. Service and help make the world better to live in. Giving merits to others shows that one is concerned for their well-being, while rejoicing with others' happiness is a great cause of peace and harmony. Listening to Dhamma one learns a good way of conduct in this life and shows this to others through one's actions. Teaching Dhamma is for the highest good of others, while, after straightening out one's views, one can tell the basic principles of Dhamma to other people.

Before going on to describe these ten ways of making merit in some detail, let us look at merit from another viewpoint. The general desire of all beings throughout their lives is to escape from painful, unwelcome experience and seek for circumstances giving rise to happiness. Many people ignorant of the true ways of gaining happiness, look for it only in the round of sensual pleasures indulged in for their own selfish enjoyment. They do not understand that by searching greedily only for happiness-giving experience, they actually bring upon themselves suffering. While one may greedily enjoy a pleasure so long as it lasts, afterwards all sorts of regrets may mar even the memory of its experience. And where there is greed, hatred is always found as well, both of these criminals being urged along by the gaoler of delusion. So, greedy indulgence is always the way to bring unhappiness upon oneself and never brings the sort of happiness so restlessly searched for. But this happiness *is* available to the person who makes an effort with merits. He notices that he is mean, so he decides to give. He sees his own envy of others' fortune, so he resolves to cultivate gladness with others. Or he becomes aware of the narrowness of his mind, so he makes an effort to develop it. People like these really win happiness not depending on the vagaries of the world but on a happiness which cannot be taken away, since it is born of merit and purity of mind. If Buddhists are happy people and if their happiness goes beyond the frail and transitory pleasures so much advertised in modern life, then it is because they know, those among them who practise, that the way to happiness lies through merits.

As the Treasure Store Discourse relates, "This store can satisfy indeed, every desire of god or man" so that whatever one aspires to, providing one's share of merits is compatible with that aspiration, that one may realise. To take but two opposing cases as illustrations of this principle. A young man sets out in the world of business determining to make his way in some venture or other. As he works, wealth and other opportunities for gain come to him freely and these he is able to utilise well for his further advantage. These circumstances show that he is in possession of merit. Another man determines upon a life which he will devote to the understanding of the mind and the thorough investigation of its workings. Set upon the direct course of action, he finds a good teacher and goes to the forest. Then he is able to follow his instructions, and attainments come to him with some ease. His finding the Way and then practising the heart of Dhamma as well as his ease of opportunity and attainment are "All that is got by merit's grace" as the refrain of the Discourse tells us.

We are also told what are the best "fields of merit." A field of merit is the person or persons to whom a meritorious deed is addressed. Just as a farmer knows that this field being fertile and of deep soil will produce a fine crop, while another field having sandy or shallow, stony soil will only give a poor yield, so some persons, by reason of their good qualities, are good fields of merit yielding a rich crop of merits, while other men poor in virtue are less worthy fields of merit. In the Discourse, we find mentioned the building of religious structures and the Sangha or Buddhist Order listed first, as most meritorious; mother, father, relatives and guests are also said to be good fields of merit. We notice too that what may be got from merit ranges "From every human excellence; any delight in godly worlds; even Nirvana's excellence; all that is got by merit's grace." Whether one requires ordinary beauty and wealth, whether one aspires to rule, to gain a birth in the celestial realms, or perhaps to pass utterly beyond all birth and death, "And that is got by merit's grace," though we should qualify this statement in respect of transcendental states, since wisdom, and not only merit, is required for their attainment.

Now we come to consider, one by one, the ten ways of making merit, beginning with giving.

1. Giving, or *dāna* in Pali, is something so basic to the practice of Dhamma that, although manifest everywhere in Buddhist countries, requires a little explanation. Worldliness is concerned with getting, with piling up so-called possessions and with increasing the sense of "I am" by proclaiming "I have." That a person gives, shows that he has some concern for others' welfare, and that he knows where his own true welfare lies. One possesses the worthwhile by giving things away, while things possessed are not possessed at all ultimately—for when one dies, to whom do all one's precious possessions 'belong'?

What then is covered by the Buddhist teaching of giving? Material gifts include medicines for the sick, food for the hungry, money for the poor and so on. Bhikkhus are given four kinds of material gifts by the lay people so that they may continue with their work. These are robes, almsfood, shelter and medicines. Whatever is a necessity of life to one who lacks it and whoever should supply that lack, is said to give material gifts. Since the giving of a gift must be connected with skill to be accounted merit, naturally the giving of the wrong sort of thing, such as a weapon, could never become meritorious. No less valuable is the gift of education or training, which is a gift highly esteemed in Buddhist tradition. The first universities in the world were the enormous Buddhist vihāras of Northern India at the height of their success over a thousand years ago. Since the Dhamma is not a system of dogmas to be believed by the blind masses, but a Way requiring understanding, it is not surprising that the Buddhist religion and education have always been connected.

A kind of giving which involves friendliness and gentleness, the giving to other beings of fearlessness, is a gift which may be given by even the poorest man. All beings fear death and one should try not to be the agent of death for them. Lord Buddha also gave the greatest gift of fearlessness, when he gave all beings who could understand the Dhamma discovered by him—for the Dhamma leads one, although surrounded by what is fearful, to dwell in the world fearless. Finally, "All gifts the gift of Dhamma doth excel" but since one aspect of merit-making concerns "teaching Dhamma," consideration of it will be postponed.

2. The next way of merit-making is through moral conduct (*sīla*); that is, by way of observing the Precepts and thereby leading a life which is not harmful to others, while one sees that it is beneficial to oneself. This is obviously meritorious since it involves the growth in one's character of compassion and wisdom. No Buddhist observes the Precepts either from fear of, nor from love or reverence towards some power outside himself. It is quite an obvious fact to him that the man of upright moral conduct has many advantages over another who leads a life crooked in some way. There is no need to wait for a future life in order to benefit from virtue, just here and now this can be found in one's own life.

One does not have to take Buddhist teachings on the subject of moral conduct on faith, since advantages are found in the present. The present indeed is the time in which we actually live, for the past has gone like a dream and to regret past misconduct is not only foolish, it is unskilful; while the future, like a mirage, is uncertain and to resolve that one will begin to train oneself sometime later is equally foolish. Only now can one practise virtue, only now be wise, only now have compassion. The various precepts established by Lord Buddha are for training the heart in the right direction, towards wisdom and away from ignorance; towards friendliness and compassion, away from enmity and callous indifference. Basically, all the precepts may be classified into actions of body, speech and mind, and a useful list of ten paths of actions (*kammapatha*) summarises them. Abstinence from the three Precepts of taking life, taking what is not given, and wrong conduct in sexual desires, make up the first three paths by way of bodily action. Verbal action is the fourth precept split into four: abstinence from lying, harsh speech, malicious tale-telling and nonsensical chit-chat. Mental action is abstinence from covetousness, ill-will and wrong views. Thus is moral conduct a way of making merit.

3. Next comes mind-development or *bhāvanā,* often called by the inadequate word "meditation." This is basically of two kinds where one either develops calm first and then gains insight or else, using mindfulness, one proceeds to develop calm out of which also grows insight. The difference is in the use of an object of meditation as with the first, or using the events of life for one's object, as in the second. Both kinds have as the result aimed at the experience of insight and the growth of wisdom. One meditates to calm the grosser mental defilements and develop the mind in such a way that it comes to know real wisdom, that which is beyond words and not the result of learning or thinking. It is this wisdom with which there is the realisation of Nirvana.

We have now to examine briefly other aspects of merit-making, which are also counted as developments of mind.

4. Reverence or respect is one of these. It is obvious that the reverent and respectful man develops his mind, for, by his attitude, he cuts down the defilement of pride and replaces it by the wise conduct of humility. The humble man also has a flexible and adaptable mind and can therefore learn, while the proud man is at a great disadvantage. Reverence runs through a Buddhist society in all ways. Children respect adults, especially elderly relations. People pay their respects to the King. They reverence bhikkhus by respectful salutation and offerings, while in the Sangha, novices pay respect to bhikkhus and the latter, if juniors, revere the seniors. All pay their respects to the Supreme Patriarch, while he together with the King and people all revere alike Lord Buddha as the Great Teacher.

5. Service in helping others is the next way of merit-making. If compassion were only the thinking of kind thoughts, it is obvious that it would be a rather insignificant exercise. The fact is that one shows, by willing and unprompted deeds, that one thinks of the comfort of other beings. Such a great range of action may be

included in this way of merit-making that we have no time here to illustrate this at length.

6. Following service, and just to show that one's good deeds are not egotistic, one gives away the merit from their performance. This is indeed intended to illustrate the paradoxical teaching that a man makes most merit when he is not thinking, "I am making merit." The action which is done spontaneously and out of the goodness of the heart, is the most meritorious action of all. Merit should be relinquished for others' benefit, because, like "my" body, it does not really belong to me at all. As Lord Buddha said, "That which does not belong to one, that give away."

7. Besides giving away even merits, one should also rejoice in the merits of others. When others have some gain or other, material or immaterial, does one become envious? If so, one needs to arouse the spirit of gladness at others' happiness. This is done by way of the third of the four Divine Abidings, called *mudita*. One rejoices at the merit of others when for instance, a bell is struck near a shrine or holy place, or when one sees merit being made or else hears about it. The traditional exclamation at such a time is '*Sādhu*!', meaning, "it is well." This is a great merit indeed.

8–9. The following two ways of merit-making are a pair, since one is listening to while the other is teaching Dhamma. Listening means concentrating one's whole attention so that there is only the voice of him who speaks Dhamma. One can go further until there is only Dhamma in one's own heart—though this requires a well trained mind not liable to stray here and there. Teaching Dhamma is not just teaching rules and dogmas for people's belief. It is dealing with the practical Way for this life here-and-now, the Way leading to the experience of the Ultimate Truth or Nirvana. It is truly said: "All gifts the gift of Dhamma doth excel." Much merit attaches therefore both to Dhamma listening and to Dhamma teaching as they are concerned with the true nature of things.

10. Last comes setting upright or straightening out one's views. This aspect of meritorious conduct counterbalances some of the other aspects described here. One should understand clearly and without self-delusion that one suffers from one's own foolishness and not because of any outside power; likewise, that one will find the path to final peace and release from birth-and-death through

one's own efforts and not through those outside oneself. Wrong views are those which lead one away from Reality, away from Dhamma, while Right View is the seeing of things as they really are. Such is a supreme merit.

For all these reasons and in all these ways one should make merit, for as Lord Buddha says in the last stanza of the Treasure-Store Discourse:

"So great indeed are its rewards,
Simply, this merit's excellence;
For that the steadfast and the wise
Commend a store of merit made."

Dasa puññakiriya-vatthu

The ten items (types or bases) of meritorious action

1. *Dāna*—Giving
2. *Sīla*— Morality
3. *Bhāvanā*—Development
4. *Apaciti*—Respect, reverence
5. *Veyyāvacca*—Service
6. *Pattānumodanā*—Giving away (or transferring) the merit
7. *Abbhanumodanā*—Rejoicing in the meritorious deeds of others
8. *Desanā*—Preaching (and teaching) the Dhamma
9. *Savaṇa*—Hearing the Dhamma
10. *Diṭṭhijjukamma*—Straightening out one's views.

The Analysis of Offerings

Whoever, moral in habit, gives to the poor in moral habit
A gift rightfully acquired, the mind well pleased,
Firmly believing in the rich fruit of kamma—
This is an offering purified by the giver.
Whoever, poor in moral habit, gives to those of moral habit
A gift unrightfully acquired, the mind not pleased,
Not believing in the rich fruit of kamma—
This is an offering purified by the recipient.
Whoever, poor in moral habit, gives the poor in moral habit
A gift unrightfully acquired, the mind not pleased,
Not believing in the rich fruit of kamma—

This is an offering purified by neither.
Whoever, moral in habit, gives to those of moral habit
A gift rightfully acquired, the mind well pleased
Firmly believing in the rich fruit of kamma—
I assert this gift to be of abundant fruit.
Whoever, without attachment, gives to those without attachment
A gift rightfully acquired, the mind well pleased,
Firmly believing in the rich fruit of kamma—
I assert this gift to be a gift abundant in gain.

(M III 257).

From the Dhammapada

Should a person merit make
Let him do it time and again
And turn his heart to delight therein,
For happy is the piling-up of merit. (v. 118)

As from a heap of flowers
Many a garland may be made,
So by one born mortal
Should many skilled deeds be done. (v. 53)

Disregard not meritorious deeds,
(Thus thinking):
'Merit will not come near to me'—
For, the constant falling of drops
Fills even a water-jar.
The sage likewise, little by little
Fills himself with merit. (v. 122)

Translated by Bhikkhu Khantipālo

— §§§ —

The Supreme Conqueror

Francis Story
(Anāgārika Sugatānanda)

Bodhi Leaves No. 39

First published: 1968

The Supreme Conqueror

I

Without beginning and without end, over unimaginable aeons of time, the rolling cycles of the cosmos unfold themselves. Worlds arise, produce their living beings, their civilisations and then fall into decay and pass away. Entire universes, planetary systems, whirling in the vastness of space, emerge from their gaseous wombs, live out their span of life and disappear.

Nowhere is there stability, nowhere peace, nowhere security. All is change, incessant, repeated—a blind whirling in the vortex of becoming. Birth, decay and death, the one following inevitably upon the other. Birth, decay, and death. Over and over again—the blind groping, the craving for being, a being that can never achieve being, because it is always becoming.

Man, caught in this blind cosmic machinery, himself a part of it, is carried onward, through life after life—a process, not a being, because he too cannot free himself from the universal flux, cannot achieve the perfect state of being, the perfect equilibrium. Driven by an insatiable thirst, he clings to his minute illusion of self as a man clutches at a floating spar in a whirlpool. He is the slave of *saṃsāra*; its slave and at the same time its creator. The vortex is also the ultimate paradox.

Blind because ignorant, man struggles pitifully, matching his puny strength against the huge impersonal forces of this cosmic process. Age after age, aeon after aeon, over measures of time beyond thought, swept along by currents of passion in a void that he peoples with the phantoms of desire, he drifts from birth to birth, from world to world.

But in this dark, chaotic night of suffering and ignorance, from time to time a light shines forth. Then men see the Truth and many of them break the chains that bind them and gain their release. From time to time, in the course of aeons, a being by his own efforts penetrates the thick veil of ignorance and teaches man the way to ultimate peace, cessation from becoming, equilibrium, fulfilment.

One destined to Buddhahood is born.

II

In this world-cycle, it took place close to the foothills of the Himalayas, for ages the home of India's great saints and teachers. A prince of the Sakyas, a race of the warrior-nobility of ancient Bharata, was born at Kapilavatthu on the borders of modern Nepal. He was named Siddhattha Gotama; his father was a Raja, Suddhodana, his mother Māyā. His race was that of the Ikshvakku, the Solar Dynasty, proud, heroic, rulers by descent and by instinct, who looked even upon brahmins with disdain.

But the prince was greater even than his lineage. For at the age of twenty-nine he abandoned his rank, turned aside from the destiny of a world-ruler that had been predicted for him, and became a wandering ascetic. The Sakyas were ambitious, but his ambition was greater than theirs; it was the greatest of which men or gods are capable. Prince Siddhattha cared nothing for earthly glory, for power or for luxury. The tears of the world were too real to him; its pain and insecurity were too vivid; he could not rest, nor could he find distraction in activity. One thing, and one thing alone, could satisfy him—absolute knowledge, absolute liberation and absolute bliss. For, having attained these, he could help the world of suffering beings.

So he renounced the world and set forth to find liberation. At first he did as all seekers do; he placed himself under a teacher, the best teacher of the time. Twice he did this, but having mastered all they could import, he left them dissatisfied. He had practised their methods, attained to the realm of Brahmas and identified himself with the highest cosmic forces, but this was not enough. He must get beyond the process of cosmic becoming, must find the last, eternal, unchanging state.

He left his teachers and embarked on the path of extreme asceticism. He lived in the forest, mortified his flesh, fasted and watched and guarded his senses, deprived his body and reduced his frame to a skeleton. For six years he continued this course with the indomitable resolution of a warrior who knows no surrender. His fair body became black, his rounded limbs mere sticks hung with withered skin through which the bones stuck sharply, his belly became hollow and close to his spinal column. His five companion ascetics watched and waited. Never had they seen anything like this, accustomed though they were to the superhuman mortifications of their kind. Surely his supreme struggles must gain the supreme reward. Surely he would be their teacher and liberator. They watched and waited.

But the prince-ascetic became weaker and weaker and still he had not achieved the final goal. He had gone beyond all of them, including many who were not his peers in spiritual attainment who had set themselves up as teachers and were honoured and claimed large followings. He could have done the same, but not for one moment did he waver in his set purpose. He had not achieved his goal and he knew it. He must go on, higher, higher.

One day he collapsed. Scarcely conscious he lay, unable to move. Yet still that fine, indomitable mind was alive, active, searching. What had he gained? Instead of becoming superhuman he was reduced to this—a pitiful victim of the insatiable body, weak, powerless, almost dead from hunger. And then suddenly he knew: this was not the way. They had all been wrong. To abuse the body is to enslave oneself to the body, whatsoever form the abuse might take. The body would take its revenge. Its conquest must take a different form from this.

He was offered food and he accepted it. Giving the body its just demands, he strengthened himself again; and once more his mind asserted itself over the body, clear and luminous and resolute. But his five companions were grieved—grieved and disappointed. He had failed them; he who was to have been their teacher, the master-ascetic, the greatest *rishi* of all time, had failed them. He had deserted his quest, had taken to easy living again, and was no more worthy to be their leader. They left him.

Alone, the prince-ascetic found himself at Gaya and once again he addressed himself to the supreme task. Seated cross-legged beneath a tree, he considered his position. He had tried so many paths, and all ended the same way. Was there no end to this quest? He summoned all the latent powers of mind and body and made the supreme resolution: "Even though my body should fall into decay and dissolution, I shall not rise from this seat until I have attained Buddhahood."

In the first watch of the night, Prince Siddhattha meditated.

III

It was the festival of spring ploughing. Already the sun was hot, but where the child sat there was shade from the sal tree that spread its branches over his head. His father, the king, was at the plough, performing the ancient, universal ritual of breaking the soil to ensure a healthy crop for the coming year. Back and forth he went, the handles of the jewelled plough glittering in the golden sunlight, and the child watched. As the rich brown earth was overturned, worms and insects were exposed and flocks of birds followed the track of the plough. Noisily they clamoured, fluttering their wings and jostling one another for the fattest worms, the largest insects. They fought and screamed at one another in their tiny bird voices, pecking at the ground, eating the living creatures as they were turned up by the royal plough.

A microcosm of the universal order. Worms, insects, born into the world to be eaten by birds. The birds, in their turn, killed and eaten by larger creatures, and the animals themselves food for one another. A universal, ceaseless round of inane carnage: the whole earth, a battle-ground and a cemetery. Pain and suffering and bloodshed, birth, decay and death. And in between birth and death, continual uncertainty, restlessness, disappointment, disease, separation from that which is pleasant, contact with that which is unpleasant. In a word, suffering.

And the cause of this suffering? The answer was there, too. It was craving, thirst for life. The craving of the worms and the insects for life, the craving of the birds for life, the craving of animals, the craving of men. They were born and reborn because they craved for the satisfaction of the senses. Their craving bound them inexorably to the wheel of becoming and so they suffered, hopelessly, endlessly, for there could be no life, no process of becoming, without this accompanying element of suffering.

A strange thought: what precisely did it mean? It must mean that suffering goes deeper than the mere superficial aspect of it that we all see. For that suffering appears to be balanced by a contrasting enjoyment. A fleeting enjoyment, it is true, but still happiness of a kind. But fleeting—fleeting. There was the answer. There could be no true happiness in fleeting sensations. Impermanence—suffering—a pattern, a relationship was beginning to emerge.

What of the material phenomena of nature? Did that know anything of this suffering? Was there a cosmic suffering, something inherent in all compounded things, an element that existed whether there was any awareness of it or not? What did the body have to say? Turn inward, concentrate the attention, get to the very foundations of physical being. Search there.

Yes. There it was. There was the agitation of the molecules, the atomic restlessness of the body, felt, perceived, the arising and passing away. So inconceivably rapid as to be imperceptible to the distracted mind, but very clear to the trained, stabilised attention that brought all its functions to bear on the object, the cosmic suffering, inalienable, an inherent part of all phenomena throughout the universe. The primordial fact.

So as long as there was the arising of compounded things that are impermanent, there must be suffering. The perceived suffering that is in grief, lamentation, pain, despair, and the unperceived suffering that is the agitation and restlessness of the atomic constituents of matter and mental formations, each one an aspect of the other. And it was all the result of craving, the thirst for sentient life.

In this process of arising and passing away was a momentary birth and death. Mind and body alike were changing from moment to moment. Where then was the stable, immutable element, the self, the *ātman*, the soul? On the one hand, there was his body, and, according to all the schools except the materialist ones, there was the immaterial element, the spirit, opposed to it and yet in some inexplicable way bound by this gross physical envelope. Of what did this spirit, the conscious element, consist? There was sensation; that was indisputable. There was also perception, awareness of the sensation. There were also the mental formations and tendencies that make up the character—were they permanent? No, they too were subject to change and transformation, because they were linked up with past and present actions, *kamma*. So what was left? Only consciousness—the sum of awareness, the knowledge that says: "I am"—and that in the very act of asserting, it is changing, flowing, perpetually in transition. So there could be no permanent entity of selfhood, no single element alone and independent of the others to constitute a self. Just five aggregates, like bundles bound together; when they were all present, there was what is called a living being. An interdependent complex of factors, with no element stable or constant and no link of self-identity from one thought-moment to another.

Void. Yet in the void, this infinite potentiality of suffering. A current passing from one phase of becoming to another—from childhood to maturity, maturity to old age, old age to death. And then a leap, a spark of the energy-potential jumping to a new manifestation, a "rebirth." Not the same, yet not another, as the man is not the same as the infant, the old man not the same as the man in his prime. All different, yet all belonging to the same sequence, the same current of actions and results. Inheritors of the *kamma* of the past: ancestors of a yet unborn futurity.

The cosmic pattern takes shape—visibly the factors arrange themselves. The vast incomprehensible machinery is seen, not from within, but from the outside. A new dimension of knowledge and experience is opening up.

The universe of phenomena, of compounded things, arranges itself in accordance with a common denominator—three characteristics which are in their final essence one, because each is the natural corollary of the others. Impermanence; and because of impermanence, suffering; and because of impermanence and suffering, the absence of self.

The lean ascetic seated under the banyan tree at Gaya—was he the same as that child who had been seated under the sal tree watching his father the king on that day of the spring ploughing so many years ago? In a sense, yes; but in a deeper sense he was not. The ascetic was the result of the child; the child was but one link in a series of beings flowing back into an infinite past.

Let the mind run back. Beyond this life, to birth before birth. Where was the beginning? Nowhere could it be found. Man, deva, animal, man again, infinitely, endlessly but no beginning to the process, no point at which it could be said, "Here is the first link in the chain, the first cause." Over hundreds of aeons the luminous, developed mind might retrace the paths of lost time, but the beginning would ever elude it. For there could be no beginning to time when this was not, no time outside the realm of conditioned things.

And there arose in his mind the knowledge of past births.

IV

With a supernormal vision in which space and time were transcended, he surveyed the world and the immensities of world upon world beyond. The relativity of all things became clear to him and he traced their relationships, above, below and across. Men, gods, in worlds of form and worlds without form, he saw distinctly in the light of a new knowledge. Only the dark frontier of ignorance hemmed them in; they came and went, chained forever to that palpable darkness which seemed to be their very substance, the fabric of their being and the atmosphere they breathed. There arose in his mind the knowledge of their present birth, their arising and passing away. Yet still the first cause hid itself, search where he would. And the second watch of the night came to an end.

Ignorance, the sleep of not-knowing, the dreams of the sleeper, acting in a trance of ignorance. And then he saw that here was its beginning; a beginning not in time but co-temporal and all-permeating. For these beings clung to life because they thought it good, believed it to be wholesome and desirable. Every thought, every word, every deed was the outcome of this ignorance. The ever-renewing consciousness, the assertive "I am," sprang from these actions, from the identification of the actions with the actor. Because there was the thought, word and deed, there was the delusion of a thinker, a speaker, a doer, but everywhere it was the same thing—a process that masqueraded as a being. From birth to birth the causal process, the relationship of dependent phenomena. Nothing more.

Out of that came the aggregates of personality, physical and mental, the fivefold group. Body, sensation, perception, tendencies and consciousness; the body equipped with six senses all on fire with craving nourished by contacts and sensations as a fire is nourished by fuel. For out of the contacts came sensation, and from sensation new craving-impulses were born from moment to moment, gathering into a force of grasping that would not let go. And that force became the current of becoming, the becoming which was the enemy of being. A life-force recharged from moment to moment and endless momentary succession of births and deaths. And when the bundles were at last torn apart and scattered, it was only a simultaneous group death, as against the separate deaths and rebirths of mind and body which, like a flowing river, preserved the seeming identity of that restless current. For on the instant of disintegration, a new mind-body complex arose, the current remanifested itself again somewhere in space and time. All causes must produce a result.

But how could this be expressed? Just as a ripple on the surface of water travels from its point of origin to some other points but the particles of the water are not displaced, so it was only the impulse, the pushing of an active force against the inert mass, imparting movement. It wasn't the water that moved, but the impulse that moved through the water, rebirth—but nothing that was reborn, nothing identical except the force and the direction.

For a long time he contemplated it, in the light of this new knowledge. How completely mistaken they had all been, blinded by the illusion of self. There was no *ātman*, no permanent, unchanging entity. There was only this current of activity functioning in the void; yet from that arose all the suffering of the world, the grief, lamentation, pain and despair of sentient beings. Still and detached he sat and contemplated it, absorbing the knowledge, seeing the reality for the first time. Plainly the pattern spread itself before his sublimated vision; not in words, not an intellectual concept but a direct realisation.

Then where was the cessation, the peace, the unshakable stillness in which becoming ended and true being took place? Twelve causal factors, and at their head, the primal ignorance. If ignorance were destroyed, then there could be no more actions prompted by ignorance—no more aggregate of kamma. The force would be neutralised. With the kamma force neutralised, there could be no more arising of consciousness, no more mind and body, no more field of sense-perceptions and therefore no more could thirst or grasping arise. That indeed would be the end of the life-process, the end of rebirth, the final end of grief, lamentation, pain and despair. It would be Nibbāna, the great cessation. There at that point, becoming would give place to being—a state that was not life nor death, existence nor non-existence, but was beyond all the opposites and dualities of relativity, the false concepts of ignorance, outside of space and time and eternal, unchanging.

So there was suffering, the cause of suffering and its cessation—three Noble Truths hitherto unrealised, now clear to his awakened insight. One thing more was needed—the way to achieve that cessation, the method by which beings might, by their own exertions—for there was no supreme deity to help them—eradicate ignorance and gain Nibbāna.

Right View must come first. For unless it is known that all things are impermanent, subject to suffering, and void of self, there can be no starting on the right direction. Without that there could only be misdirected energy. Kālāma, who taught that the atman was permanent and unchanging, and so could never get beyond the sphere of sublimation and self-identification. Or the unending struggle with kamma of Uddaka Rāmaputta, who could never free himself from the entanglements of metempsychosis. With Right View established, Right Resolution must follow—the thought free from lust, free from ill-will, free from cruelty. The pure, untainted thought of benevolence directed without distinction toward all beings, the resolution to gain Nibbāna. And from that, Right Speech, truthful, sincere, uttering whatsoever was good for gods and men, beneficial, free from trivialities, from malice and from harshness. Then Right Action, gentle, non-violent, pliant towards others, but rigid towards the self, restrained and controlled. Also Right Livelihood—the livelihood gained by work beneficial to living beings, by one who has put away violence in all its forms, who will not encourage violence in others. Then would the character be formed for Right Effort—the fourfold great effort, to avoid the arising of impurities and demeritorious states, and to bring to an end those that have already arisen—to avoid and to overcome. Furthermore, to develop states of purity and merit that have not yet arisen, and to encourage and establish those that have already arisen—to develop and to maintain.

This, then, was the teaching of all the Buddhas: to put away evil and to fulfil all good—to purify the heart. Then the way would be made clear for the supramundane path: clear and luminous in the light of virtue which is power. Cultivation of a mind that can see through illusion; Right Attentiveness, the awareness of the functions, the detached, impersonal regard of body, feeling mind and phenomena, knowing them to be but a part of the cosmic order, not "I," not "mine," not "myself." Then, with the breaking down of the limitations of personality, would come the great psychic powers and the release from pleasure and pain, fear and mundane hope, and the calm, unshakable equilibrium of mind would be realised. And lastly, Right Concentration, the opening up of new dimensions of experience, the *jhānas*. Detached from sensual objects, from all impure contacts, the mind enters upon the first sublime state, with thought and discursive rumination, distinguished by rapture, happiness and concentration. From thence, overcoming thought and rumination, it enters the second sublime state, free from the activities of discursive thought, the state filled only with rapture and happiness.

And further, overcoming rapture, the mind enters into the third sublime state, the sphere of equanimity, attentiveness, clear consciousness, and dwells there in the enjoyment of pure happiness. But then, giving up pleasure and pain, joy and grief alike, it enters the fourth sublime state, which is beyond these—the state for which it can neither be said that it is consciousness nor unconsciousness, nor does it admit any of the categories of normal experience. And from there the gate of the deathless is open.

This is the Middle Path that the All Enlightened One discovered, that enables one both to see and to know, that leads to peace, to discernment, to enlightenment, to Nibbāna.

Then the glad cry of the conqueror rang forth from the prince-ascetic who had become the Buddha of this world-cycle: "Long have I sought you, O builder of the house of this body. Now I have found you. Your beam is cast down, your ridge-pole broken. Never again will you build the house. For good, birth and death are ended; I have done what had to be done. The path of virtue is fulfilled. I behold Nibbāna face to face."

V

The long night was ended and a new light flooded the world. The All Enlightened One began his ministry of teaching, which he was to continue for forty-five years. Great were his supernormal powers, gained that night under the bodhi tree at Bodh Gaya when he attained omniscience; but first and greatest of all, he placed the power of teaching the Dhamma. He rarely performed miracles, but when he did they were of such kind as to stagger the mind and confound his opponents. Most of all, he desired to convince people by the power of truth alone, so that of their own free will they would accept what he had to tell them and act upon it. His Dhamma is "*ehi passiko*"—that which bids us, "Come and see for yourself." He taught it in the sequence in which it had been discovered by him, beginning with the three signs of being: impermanence, suffering, and non-self. From this came the Four Noble Truths: the truths concerning suffering, the arising of suffering, the cessation of suffering and the way leading to that cessation.

The cause of suffering is craving and the process of its arising is shown in the twelve factors of *paṭicca-samuppāda* (dependent origination). Its cessation is Nibbāna, the unborn, unoriginated, the state free from any possibility of the re-arising of conditioned existence, the ultimate peace. The Supreme Buddha did not attempt to define Nibbāna in words because words relate to concepts, being relates to non-being as day relates to night, and Nibbāna is neither being nor non-being as we understand these words. It is altogether outside all categories or experience; it must be known to be understood.

In his teaching, there is no metaphysic (except where later men and lesser minds have manufactured one); it is a practical way, a path to be trodden. Speculation is useless, a hindrance on the path, and as such the Buddha condemned it. All he asked was that his disciples should examine the factors of phenomenal existence, satisfy themselves that what he taught of it was true, and from there go on to discover by direct insight the real truth that lies beyond phenomena. The way itself, the Middle Way between all extremes, is the Noble Eightfold Path (*ariya-aṭṭhaṅgika-magga*). From this nucleus of teaching, all further developments of ethic-psychology followed in natural and logical sequence, from the Five Precepts of the layman to the intricacies of Abhidhamma, the detailed analysis of mental phenomena.

Very soon after the attainment of enlightenment, the Buddha founded the Order of Monks, containing the four groups of ariyan disciples: the stream winners, or those who had entered the path; the once-returners, those of the second stage of purification who, if they passed away before gaining arahantship, would only be reborn once; the non-returners, those destined to achieve rebirth in a Brahma-realm from whence they would pass into Nibbāna, and the arahants, the fully perfected and purified for whom there would be no rebirth after this present life. "In whatsoever discipline, O monks, there are the Four Noble Truths and the Noble Eightfold path, there will be found those of the four degrees of saintliness. But in whatsoever discipline the Four Noble Truths and the Noble Eight-fold path are not found, they cannot be disciples of the four degrees of saintliness." And the Exalted Buddha sent forth his perfected disciples to preach the doctrine. "I, O monks, have seen suffering and the destruction of suffering and the way leading thereto. I have freed myself of the impurities. You too, O monks, are freed from the impurities. Go forth, then. Proclaim the Doctrine perfect in its beginning, in its continuation and in its end, for the good, the benefit and the welfare of gods and men."

So it came about that the Doctrine was established and propagated in the world. The noble Order of Monks increased and spread throughout India and beyond, and the gospel of mercy and liberation became known to all those "whose eyes were but lightly covered with dust." The ariyan discipline followed by the monks in their yellow robes was austere but not extreme; it looked more to the mind than to the body, for in the mind is the seat of craving. "*Mano pubbaṅgamā dhammā manoseṭṭhā manomayā,* mind is the forerunner of all phenomena; mind is chief, they are all mind-created." "Guard therefore the mind, purify the mind, for out of the intention all things come to be." Neither do you look to any external aid, for "Self is the master of self. What other master could there be?" Put aside all vain beliefs, all faith in rituals and religious performances, for these things avail not against ignorance, being themselves products of ignorance. "In this fathom-long body, O monks, equipped with sense and sense-perceptions, I declare to you is the origin of suffering, the cessation of suffering and the way leading to that cessation." Never before in a world bewitched by superstition and priestcraft had such a challenging message resounded. The followers of the Supreme Buddha no more resorted to the sacrificial fires, to holocausts of men and beasts to appease the personified force of nature, no more cultivated magic or submitted their bodies to unavailing self-torture. Instead, they cultivated a mind of boundless loving-kindness, lived righteously and fearlessly and found a happiness hitherto unknown to them.

VI

"I promise to observe the precept to abstain from taking life. I promise to observe the precept to abstain from taking that which is not mine. I promise to observe the precept to abstain from adultery. I promise to observe the precept to abstain from untruthful speech. I promise to observe the percept to abstain from intoxicants and drugs."

To the laymen and women who came to him the Buddha gave these five simple precepts. He did not command, did not take upon himself the authority of a creator-god to punish and reward. He was greater than this. He was the Supreme Teacher, above all beings spiritual and terrestrial, himself having seen, with direct insight, the working of cause and effect. He prescribed the course of conduct that would eliminate evil results and lead upwards. "Take these precepts," he said in effect, "for by observing them you will avoid the lower courses of rebirth, will diminish suffering which men bring upon themselves by unskilful action. These precepts of mine are a medicine for your sickness. Take them and become safe from sorrow. All fear the rod; all fear death. Putting oneself in the place of another, one should neither strike nor kill." And the people, reverently receiving the precepts from the lips of the Master, assenting to the undeniable truth of his words, bowed themselves in homage: kings, ministers, treasurers, artisans, householders, hetaerae and beggars. Many were the ascetics of other faiths who embraced the Doctrine of the Buddha with the simple formula: "I go for refuge to the Buddha. I go for refuge to the Dhamma. I go for refuge to the Sangha." The Teacher, the Teaching and the Taught were their refuge but they themselves had to effect their own liberation. "You yourself have to tread the Path; the Buddhas can but show the way"—it was the supreme test of self-reliance, the greatest assertion of human freedom, so that in accepting the discipline they were proving the triumph of men's free will in its highest and ultimate sense, taking upon themselves the mastery of their own destiny.

VII

"Profound and difficult to understand is this Ariyan Doctrine, O bhikkhus, only to be understood by the wise; deep and unfathomable as the ocean. But like the vast ocean, it has but one flavour throughout—the flavour of liberation." So it was that some failed to follow the Teaching, while others, like the great disciple Sāriputta, perceived its truth on hearing just one verse from the lips of a monk who was himself not completely a master of it. Others there were who started well, but fell by the wayside like the unfortunate Devadatta, intoxicated by his mastery of the psychic powers, who became maddened by pride and ambition and so cast himself down into hell. But with unchanged serenity the Master smiled, knowing that Devadatta too, in course of time, would expiate his evil deeds and attain enlightenment. To a Buddha, the enormous cycles of time are but as a moment: with his divine eye he surveyed the world, the seen and unseen, to the furthest limits of space, and knew the nature of gods and men—what past deeds had produced them and where their destinies lay. For the potentialities of a man's nature are deep hidden in his past; he is the heir of a countless succession of dead selves and only a Supreme Buddha can know when the moment of fruition, the ripening of wisdom, is about to take place.

There was, for instance, the ruthless murderer Aṅgulimāla, who wore about his neck a grisly garland of the fingers of his victims. Surveying the world with his divine eye of infinite compassion, the Buddha one morning saw this outlaw and he perceived that an atrocious crime was about to take place. To complete his garland the murderer needed one more finger; and Aṅgulimāla's mother was on her way to visit her son.

Instantaneously, as a strong man reaches out his arm, the Buddha was upon the scene, for to one who has conquered life and death, space no longer exists. He stood before Aṅgulimāla, radiant and majestic, and barred his way. But one thought alone possessed the murderer's mind—he must obtain the finger. He drew his knife and leaped towards the Buddha.

He leaped, but the same distance remained between them. Calmly the Buddha surveyed him, compassion in his eyes. Aṅgulimāla started running towards him, but although the Buddha remained motionless, the distance between them was not decreased. Aṅgulimāla ran, and as he ran he cried out, "Stop, Ascetic! Stand still!"

"I am still, Aṅgulimāla," the calm voice replied. "It is you who is running."

Panting and frenzied, the murderer strove to reach his objective, but no matter how fast he ran, the figure of the Buddha remained motionless before him, still, remote, imperturbable.

And the voice was speaking again, penetrating into the depths of his consciousness. "I am still, Aṅgulimāla. For he who is still, goes; but he who goes is still."

Exhausted and confused then, the murderer came to a halt. And as ever, the Buddha stood before him. Waves of tremendous force struck against the murderer, enveloped him and rendered him powerless. But they were waves of compassion, vibrations of an infinite, indescribable power and beatitude that flowed over and through him, and he was aware of a super cosmic light that seemed at first terrible but when, giving way to his weakness, he surrendered himself to the light, it was more tender and comforting than anything he had ever known. He fell on his knees and stretched out his arms towards that glorious light, towards that all-embracing compassion. And the heat and frenzy of his heart was calmed.

"I am still, Aṅgulimāla. For he who is still, goes; but he who goes is still."

In that moment Aṅgulimāla understood. "I take refuge in the Buddha: in the Dhamma: in the Sangha." And so the former murderer, whose pride had been the garland of fingers hung about his neck, took the yellow robe of a bhikkhu and in no long time attained arahantship.

Many are the ways whereby a man may be brought to realise the truth. The Supreme Buddha was master of them all. If the potentiality for understanding were present, the Buddha could awaken it, bring it to perfection. Where a demonstration of power was called for, he exercised power. Where wisdom was called for, he exercised verbal skill, yet always with gentleness, forbearance and compassion. There was a philosopher skilled in dialectics who swore to overcome the Buddha in argument. Although the Buddha did not value dialectics, rarely resorting to argument, before long the sophist was reduced to confusion. He contradicted himself, became entangled in his own theories, and became alarmed for his reputation. Sweat poured from his body and his mind became dazed; and in the end he crept away, leaving the Buddha serene and calm as ever. For who can refute truth?

But those, often people of simpler minds, who listened to the Teaching and allowed it to sink into deeper consciousness, or who tested it by the touchstone of their own experience, knew the awakening of confidence and pursued the Path to the glorious goal. For wisdom does not always consist in learning or scholarship; it is something that may, and often does, exist independently of these.

VIII

"All compounded things are impermanent."

For forty-five years, the exalted Buddha taught the incomparable Doctrine until his *sāsana* became established. Then, in his eightieth year, the time came for him to give up his existence. To the arahant who has seen Nibbāna in this very life, death is of no account. He suffers the continuation of his earthly existence only for the good of others, knowing all the time the process of arising and passing away, the continual agitation of the elements which men call "life" to be but a flux of energies, without stability and without permanence. And so a day came when, at the small town of Kusināra, the Supreme Buddha laid himself down for the last time. None can escape the pains of existence, and the Buddha's body was old and enfeebled by sickness. But not so his mind. Alert, composed and tranquil, he continued to survey the world. He was about to leave. His robe had been spread for him by his devoted attendant, Ānanda, between twin sal trees. And the bare branches of the sal trees blossomed over his head and broke into glorious bloom in the season of bareness.

A wandering ascetic of another faith, hearing of the Buddha's greatness, came and begged to talk with him. "The Blessed One is sick," he was told, "Please do not disturb the Blessed One. He is resting."

But the Buddha called out, "Who is there?" And when they told him, he said, "Let the wandering ascetic approach. Do not forbid him."

So the wandering ascetic approached, and saluting the Blessed One, he seated himself respectfully on one side. And the Blessed One discoursed to him for a long time. At the end of the discourse the wandering ascetic acknowledged the Teacher and begged admission to the Order. He was the Buddha's last convert.

Rapidly the news spread that the Supreme Buddha was about to pass away, and from far and wide came the sorrowing people to pay their last homage to the beloved Teacher. From the adjoining kingdoms came the brahmins and nobles of the warrior caste together with the people, and assembled about the Buddha's last resting place. From the heavenly realms also, the devas and Brahmas gathered together and heavenly music was heard from invisible minstrels. At the same time, divine perfumes filled the air and petals from flowers of more than earthly beauty were scattered on the Buddha's couch. And seeing this, the Blessed One spoke to Ānanda and those about him, and what he said was this: "It is right and fitting that the passing of a Tathāgata should be honoured by divine music, divine perfumes and flowers of celestial beauty. But not thus is the Tathāgata most truly honoured. The layman or woman who fulfils all the greater and lesser duties, who observes the Precepts and follows the Noble Eightfold path, he or she it is who renders the greatest reverence and truest homage to the Teacher."

And when the sorrowing Ānanda, who had not yet attained arahantship, gave way to his grief, the Buddha reminded him of the Doctrine. "Have I not told you Ānanda, that all compounded things must pass away? Then grieve not, but apply yourself with determination. The Teacher must pass away, but the Teaching remains. I leave you the Doctrine; when I am gone, let that be your guide and refuge."

Calm, tranquil and in full possession of his great faculties, the Buddha continued to advise and instruct and encourage his followers to the last. Just before the end, he gave his final exhortation: "Let the Dhamma be to you a lamp and a refuge. Seek no external refuge. Strive with earnestness."

Then, with faculties collected and intent, he entered into the first jhāna. And rising out of the first stage he passed into the second. And rising out of the second stage he passed into the third. And rising out of the third stage he passed into the fourth. And rising out of the fourth stage of deep meditation, he entered into the sphere of the infinity of space. And passing out of the consciousness of the infinity of space, he entered into the sphere of the infinity of consciousness. And passing out of the sphere of the infinity of consciousness, he entered the sphere of nothingness. And leaving behind the stage of nothingness, he entered into the realm of neither-perception nor non-perception. And leaving the realm of neither-perception nor non-perception, he entered into the attainment of the cessation of perception and feeling. Then the Venerable Ānanda said to the Venerable Anuruddha; "O Venerable Sir, O Anuruddha, the Blessed One is dead."

"Not so Brother Ānanda," replied the Venerable Thera. "The Blessed One is not dead. He has entered into the attainment of the cessation of perception and feeling." Then the Blessed One, passing out of the attainment of the cessation of perception and feeling, entered into the sphere of neither-perception nor non-perception. And passing out of the sphere of neither-perception nor non-perception, he entered into the sphere of nothingness. And passing out of the realm of nothingness, he entered into the sphere of the infinity of consciousness. And passing out of the sphere of the infinity of consciousness, he entered into the sphere of the infinity of space. And leaving the sphere of the infinity of space he entered into the fourth jhāna; and leaving the fourth stage he entered into the third; and leaving the third stage he entered into the second; and passing out of the second he entered into the first jhāna. Then, passing out of the first jhāna, he entered into the second. And passing out of the second jhāna, he entered into the third. And leaving the third jhāna, he entered into the fourth stage of deep meditation. And passing out of the last stage of deep meditation, he immediately expired. And when the Blessed One expired there arose, at the moment of his passing out of existence, a mighty earthquake, terrible and awe-inspiring and the thunders of heaven burst forth. When the Blessed One expired, Brahma Sahampati, at the moment of his passing away from existence uttered this stanza:

"All beings that have life must lay aside
Their complex form, the mind and body compound
From which, in heaven or earth, they draw their brief
And fleeting individuality—

Even as the Teacher, such a one as he,
Unequalled among all the sons of men.
Successor to the Buddhas of the past.
In wisdom mighty and in insight clear—
Even as he hath passed beyond our ken."

And when the Blessed One expired, Sakka, king of the gods, at the moment of his passing away, uttered this stanza:

"Transient are all beings, their parts, their powers:
Growth is their nature, and with growth decay.
Produced are they, and then dissolved again.
And best it is when they have sunk to rest."

When the Blessed One expired, the Venerable Anuruddha, at the moment of his passing away, uttered these stanzas:

"When he who from all craving was released,
Who to Nibbāna's tranquil state attained,
When the great Sage his life's span had fulfilled,
No breathless struggle shook that steadfast heart.

All resolute, with firm, unshaken mind,
He calmly triumphed o'er the pangs of death;
Even as a bright flame dies away, so he gained
His deliverance from the bonds of life."

When the Blessed One expired, the Venerable Ānanda, at the moment of his passing out of existence, uttered this stanza:

"Then was a mighty fear!
The hair uprose,
When he, possessed of all perfection,
He, The Supreme Enlightened One, expired."

Thus, having taught the sublime doctrine of deliverance, the beloved Teacher passed out of *saṃsāric* conditions forever. He left behind him, bound up with his Teaching, the memory in men's minds of a personality absolutely unique in human experience. The virtues towards which others had striven, in him were exemplified in their fullest perfection, effortlessly with unwavering assurance. Freed for ever from internal conflicts that mark our human condition, the alternations between selfishness and altruism, the loves and hates, doubts and fears that beset even the best of men. He trod a path trackless as the flight of birds in space, and only one who was his equal could fully understand him. Men judge and evaluate one another by their own standards, the standards set by self and the degree to which self-interest motivates them. The Exalted Buddha had destroyed this illusion of self, had become identified only with the Dhamma, for he had said: "One who beholds the Teacher beholds the Doctrine: and in beholding the Doctrine he beholds the Teacher." All limitations of phenomenal personality transcended, the Buddha had no peer save in the Buddhas of former ages, and will have none until the next Buddha, Maitreya, walks the earth.

IX

Two thousand five hundred years have passed away since that day when the Supreme Buddha entered into final Nibbāna. The Doctrine was then only preserved by word of mouth, memorised and passed on from teacher to pupils. But while the arahants who had heard it from the lips of the Master were yet alive, a great meeting was convened to recite the Teaching. Each point was then carefully checked and confirmed and the body of the Doctrine was consolidated. During the reign of Asoka, another meeting was held for the same purpose, and by that time it had become necessary to correct certain heretical versions that had become current. After that, it was put into writing, and the present Pali Tipiṭaka of three divisions, the Sutta, the Vinaya and the Abhidhamma, represents this authentic Theravāda tradition. Generations have come and gone, but the *sāsana* of the Buddha still stands. And although the greater part of the world yet remains in the dark night of ignorance, there has been a strong historic current from Buddhism that has affected the whole of human thought, lifting and ennobling it. Our present age is a paradox. While it is highly materialistic in the sense that all the emphasis has come to be laid on material achievements and activities centred about the world, it shows at the same time a growing tendency towards higher aspiration. Men on the whole are more humane, their laws more just, their relationships more equitable, than in the past. There are many dark blots upon our civilisation, survivals from a barbaric past, but they stand out the more clearly because of the progress we have made elsewhere. We are more aware of the shadows in contrast to the light and cruelties and injustices that only a few generations ago were accepted as part of the natural order of things, now stand out with shocking clarity.

Together with this, there is a widening of mental and spiritual horizons. More and more people are turning, often unconsciously, towards a Buddhist interpretation of life. Warped and distorted this may have become in its progress from East to West, yet the spirit is there revealing itself in modifications of traditional thought, in a broader and more tolerant view of the conflict which is life.

Many are the creeds that men have followed, many the idols before which they have abased themselves, many the dogmas to which they have prostituted their understanding. And inasmuch as in every thinking man there lurks a vestige of knowledge gathered painfully from his past lives, which speaks to him of moral law and a beauty to be realised, these creeds have moulded themselves to this faith imperfectly; perhaps, because they could not reach the ultimate understanding of life which alone can give actuality to man's dreams of perfection, but still containing in themselves something of this knowledge, the knowledge that as ye sow, so shall ye reap—and so have helped to raise this human nature which is midway between the animal and the divine. But above and beyond them all stands the supreme Truth, the Truth discovered and taught by him who was Prince Siddhattha of the Sakyan clan. Who became the Supremely Enlightened One, Teacher of gods and men, and around whose funeral pyre, because he was a Khattiya and the greatest warrior of all—the conqueror of self, who shed no drop of blood—the warrior nobles raised a palisade of spears.

— §§§ —

Right Understanding

Bhikkhu Sīlabhadra

Bodhi Leaves No. 40

First published: 1968

Right Understanding

Namo tassa bhagavato arahato sammā-sambuddhassa

It has long been the custom to place on the opening page of books treating the Dhamma of the Buddha, this ancient Pali formula expressive of homage to the holy, the Exalted, the Supremely Awakened One. The old time-honoured practice is eminently commendable, for who is there worthier of the world's homage than he through whom has come to mankind of this era the knowledge of Nibbāna and the way thither?

But if it be well thus constantly to signify a grateful recognition of the bringer of the knowledge, surely it were no less well if with equal frequency mention were made of that wherein the knowledge consists, so that Teacher and Teaching might always be associated the one with the other and no opportunity given for mistake or misapprehension as to the meaning and function of either. Surely it were well if every leaflet, pamphlet, treatise, or book dealing with the Dhamma of the Buddha also bore on its first page in the boldest, most striking characters procurable, that saying in which the Buddha himself sums up the entire purport of his Teaching: "One thing only do I teach—ill and the ending of ill."

"One thing only do I teach," he says. He does not say: "One thing only do I know." Quite the contrary, for upon one occasion, as he was passing through a forest attended by a company of his disciples, he picked up a handful of leaves from the ground, and holding them out, asked his followers then with him which in their opinion was the greater, the bunch of leaves in his hand or all the remaining leaves in the wide forest. The bhikkhus, of course, replied that the remaining leaves in the forest were greater in number by far than those the Master held in his hand.

"Even so," was his impressive reply, "is that which I have not told you far greater than that which I have told you. But what I have told you is sufficient unto deliverance—this, namely, ill, its arising, its ceasing, and the way that leads to its ceasing." Clearly then, in any discussion of the Buddha's Teaching, whether by friend or foe, what must always be borne in mind is that which the Teacher taught only, to the exclusion of anything else that he might and could have taught; and what he taught was just the existence of a disease and its cure, the presence of an evil and the method whereby evil might be removed, nothing more.

The first of the eight divisions of the Path that leads to the ceasing of ill is called Right Seeing or Understanding; and in consonance with what has just been said as regards the essential nature of the Buddha's teaching, this seeing or understanding is not any one of the thousand things the restlessly busy, the actively curious and contriving minds of men are only too apt to conceive. To see and understand rightly, in the Buddha's sense of the words, does not mean, for instance, to see and understand that the world is eternal; no more does it mean to see and understand that the world is not eternal. The world may be eternal, and again it may not be eternal; however the case may be, it has no bearing on the only thing with which the Buddha is concerned—ill and its ending. Neither, in the Buddha's acceptation of the words, do seeing and understanding rightly mean seeing and understanding that the universe is finite, any more than it means seeing and understanding that it is infinite. The universe may be either the one or the other without in any way affecting the Buddha's sole business—the relief, final and complete, of suffering.

Put in its most succinct, its briefest possible form, Right Understanding may be defined as the simple understanding that everything that has arisen, without any exception, has done so in dependence upon some immediately pre-existing condition, and that with the abrogation, the removal of this condition, the thing arising in dependence upon it is also abrogated, removed, ceases to be. Or, as the Buddha himself puts it, yet more briefly and succinctly: it is to see "That being, this is; that arising, this arises. That not being, this is not; that ceasing, this ceases."

This, of course, is only a particularly terse way of formulating the law of causation upon which the methods of modern physical science are based, for that science does not seek for causes in any real sense of the term but only, strictly speaking, strives to ascertain the antecedent conditions under which any given phenomenon arises.

The Buddha, however, is something more than a physical scientist and albeit his formula holds good of physical phenomena and of the sequence of change observable in physical matter; on his lips it embraces a wider and somewhat different purview.

Concerned as he is only with ill and its ending, his definition of the law of causation is set forth only with reference to ill. This ill is ill as felt and known by each man immediately, in his own person. Hence the understanding of ill and its ceasing and the application of the law of causation thereto, means the application of the law of causation to man and his various psychical states, to all human states of feeling and emotion and mentality. In other words, it means the understanding that such and such an ill and undesirable state has arisen in dependence upon a certain foregoing state, and that with the ceasing of the antecedent state the succeeding untoward state will also cease.

What then is the cause of ill, of the sum of suffering, the total mass of misery that in one form or another afflicts and distresses man? How comes it at all that man is subject to ill? What, in short, is the immediately preceding condition following upon which ill for living creatures comes to be? To this question the answer, the obvious answer, is that it is through his having been born that a man becomes subject to whatever ill may affect him; had he never been born, ill, of no matter what kind, could never befall him. A self-evident proposition. The immediately preceding condition then, in dependence upon which the entire sum of suffering arises for living creatures is birth. Seeing and understanding this, one sees and understands rightly; one is by so much possessed of Right Understanding.

But our inquiry into the arising of ill cannot stop here. That we have been born, have come into manifested life, is beyond denial the immediate cause that we are subject to all the ills that visit living creatures, and to the final pangs of dying and parting in pain from all we loved and clung to; but whence comes it that we have been born? We and all creatures that come into life and fall heir to its ills, do so, says the Buddha, because of the existence of the huge, all-comprehending, and—so far as we can see—never-ending process of becoming that makes, and in fact is, our world. Men are born into existence so he teaches, because of the ceaseless actions of the great process of *kamma* (volitional action) and *vipāka* (moral results), an ever-present fact to be accepted with what grace we may, not to be explained away or rejected by any subtlety of reasoning, since it is the very world-process wherein we and all creatures at each moment of our existence are involved beyond possibility of denial or appeal. To see and understand that this is so is a part of Right Understanding.

But through what arises this process of becoming that in its ceaseless working brings to birth beings that suffer ill? What is the fuel that sustains this mighty fire? For to nothing so much as to a fire is to be compared the unceasing procession of cause and consequence that is our world, a fire constantly consuming and ever as constantly renewing itself, so long as is present any fuel upon which to feed. The answer is: the fuel that feeds the fire of becoming and in its burning brings to birth each new being, is attachment, cleaving life as cleaves the snake to the prey it has seized in its jaws. For in the Buddha's view—and, in that of all Indian thought, it may be added—the whole process of the universe of life is based upon mind, kept going by mind and its impulsions. The physical is always and only the manifestation of the mental; it is merely the mental made visible. That which is seen with the physical eye, which takes place in the external world of things perceived by physical sense, is only the belated outcome of what has already taken place in the inner world of things thought of, things conceived and formed in the mind. Already, in the past, mind has clutched at and held fast to its own objectified creations, things visible, audible, gustable, and so forth; and that clinging and cleaving, now in the present takes visible form as a flesh being bound by that same cleaving upon the wheel of birth and death. It is the attachment of the mind in a former existence which has maintained the process of becoming as that process now expresses itself in the birth of a new creature. Thus, to see and understand is another part of Right Seeing and Understanding.

And where does this cleaving that feeds the flame of becoming take its rise? The Buddha's reply is: such cleaving arises through craving, through the thirst of the mind after the objects of sense. Because of this eager craving, which is even as that of the snake for the bird it finally snatches and holds, does the mind come to seize and cleave to the things of a sense world. The seeing and understanding of this is another part of Right Seeing.

And how does this craving arise? Upon what does it depend for its coming to be? As is easily seen, craving is made possible by and arises directly from the fact that there is such a thing as sensation. Only because there is an affection of the various organs of sense by the object of sense corresponding to them, only because there is an agreeable stimulation of the sense organs by pleasurable delightful sights and sounds and odours and savours and contacts and ideas, only because of this does craving for these pleasure-giving objects arise. Thus seeing and understanding, again one is possessed of Right Seeing, of Right Understanding.

But how does the thing called sensation come to be? The answer is: sensations come to be through contact between sense organ and corresponding sense-object, whether, as in the case of touch, that contact be immediate, or only mediate, as in the case of sight, for without such contact, sensation could never arise. To see this again is to see rightly, to have Right Seeing.

And what makes possible this contact between sense and object of sense? The answer given is: contact is possible between each of the six senses (mind being classed as the sixth sense) and their corresponding six classes of objects (ideas, corresponding with mind, making the sixth class), because of the existence of senses, of objects of sense. In the strict analysis we are here pursuing, this obvious step, for all its obviousness, may not be omitted. This understanding also belongs to Right Understanding.

But how have the six senses and their corresponding classes of object come to arise? The answer to this is: the six senses and their corresponding objects arise in dependence upon subjects and objects. That is to say: because of the existence of the great line of demarcation which separates off all that is into subject and object, there exists this lesser division—senses and things which affect those senses. The distinction of sense and sense-object, in effect, is only a variation of the larger, all-inclusive distinction, subject and object. Thus to see and understand pertains to Right Understanding.

And upon what depends the existence of the distinction, subject and object? The existence of subject and object depends upon the existence of consciousness, is the Buddha's reply. Consciousness is that which makes possible the distinction between subject and object. All consciousness is consciousness of something, hence arises the distinction between knower and thing known, between perceiver and thing perceived—in a word, between subject and object. To see and understand this constant dependence of the fact "subject and object" upon the fact "consciousness" is another constituent of Right Seeing and Understanding.

And what is that upon which depends the arising of consciousness, the real starting point of any new individual, of any new subject, or—as the Buddha calls it, and as it ought rather to be called—subject-object, seeing that there never can be a subject without an object, just as there never is and never can be an object without a subject, subject meaning nothing more than the condition of the perceiving of an object, while object means nothing more than the condition of being perceived by a subject? The answer that the Buddha provides to this important question is: consciousness, the nucleus around which crystallises the new being that is arising, comes to be by reason of the life-affirming psychical activities of the being in this particular causational series which last appeared upon the stage of visibly manifested life. These activities, according to the Buddha, reach over from that existence into the present not in any wise as a travelling entity but rather as a communicated vibration, a transmitted impulsion that takes present shape and form—so to speak—as the consciousness of the nascent individual of the present. To see and understand this arising of a new consciousness, a new "individual" as taking place in dependence upon, by reason of, the life-affirming activities of the "individual" which preceded it in the same line of cause and consequence—is again to see and understand rightly.

But how has this life-affirming activity come about? What is that upon which depends the arising of the activity that results in the formation of a new conscious being, and all the limitation and consequent imperfection and ill involved in the existence of such a being? To this last pertinent question the Buddha replies: life-affirming action and all it involves of subsequent ill arises through *avijja*, comes to be because of ignorance. The ignorance, however, that here is branded as the source of the sequence of ill is no vague, vast something hid in the dark womb of the past, no huge primeval chaos or "old night" conceived of as mother of this or any other cosmos. Such a conception of ignorance, source of ill, compared with the Buddha's is as the fancy of a child set beside that of a grown man. The child loves the vague and the mysterious; the man prefers the definite and intelligible. And so it is not in any imagined inchoative past, but in the actual, palpitating present, the present that is always coming to be with each fresh moment that the Buddha bids us look for the fount of things. And the ignorance with which alone he seeks to deal is ignorance as it is found here and now in living beings—ignorance of ill, ignorance of the root of ill in craving, ignorance of the ceasing of ill through the ceasing of craving, and ignorance of the path that leads to the ceasing of ill; all four of them found where they always have been found and always are to be found, in the ever present now. Not in any kind of excogitated cosmology but in the data supplied by a closely analytic psychology does the Buddha find the light he has to throw upon the origin of imperfection we call a world. And this to see and understand, once more is to see and understand rightly.

Here the tracing out of the sequence of ill comes to an end. Further than this we cannot hope to go, for this ignorance we are. Each living creature that walks the earth is only another example of this ignorance corporealised, made visible, given local habitation and a name, and to attempt to get behind it is as vain to seek to climb a height by mounting upon one's own shoulders. Here only one thing is to be done—without delay to set to work and remove the ignorance that is productive of the undesirable thing. For where ignorance of ill is removed, where knowledge of the ill of limited, imperfect existence is fully overcome, there all motive for life-affirming action is withered at the root, and so all such action comes to an end. And where life-affirming activity is wholly at an end, consciousness, the central nucleus of a "self" of a fresh being, no longer can arise. Where consciousness does not arise, subject and object are not to be found, for these are only the inseparable corollaries of consciousness. Where subject and object are not, the six senses and their corresponding fields of action, the six classes of sense-objects, have no existence, since they are nothing but an expression of subject and object. Where senses and sense-objects do not exist, there can be no talk of contact taking place between them. Where there is no such contact there can be no sensation; where there is no sensation of any kind, no craving, there no thirst for pleasurable sensation can arise. Where no craving for sensation arises, there can be no grasping at, no clinging to sensation, or to objects, the external agents in sensation. Where there is no grasping, no clinging to sensation or sense-objects, there the process of becoming is deprived of its motive impulsion, and so comes to an end. And where there is no more becoming, there is no more birth and no more of all that follows birth to beings born—pain, distress, disease, old age, and death. Thus in strict logical sequence does ill come to an end through the ending of ignorance, and who so sees and understands this, he sees and understands rightly.

And the final component of Right Understanding in respect of ill is to understand that its untoward chain of succession is broken, its several links sundered and destroyed forever by the following of the excellent Eightfold Path made known by a Buddha.

The four chief elements that make up Right Understanding are thus these: the understanding that here is ill; the understanding of the sequence in which that ill arises; the understanding of the sequence in which that ill is caused to cease; and the understanding of the Path through which the sequence of ill is caused to cease. But it is not given to any of the sons of men to attain to a full and complete measure of this understanding upon the first occasion of its being put before him in words. The approach to fullness of Right Understanding can only be gradual, proceeding by slow degrees from a bare intellectual assent to the truth of its terms, to a conviction of the whole man that the case veritably is as said and the final absorption of the being of the man himself in the truth he has realised. Such absorption is really the goal towards which the Buddha's teaching points the way, the final achievement of him who follows that way to its ultimate end. Needless to say, that end can only be reached after long effort along the road that leads thither. And one of the stages along this road is that elementary measure of Right Understanding that consists simply in understanding what is evil and what is good—that is to say, what is that course of conduct that thwarts, hinders, retards progress towards the deliverance of the mind from attachment to existential life, and what is that course that promotes, conduces to, makes for that deliverance; as also in understanding what is the root that nourishes these two modes of behaviour, from what root springs that mode of behaviour that hinders deliverance, from what root grows that which helps towards it.

Who so has attained to this initial measure of Right Seeing and Understanding, he sees that killing and stealing and lying and lasciviousness and the drinking of strong drinks are things that present obstacles and hindrances upon his path towards deliverance from ill. He understands that they clog and hamper his feet so that they scarcely can move forward upon that path: and so seeing, so understanding, he eschews and shuns them to the end that his progress towards the goal may not be uselessly delayed. Such a one also sees the root that nourishes these hindering evils, understands that it has three roots or sprouts. First: selfish craving, the desire to have and to hold for oneself alone. Second: hatred, anger, aversion to one's fellow creatures in any of the manifold forms such aversion may assume. And third: delusion, the delusion that one is possessed of a self separate and distinct from that of every other creature, which delusion may be said to be the shoot that bears the other two, since craving to possess for self and hatred of others obviously are possible only where reigns the delusion that there exists a separate self.

And the man who has attained to this earlier measure of Right Understanding, he also understands what is good, what is that which makes for deliverance from all ill. He understands that it consists in abstaining from killing and stealing and lasciviousness and lying and the drinking of drinks that take the wits away, and shapes his life accordingly. He likewise sees and understands that the root of good, the root of all that makes for liberation, for freedom, for salvation from suffering and distress, lies in selflessness, in the cessation of all longing and striving for self alone; in love to all that lives, ceasing from every form of hatred and ill-will; and finally in wisdom, in clear-eyed perception of the utter baselessness in truth or fact, of the notion of separate selfhood. He sees and understands that in this clear-eyed perception, which once attained can never be lost, lies the sure source of all deeds of kindness and good will, all deeds that have for their object never the heedless aggrandisement and gratification of self alone, but always the good, the advantage and benefit of others simultaneously.

Such Right Understanding, when come to full fruition, becomes realisation, even as the other, is the last achievement of Buddhist effort; it too means and is final deliverance from the round of birth and death. And it also is to be realised through an approach made up of many slow and gradual stages. At first glimpsing but faintly comprehending only dimly what deeds are good and what evil, what deeds further and what delay his deliverance, a man begins, half-heartedly it may be and by no means at all times, to endeavour to do only such deeds as are good and to shun those that are evil. The effort put forth is not very great, so that result achieved is not very great either. But such as it is, it is not without its due effect. The slight degree of success in right doing thus achieved reacts upon the slight degree of Right Understanding that led to the effort made in that direction; in duly corresponding slight measure, it strengthens and clarifies that understanding, makes what was little a tiny degree less little, makes the little to be somewhat more. And now with Right Understanding thus in some small measure become clearer and stronger than it was before, the next effort of the man towards good and away from evil is by so much a less half-hearted, a more vigorous and determined effort, and hence achieves a greater degree of success. This success again reacts upon the understanding so as to clarify and strengthen it yet more, and again the understanding thus endowed with this fresh accession of clarity and strength makes possible a still higher degree of effort after right conduct. The whole procedure is like that of the cleansing of hands or feet. "As hand washes hand and foot washes foot," says a sutta, "so Right Conduct is purified by Right Understanding and Right Understanding by Right Conduct." Thus on and on these twain, conduct and understanding, by the mutual strengthening influence of each upon the other, gain depth and fullness in increasingly larger degrees until at length the highest possible degree of both is reached, the supreme summit of Right Understanding attained, and the mind delivered "with the deliverance that comes of wisdom;" that which in its feeble, elementary beginnings was the first step upon the Path, having become in its final perfection the last step, the winning to the goal.

Thus from lowliest levels does the Path lead on to the loftiest heights. Thus may each man just where he is, and as he is, begin to take those steps which, only maintained and persisted in, will bring him at length whither all the great and noble of the earth have made their way. For they too once stood where we now stand in the climb up the mound of perfection. But by patient, continuous endeavour they have attained; and even so we also may attain through the perfection of Right Understanding.

Applications of Dhamma

Siri Buddhasukh

Bodhi Leaves No. 41

First published: 1968

Applications of Dhamma

Transcendence

Transcendence is the chief characteristic virtue of Buddhism. In our daily devotions we remind ourselves of the Buddha's transcendental wisdom, which implies knowledge of all and attachment to none. Then we call to mind his purity, which, being absolute, surpasses the realm of all defilements (*kilesa*) and outflows (*āsavā*). Again, we focus our thoughts on his untrammelled loving kindness, which embraces all living beings, extending beyond the barriers of caste, creed, nationality and the like. In fact, we can think of him in countless other ways, but those ways may be summed up under the above-mentioned Threefold Nobility, which is the synopsis of his virtue and which intrinsically reflects one and the same characteristic virtue: transcendence.

For how could wisdom be full and final or, in Buddhist terminology, supramundane (*lokuttara*), without transcending the mundane conditions?

Again, how could purity be absolute without transcending once and for all the realm of passions and defilements?

And lastly, how could compassion or loving-kindness be untrammelled or all-embracing (*appamañña*) without transcending the barriers of pride and prejudice based on caste, creed, nationality, race, and the like?

But it is a sad fact that many people, including some Buddhists, have misunderstood, and thereby misinterpreted, this characteristic virtue of transcendence to the detriment of their own progress on the Buddha's Path. They often regard the virtue of transcendence as permitting negligence at the lower stages of development, treating it with cynical contempt, and only considering whatever is to be transcended at the highest stage. The following facts will serve to indicate the relevance of the virtue of transcendence at all stages in the practice of Buddhism and clarify the Buddhist attitude as far as the characteristic virtue of transcendence is concerned.

1. Three Steps of Advantage

Obviously, the ultimate goal of Buddhism is renunciation of the fleeting world, pleasure and enjoyment, for the sake of the unshakable and deathless condition of Nibbāna. But the Buddha knew how widely different sentient beings are with regard to their environment as well as their spiritual capacity for understanding and following his teaching. So he laid down two other, although lower steps of advantage, viz., the advantage obtainable in the present life (*diṭṭhadhammikattha*) and the advantage obtainable in the future life or lives (*samparāyikattha*). The first is purely earthly, whereas the second is half earthly and half spiritual. These two, however, are still on the mundane plane (*lokiya*), being conducive to rebirth (*vaṭṭagāmi*), and are the elementary and intermediate stages suitable for most people, whereas the third advantage aims at the supramundane (*lokuttara*) or breaking the circle of rebirth (*vivaṭṭagami*), and is reserved for the strong in heart and mind and will. With these three steps of advantage or practice well defined and distinguished, it is plain to see that Buddhism does not force the life of renunciation upon anybody who is not mature enough for such an advanced course of self-training.

2. Body and Mind

Buddhism being a system of practice for spiritual development, emphasis is laid more on the mind than on the body. But this does not mean that the body is to be totally neglected. It is by giving it proper care and attention, neither indulging its carnal desires nor neglecting its natural, purely physical needs, that real spiritual growth can be expected. This is maintaining the point of balance or, in Buddhist terminology, the Middle Way. Thus we can conclude that Buddhism does not neglect the proper care and attention given to the body.

Mindfulness regarding the body is the only way to ensure that neither of the two unskilful extremes is adopted when dealing with it. These two extremes—sensual indulgence and mortification of the flesh—were mentioned by the Buddha in his first discourse and thereafter he frequently explained their shortcomings as ways of action. The Middle Way is mindful attention towards the body, realizing thereby that it is conditioned and compounded of different elements, as well as being a collection of organs certain to decay sooner or later.

Instead of trying, ostrich-like, to disregard the hell of bodily ageing, death and dissolution, the Buddhist tradition insists that one must not attempt to repress awareness of these inevitable facts but bring them into the focus of the fully conscious mind by deliberately meditating upon them.

Then, having to some extent attained a detachment from the body, having lessened self-identification with it, the body may then be regarded as an "instrument of Dhamma." It will then become most precious and valuable a thing with which one is enabled to practise the Dhamma for one's own and others' benefit. But at first it cannot be regarded in this way; otherwise the dangers of conceit and the wrong view of "my body" may be strengthened.

3. *Economic Aspects of Living*

The Buddhist goal transcends that of economics, it is true, for whereas economics caters for the increase of wealth and gratification of desires, Buddhism advocates as its highest goal a life of simplicity and paucity of wants, and preaches the method of subduing and eliminating desires. But in the first step of advantage, which is purely worldly, Buddhism also stresses the acquisition of wealth through diligence and the safeguarding of the acquired wealth through being economical. This shows that the Buddha understood how indispensable money is to worldly matters and thus how important are the acquisition and the safeguarding of wealth, which is nothing but the economic aspect of the life of those who cannot as yet renounce the world altogether. So it is clear that Buddhism does not ignore the economic aspect of living.

This may be seen from the lives and laws of such great Buddhist rulers as the Emperor Asoka in India, or more recently King Mongkut in Thailand. They clearly desired the welfare of their subjects and led the way by showing them the practical application of loving-kindness, compassion, and sympathetic joy (*mettā, karuṇā, muditā*) to everyday life.

The modern concept of the welfare state that dispenses from its material wealth numerous benefits to the old, the poor, and the sick, remains an empty and bureaucratic idea unless its charities are given in the spirit of loving-kindness and so forth. Unfortunately this is not always the case and, therefore, many are found who express a preference for acts of benevolence performed by individuals who really desire the welfare of those whom they benefit.

4. *Worship with Flowers and Offerings*

Buddhism transcends the idea of clinging to the conventional methods of worship as the ideal way of showing love and respect towards the Buddha. We know this from the Buddha's attitude manifesting throughout his life and especially from his own words just before he passed away to the effect that the embodiment of his teaching into our daily lives and affairs is the highest worship his disciples can hope to offer to him. But it does not mean that the kind of worship with flowers and offerings is to be banned. For it is the proper evaluation of each method of worship that will prevent Buddhists from extolling one and condemning another. Thus the Buddhist method may transcend, but it does not ban, the kind of worship performed with flowers and offerings.

Many Buddhists, at the time of making these traditional offerings, use the occasion for a little discursive meditation. Thus, the Buddha is remembered when lighting the candle or lamp, while the Dhamma which is fragrant with good conduct and other fair qualities is thought of when the incense sticks are offered. The offering of flowers is then made recollecting the bright and beautiful virtues of the ariyan (noble) Sangha.

Besides offerings, worship is traditionally made by the triple prostration of the body as well as by placing together one's palms. These are attitudes of reverence recognized in many religions. In Buddhism, it is well understood that provided that they are accompanied by mindfulness, they help to promote faith, humility and gentleness in the individual performing them and are thus for his own spiritual benefit. Of course, they have nothing to do with the worship of an idol. Much the same may be said of the verses and passages chanted by Buddhists at this time. They are often in Pali and describe the virtues of the Triple Gem, thus expressing the devotion and gratitude of the follower and his inward recollection of them.

5. *Two Grades of Truth*

Again, the Buddhist ultimate truth (*paramattha-sacca*) transcends the realm of worldly apposition (*loka-sammuti*), worldly definition (*loka-paññatti*) and worldly ways of expression (*loka-vohāra*), but never does Buddhism deny the value and truth of those worldly attributes on their own plane. The Buddha introduced the *anattā* (non-self) doctrine as the unique aspect of Buddhism, but in matters of everyday life he also spoke in terms of *attā* like other people, when it concerned non-philosophical, practical affairs. The Buddha analysed man into the five aggregates of existence (*khandha*), void of such designations as "father," "mother," "I," "mine," and the like, but he never rejected the relative validity of such designations in the realm of conventional truth (*sammuti-sacca*). Hence the vital and irreconcilable difference between Buddhism and the various doctrines of idealistic nihilism which categorically deny the relative truth in the relative sense of these terms on the relative plane to which they belong. Here again, it is beyond doubt that Buddhism transcends, but does not deny, the relative or suppositional truth (*sammuti-sacca*) on its own plane. On the other hand, it does not regard relative truth as being the only reality, as does materialism.

6. *Two Steps of Merit*

With all these aforementioned facts at hand, it is now fairly safe to conclude that the transcendental virtue of Buddhism never implies negligence or contempt of the lower stages of development that cannot be ignored if one wishes to attain to the higher stages and the final goal. For everything has its own value in its own place, and a wise man is he who knows how to evaluate things justly, neither overrating nor underestimating anything. The first step of a ladder is lower than the second, it is true, but its value as a means by which a person is helped to the second can by no means be ignored and nobody in his right mind would ever dream of treating it with contempt even though he has already risen to the second or a higher step.

Hence merit (*kusala*) in Buddhism is in a sense of two grades: viz., *vaṭṭagāmī* and *vivaṭṭagāmi*. The former, being comparatively easy, leads a person to a better rebirth with more felicities of life and may be called mundane merit (*lokiya-kusala*), whereas the latter, which is more difficult, is conducive to transcending the cycle of rebirth and may be called supramundane merit (*lokuttara-kusala*).

In the realm of the former, there is no objection or prohibition that a person should seek for prestige and power for himself or for his country or for both, provided that he uses means that are consistent with Dhamma or the law of righteousness on the mundane level.

The teaching of Buddhism is that one's deliberate action (*kamma*) will very likely be followed by experiences resulting therefrom (*phala, vipāka*). Skilful action (*kusala*) is productive of pleasurable resultants, while pain will follow him who acts against Dhamma or the Law of Righteousness. A bhikkhu or other person living a life of renunciation is naturally spared a great many of the conflicts which arise for the layman. The layman especially has therefore to act in such situations by bearing *kamma* and its fruits in mind while measuring his actions against the high standard set by Buddhist wisdom (*paññā*) and compassion (*karuṇā*). Naturally, the Buddhist who deeply appreciates and practises the precepts formulated by his Teacher, avoids killing and therefore warfare, whenever possible. Any decision to take part in armed combat that he may make, as in defence of his country against invaders, is his own responsibility and he must be prepared to shoulder the burden of any unskilful actions (such as killing) that he may commit.

To sum up then, the following facts may serve to remind Buddhists, and non-Buddhists as well, of how in Buddhism the virtue of transcendence never implies negligence or a sweeping condemnation of what is to be transcended except that at the highest stage, for:

1. Buddhism transcends, but does not condemn, the life of a layman.
2. Buddhism transcends, but does not neglect, proper care and attention given to the body.
3. Buddhism transcends, but does not ignore, economic aspects of living.
4. Buddhism transcends, but does not prohibit, worship with flowers and offerings.
5. Buddhism transcends, but does not deny, conventional or suppositional truth.
6. Buddhism transcends, but does not censure, the love of and devoted service to one's own country.

— §§§ —

Buddhism: A Method of Mind Training

Leonard Bullen

Bodhi Leaves No. 42

First published: 1969

Buddhism: A Method of Mind Training

When you hear something about Buddhism in the daily news you usually think of it having a background of huge idols and yellow-robed monks, with a thick atmosphere of incense fumes. You never feel that there is anything in it for you, except, maybe, an exotic spectacle.

But is that all there is in Buddhism? Do the news photographers take pictures of the real Buddhism? Do the glossy magazines show you the fundamentals, or only the externals?

Let us see, then, what Buddhism really is, Buddhism as it was originally expounded and as it still exists underneath the external trappings and trimmings.

Although generally regarded as a religion, Buddhism is basically a method of cultivating the mind. It is true that, with its monastic tradition and its emphasis on ethical factors, it possesses many of the surface characteristics that Westerners associate with religion. However, it is not theistic, since it affirms that the universe is governed by impersonal laws and not by any creator-god; it has no use for prayer, for the Buddha was a teacher and not a god; and it regards devotion not as a religious obligation but as a means of expressing gratitude to its founder and as a means of self-development. Thus it is not a religion at all from these points of view.

Again, Buddhism knows faith only in the sense of confidence in the way recommended by the Buddha. A Buddhist is not expected to have faith or to believe in anything merely because the Buddha said it, or because it is written in the ancient books, or because it has been handed down by tradition, or because others believe it. He may, of course, agree with himself to take the Buddha-doctrine as a working hypothesis and to have confidence in it; but he is not expected to accept anything unless his reason accepts it. This does not mean that everything can be demonstrated rationally, for many points lie beyond the scope of the intellect and can be cognized only by the development of higher faculties. But the fact remains that there is no need for blind acceptance of anything in the Buddha-doctrine.

Buddhism is a way of life based on the training of the mind. Its one ultimate aim is to show the way to complete liberation from suffering by the attainment of the Unconditioned, a state beyond the range of the normal untrained mind. Its immediate aim is to strike at the roots of suffering in everyday life.

All human activity is directed, either immediately or remotely, towards the attainment of happiness in some form or other; or, to express the same thing in negative terms, all human activity is directed towards liberation from some kind of unsatisfactoriness or dissatisfaction. Dissatisfaction, then, can be regarded as the starting point in human activity, with happiness as its ultimate goal.

Dissatisfaction, the starting point in human activity, is also the starting point in Buddhism; and this point is expressed in the formula of the Four Basic Statements, which set out the fact of dissatisfaction, its cause, its cure, and the method of its cure.

The First Basic Statement can be stated thus: "Dissatisfaction is inescapable in en-self-ed life."

In its original meaning, the word which is here rendered as "dissatisfaction" and which is often translated as "suffering" embraces the meanings not only of pain, sorrow, and displeasure, but also of everything that is unsatisfactory, ranging from acute physical pain and severe mental anguish to slight tiredness, boredom, or mild disappointment.

Sometimes the term is rendered as "dissatisfaction" or "unsatisfactoriness;" in some contexts these are perhaps more accurate, while at other times the word "suffering" is more expressive. For this reason we shall use both "suffering" and "dissatisfaction" or "unsatisfactoriness" according to context.

In some translations of the original texts it is stated that birth is suffering, sickness is suffering, old age is suffering, and pleasure is suffering. In English, this last statement fails to make sense; but if we restate it as "pleasure is unsatisfactory" it becomes more readily understandable, for all pleasure is impermanent and is eventually succeeded by its opposite, and from this point of view at least it is unsatisfactory.

Now the Buddha-doctrine teaches that dissatisfaction or suffering is inescapable in en-self-ed life; and the term "en-self-ed life" needs some explanation. In brief, the doctrine teaches that the self, considered as a fixed, unchanging eternal soul, has no reality.

The central core of every being is not an unchanging soul but a life-current, an ever-changing stream of energy which is never the same for two consecutive seconds. The self, considered as an eternal soul, therefore, is a delusion, and when regarded from the ultimate standpoint it has no reality; and it is only within this delusion of selfhood that ultimate suffering can exist. When the self-delusion is finally transcended and the final enlightenment is attained, the ultimate state which lies beyond the relative universe is reached. In this ultimate state, the Unconditioned, suffering is extinguished; but while any element of selfhood remains, even though it is a delusion, suffering remains potentially within it.

We must understand, then, that the First Basic Statement does not mean that suffering is inescapable; it means that suffering is inescapable in enselfed life, or while the delusion of selfhood remains.

We can now move on to the Second Basic Statement, which says: "The origin of dissatisfaction is craving."

If you fall on a slippery floor and suffer from bruises, you say that the cause of your suffering is the slippery floor. In an immediate sense you are right, of course, and to say that the cause of your bruises is craving fails to make sense.

But the Second Statement does not refer to individual cases or to immediate causes. It means that the integrating force that holds together the life-current is self-centered craving; for this life-current—this self-delusion—contains in itself the conditions for suffering, while the slippery floor is merely an occasion for suffering.

It is obviously impossible, by the nature of the world we live in, to cure suffering by the removal of all the occasions for suffering; whereas it is possible in Buddhism to strike at its prime or fundamental cause. Therefore the Third Basic Statement states: "Liberation may be achieved by destroying craving."

It is self-centered craving that holds together the forces which comprise the life-current, the stream of existence which we call the self; and it is only with self-delusion that unsatisfactoriness or suffering can exist. By the destruction of that which holds together the delusion of the self, the root cause of suffering is also destroyed.

The ultimate aim of Buddhist practice, then, is to annihilate the self. This is where a great deal of misunderstanding arises, and naturally so; but once it is realized that to annihilate the self is to annihilate a delusion, this misunderstanding disappears. When the delusion is removed, the reality appears; so that to destroy delusion is to reveal the reality. The reality cannot be discovered while the delusion of self continues to obscure it.

Now what is this reality which appears when the delusion is removed? The ultimate reality is the Unconditioned, called also the Unborn, the Unoriginated, the Uncreated, and the Uncompounded. We can, inadequately and not very accurately, describe it as a positive state of being. It is characterized by supreme bliss and complete freedom from suffering and is so utterly different from ordinary existence that no real description of it can be given. The Unconditioned can be indicated—up to a point—only by stating what it is not; for it is beyond words and beyond thought.

Hence, in the Buddhist texts, the Unconditioned is often explained as the final elimination from one's own mind, of greed, hatred and delusion. This, of course, also implies the perfection of the opposite positive qualities of selflessness, loving-kindness, and wisdom.

The attainment of the Unconditioned is the ultimate aim of all Buddhist practice, and is the same as complete liberation from dissatisfaction or suffering. This brings us to the last of the Four Basic Statements: "The way of liberation is the Noble Eightfold Path."

The eight factors of the path are these:

1. Right Understanding, a knowledge of the true nature of existence.
2. Right Thought, thought free from sensuality, ill-will and cruelty.
3. Right Speech, speech without falsity, gossip, harshness, and idle babble.
4. Right Action, or the avoidance of killing, stealing and adultery.
5. Right Livelihood, an occupation that harms no conscious living being.
6. Right Effort, or the effort to destroy the defilements of the mind and to cultivate wholesome qualities.
7. Right Mindfulness, the perfection of the normal faculty of attention.
8. Right Concentration, the cultivation of a collected, focused mind through meditation.

Now you will see that in this Noble Eightfold Path there is nothing of an essentially religious nature; it is more a sort of moral psychology.

But in the East as well as in the West, people as a whole demand external show of some sort, and—on the outside at least—the non-essentials have assumed more importance than the essentials.

While some external features in the practice of Buddhism must of necessity vary according to environment, the essential and constant characteristics of that practice are summed up in the following outline of the Noble Eightfold Path, the Middle Way between harmful extremes, as taught by the Buddha.

Although it is convenient to speak of the various aspects of the Eightfold Path as eight steps, they are not to be regarded as separate steps, taken one after another. On the contrary, each one must be practised along with the others, and it might perhaps be better to think of them as if they were eight parallel lanes within the one road rather than eight successive steps.

The first step of this path, right understanding, is primarily a matter of seeing things as they really are—or at least trying to do so without self-deceit or evasion. In another sense, right understanding commences as an intellectual appreciation of the nature of existence, and as such it can be regarded as the beginning of the path; but, when the path has been followed to the end, this merely intellectual appreciation is supplanted by a direct and penetrating discernment of the principles of the teaching first accepted intellectually.

While right understanding can be regarded as the complete understanding of the Buddha doctrine, it is based on the recognition of three dominating characteristics of the relative universe, of the universe of time, form and matter. These three characteristics can briefly be set out in this way:

1. Impermanence: all things in the relative universe are unceasingly changing.
2. Dissatisfaction: some degree of suffering or dissatisfaction is inherent in en-selfed life, or in life within the limitations of the relative universe and personal experience.
3. Egolessness: no being—no human being or any other sort of being—possesses a fixed, unchanging, eternal soul or self. Instead, every being consists of an ever-changing current of forces, an ever-changing flux of material and mental phenomena, like a river which is always moving and is never still for a single second.

The self, then, is not a static entity but an ever-changing flux. This dynamic concept of existence is typical of deeper Buddhist thought; there is nothing static in life, and since it is ever-flowing you must learn to flow with it.

Another aspect of right understanding is the recognition that the universe runs its course on the basis of a strict sequence of cause and effect, or of action and reaction, a sequence just as invariable and just as exact in the mental or moral realm as in the physical. In accordance with this law of moral action and reaction, all morally good or wholesome will-actions eventually bring to the doer happiness at some time, while unwholesome or morally bad will-actions bring suffering to the doer.

The effects of wholesome and unwholesome will-actions—that is to say, the happiness and suffering that result from them—do not generally follow immediately; there is often a considerable time-lag, for the resultant happiness and suffering can arise only when appropriate conditions are present. The results may not appear within the present lifetime. Thus at death there is normally a balance of "merit" which has not yet brought about its experience of happiness; and at the same time there is also a balance of "demerit" which has not yet given rise to the suffering which is to be its inevitable result.

After death, the body disintegrates, of course, but the life-current continues, not in the form of an unchanging soul, but in the form of an ever-changing stream of energy. Immediately after death a new being commences life to carry on this life current; but the new being is not necessarily a human being, and the instantaneous rebirth may take place on another plane of existence. But in any case, the new being is a direct sequel to the being that has just died.

Thus the new being becomes an uninterrupted continuation of the old being, and the life-current is unbroken. The new being inherits the balance of merit built up by the old being, and this balance of merit will inevitably bring happiness at some future time.

At the same time, the new being inherits the old being's balance of demerit, which will bring suffering at some time in the future.

In effect, in the sense of continuity, the new being is the same as the old being. In just the same way—that is, in the sense of continuity only—an old man is the same as the young man he once was, the young man is the same as the boy he once was, and the boy is the same as the baby he once was. But the identity of the old man with the young man, and with the boy, and with the baby, is due only to continuity; there is no other identity.

Everything in the universe changes from day to day and from moment to moment, so that every being at this moment is a slightly different being from that of the moment before; the only identity is due to continuity. In the same way, the being that is reborn is different from the previous one that died; but the identity due to continuity remains as before.

These teachings are basic to the Buddha-doctrine—the illusory nature of the self, the law of action and reaction in the moral sphere, and the rebirth of the life-forces—but there is no need for anyone to accept anything that does not appeal to his reason. Acceptance of any particular teaching is unimportant; what is important is the continual effort to see things as they really are, without self-deceit or evasion.

So much for a brief outline of the doctrine under the heading of right understanding. The second step, right thought or aim, is a matter of freeing the intellectual faculties from adverse emotional factors, such as sensuality, ill-will, and cruelty, which render wise and unbiased decisions impossible.

Right speech, right action, and right livelihood together make up the moral section of the path, their function being to keep the defilements of the mind under control and to prevent them from reaching adverse expression. These defilements, however, cannot be completely eradicated by morality alone, and the other steps of the path must be applied to cleanse the mind completely of its defilements.

Now in the next step—right effort—we enter the sphere of practical psychology, for right effort in this context means effort of will. In other words, the sixth step of the path is self-discipline, the training of the will in order to prevent and overcome those states of mind that retard development, and to arouse and cultivate those that bring about mental progress.

The seventh step of the path is also one of practical psychology; this is the step called right mindfulness, and it consists of the fullest possible development of the ordinary faculty of attention. It is largely by the development of attention—expanded and intensified awareness—that the mind can eventually become capable of discerning things as they really are.

The primary function of the seventh step, right mindfulness, is to develop an increasing awareness of the unreality of the self. However, it functions also by continually improving the normal faculty of attention, thus equipping the mind better to meet the problems and stresses of the workaday world.

In the Buddha-way, mindfulness consists of developing the faculty of attention so as to produce a constant awareness of all thoughts that arise, all words that are spoken, and all actions that are done, with a view to keeping them free from self-interest, from emotional bias, and from self-delusion.

Right mindfulness has many applications in the sphere of everyday activities. For example, it can be employed to bring about a sharpened awareness, a clear comprehension, of the motives of these activities, and this clear comprehension of motive is extremely important.

In right concentration, the last of the eight steps, the cultivation of higher mind-states—up to the meditative absorptions—is undertaken, and these higher mind-states serve to unify, purify, and strengthen the mind for the achievement of liberating insight.

In this ultimate achievement the delusion of selfhood, with its craving and suffering, is transcended and extinguished.

This penetrating insight is the ultimate goal of all Buddhist practices, and with it comes a direct insight into the true nature of life, culminating in realization of the Unconditioned. While the Unconditioned is the extinction of self, it is nevertheless not mere non-existence or annihilation, for the extinction of self is nothing but the extinction of a delusion. Every description of the Unconditioned must fail, for it lies not only beyond words but beyond even thought; and the only way to know it is to follow the Noble Eightfold Path to its end.

This, then, is the original Buddhism; this is the Buddhism of the Noble Eightfold Path, of the path that leads from the bondage of self to liberating insight into reality.

— §§§ —

The Relevance of Buddhism in the Modern World

Princess Poon Pismai Diskul

Bodhi Leaves No. 43

First published: 1969

The Relevance of Buddhism in the Modern World

Throughout history, the practice, adherence and belief in religion has been a virtually universal aspect of human society. And as a rule, the increase in complexity and sophistication of a given culture has borne with it an accompanying increase in the level of ethical and philosophical development of that society's religious thought.

Today, however, the world witnesses a level of civilization and social complexity far surpassing that of any previous era. Yet out of the great thoughts and discoveries of our time, no new major religion has evolved. Whatever new religious concepts may have appeared, they have failed to reach the masses of humanity in the form of altering basic beliefs and practices. Most of the new reforms that modern institutions sometimes announce with pride are actually negative in character; that is, the termination of outmoded practices and the relinquishment or reinterpretation of embarrassing dogmas.

Rather than new religions, we find for the first time mass atheism, scepticism, pragmatism, and indifference. True, these anti—or non-religious—attitudes existed in earlier times, even back into ancient Greece and India. But in olden times they were largely confined to select groups of philosophers or other exclusive minorities. Today these ideas have penetrated to nearly all social levels, regardless of education, among the advanced nations of the world. They are virtually an instituted dogma in the communist nations, while in Europe and America they have insidiously encroached upon the traditional forms of religion. Educated members of the free Asian nations have begun to follow in the same direction.

It is not religion alone that seems threatened. Ethics, philosophy, metaphysics and mysticism also appear to wither before the onslaught of technology, industrialization, science and psychology. Such concepts as justice, virtue, infinite being and transcendental absolute that occupied the minds of the ancients are now challenged as being hypothetical at best. At worst they are said to be pure verbiage and syllogisms lacking empirical and experimental verification. And at this point the essential ingredients of metaphysics become lost. Mystical experiences, once regarded as communion with the infinite, now take the status of psychological phenomena, altered states of the nervous system better induced by chemistry than by meditation or prayer. Ethics as a philosophy suffers the same fate as metaphysics. Ethics as behavioural codes for conducting one's life are, in the eyes of traditional moralists, becoming mocked and disregarded. To those with less rigid standards they are becoming radically altered with new values appearing.

Such are the features of the modern age. What then of religion? Even the newest of the existing major religions, Islam, is well past its first millennium. Christianity, rapidly approaches its two-thousandth birthday, while Taoism, Buddhism, Confucianism, Zoroastrianism and Jainism all share roughly contemporary origins dating around 500 BC. Judaism and Hinduism extend even further back into antiquity.

Our religions, then, are all products of bygone eras. They arose at a time when men thought in terms of magic, spirits and myths. Insanity was demon possession; hallucinations, messages from the divine. The sun moved around a stationary world, and one's fate could be altered by magic and rituals or by flattery and offerings to supernatural powers.

Banana leaves as wrappings and thatched grass for roofs were used for centuries. With the advent of paper, plastics and sheet metal they quickly fell into relative disuse. Will the same happen to religion as men learn to modify and control their environment and unlock the mysteries of creation? Will devout congregations be sought out and scrutinized by anthropologists and psychologists in the same manner that these scholars now pursue the Australian aborigines?

Only history will tell. Religion may not necessarily die. In Japan, one of the most modernized nations in the world, new and well organized sects with radical teachings have in a period of 20 or 30 years mushroomed to firmly embrace many millions of converts. Yet the nature of these sects appears to specifically relate to the emotional needs of certain segments of Japanese culture, and their impact outside of Japan has to date been negligible. Is religion anything more than a formalized displacement of human frustrations and insecurity, reinforced by indoctrination, utilizing the human capacity to feel and shun guilt, and offering hope when human endeavours have reached their limits? In the words of Marx, "the opiate of the people." In the words of psychiatry, a formalized cultural neurosis.

Each religion must endeavour to answer these questions and challenges on its own. To do so honestly requires a detachment from vested interests and the courage to avoid rationalization under the guise of reinterpretation. As a Buddhist, I shall endeavour to answer these questions within the framework of Buddhist thought, and such will occupy the remainder of this writing.

First of all, before any meaningful approach can be taken towards a so-called Buddhist position, one must clarify what form of Buddhism one is considering. The religious movement started in the Fifth Century BC by Gautama Buddha has, in the intervening centuries, taken on diverse forms and paths of development as it spread to new lands and cultures and intermingled with local beliefs and practices. Thus today we find different schools of Buddhism as unlike one another as they are from non-Buddhist religions. A Theravadan Buddhist monk may find himself closer in thought and spirit to a western psychologist than to a priest of the Japanese Jodo-Shin Shu sect. And the Jodo priest, if one could disregard name and form, would share much in common with many American clergymen on points where he would differ with Southeast Asian Buddhism.

I wish then to confine my discussion to the oldest known form of Buddhism that is, Theravada Buddhism which is the prevailing religion of Burma, Thailand, Cambodia, Laos and Ceylon. But I must be even more specific than this for I do not wish to discuss the various local traditions, ceremonies and later schools of thought that have become attached to Theravada. Rather I shall discuss the earliest known form of Buddhist thought—the teaching of the Buddha as recorded in the Pali language scriptures known as the Suttas and Vinaya. If one confines his attention to these earliest known Buddhist scriptures, the Western reader is often surprised by the contemporary ideas contained in writings that date back over 2000 years.

Perhaps most appealing to the modern mind (whether scientifically oriented or not) was the Buddhist emphasis upon free and rational inquiry. "Do not believe out of blind faith, do not believe merely on scripture, do not believe on mere tradition," said the Buddha. "Do not believe me just because it is I who speak. But when you have seen, examined and experienced for yourself, then accept it." Only the mind freed of vested interests and prejudices will really be able to so see and truly understand. Thus we read: "If others speak against me or against our order, be not angered or dejected. If they praise us, be not elated. Rather analyze what has been said and weigh its merits." The Buddha made full use of logic, debate and reasoning, and in so doing revealed a remarkable ability to resolve philosophical dilemmas that were purely semantic in origin. This he could do because his logic was based upon experiential data rather than metaphysical. He placed experience before logic in his quest for truth, and when he did use logic, it was based upon facts readily admitted by all. Instead of commenting upon ultimate reality, he spoke of craving and sorrow. He frequently declined to expound upon ultimate origins and post-mortem existence and instead spoke of ordinary human experience in the immediate present. For, he explained, it is only in the here and now that we can act and thus affect our destinies.

Thus the Buddha taught no concept of a sin of disbelief. One is not damned because of a lack of faith, but rather suffers by one's own ignorance when one acts contrary to natural law. The Buddha never claimed divinity or a monopoly on truth. The truth was there for any man to find. His authority lay only in the fact that he had discovered it and could show others the way to this discovery.

In order to explain the central concepts of Buddhist teaching and practice we should first note the way in which Buddhism views man and his relationship to the world about him. For regardless of the oft-noted discrepancies between belief and conduct, our world view cannot help but influence the way in which we approach life's problems. For example, a man who firmly believes that all things are made by and governed by a personal and loving God will most likely direct a large part of his efforts towards beseeching that God in times of crisis, if not at all times.

Buddhism has no such personal God. The Buddha regarded the question of ultimate beginnings as irrelevant to the problems of life in the present. Change and cause and effect are the paramount features of the Buddhist concept of the universe. All things mental, physical and social go through an unending process of birth, growth, decay and death. Nothing finite is static, immortal or unchanging. Whatever has an origin is subject to cessation, be it man or mountain, consciousness or constellation. And what is it that regulates this unending flow of flux and mutation? The answer is cause and effect. Each existing condition becomes the cause of future conditions and these effects in turn become the causes of conditions which arise after them. Even the world itself will, after many eons of time, wear away. But other worlds have existed before, and others will continue to arise into the unending future. There need not then be a beginning or an end to time but rather eternal cause and effect with world evolutions and dissolutions stretching back into the infinite past and continuing into the infinite future. All of these concepts are clearly stated in the Pali scriptures and require no degree of alteration or reinterpretation to find compatibility with the views of modern science.

Against such a philosophical background, Buddhist psychology takes an extremely radical position among the ancient schools of thought but a position that is quite modern when compared to contemporary psychology. Mind and body are not seen as a dichotomy but rather are regarded as interacting and interdependent phenomena that together comprise the individual. Mind does not arise without body or body without mind. And that aspect of the personality that we call the psyche is not itself a single, self-willed and independent entity. Rather it is an aggregate of memories, sensations, thoughts, desires and perceptions that continue to change from moment to moment throughout each waking day and continually adopt new attributes or components while abandoning or modifying old ones during the course of a lifetime. In Buddhism, this is referred to as *anattā* or "soullessness"; that is, man is not a soul or immutable spirit but instead is a dynamic, ever-changing psycho-physical process.

Such is the way in which Buddhism views man and the world.

How does this relate to the religion as lived and practised?

In Buddhist thought the central issue in life is neither philosophical in the sense of resolving ultimate mysteries nor religious in the sense of worship, grace and salvation. Rather, the prime concern is happiness and sorrow. There are moments of true happiness and fulfilment and moments of sorrow, frustration, irritation and despair. Whether it be the delights of heaven, the satisfaction of a task well done, the joy of unselfish love or the sweet taste of good foods, it is some sort of pleasurable experience or the expectation of such that makes life worthwhile and gives positive value to our existence. Conversely, be it the agonies of hell, the loss of loved ones, humiliation, physical illness or the dread of such things, there are moments of negative value that we continually struggle to avoid.

As already stated, the Buddha's teachings resemble those of science in that all things mental or physical come about through cause and effect, and pleasurable and painful mental states are no exception. Thus the solution to living is to understand those factors that produce desirable or undesirable states of mind and with such understanding guide our lives in such away as to minimize the unwholesome while developing the wholesome to its maximum possible realization. Consequently the central teaching of Buddhism is the Four Noble Truths.

The first of the Four Noble Truths simply states that suffering, frustration, discomfort and unwanted experiences in general are an inherent aspect of life. The second states that the primary cause of such discomforts is desire. Third we are told that suffering can be overcome, and fourth is the means by which this is done.

The last of these Four Noble Truths, known as the Eightfold Path, thus forms the basis of Buddhist practice. It includes the disciplines, the practices and the insights by which one attempts to grow spiritually.

Impulses, feelings and desires determine our behaviour and also our relative happiness or sorrow. Therefore, the purpose of the Eightfold Path is to produce by means of discipline, self-understanding and intellect a new and better human being and to enable one to progressively mature towards the relative or absolute realization of specific psychological goals. These goals are both negative and positive. On the negative side one seeks the eradication of greed, hatred, egoism, delusion, apathy and anxiety. The positive goals are to cultivate and develop love, compassion, equanimity, wisdom and insight. Greed, hatred and other unwholesome mental states are not only predisposed to sorrowful consequences; in addition they are in and of themselves agitating and discomforting. Conversely, love and compassion are more than forerunners of happy conditions; by their very nature they are meaningful and rewarding experiences.

As I have already stated, Buddhism regards the human mind as a compounded phenomenon of various attributes and qualities.

Consequently, the techniques for development and purification of the mind must likewise be multidimensional and varied in accordance with individual needs. Educating the mind to right understanding; guiding speech, habits and profession into harmonious life patterns; cultivation of discipline and energy, and meditative stilling of the mind to bring about awareness of subtle thoughts and feeling that normally escape awareness; these are the techniques and practices by which one progresses along the Eightfold Path. This is the practice of Buddhism, the living of Buddhism as originally taught by the Buddha himself.

Thus, one can question whether or not Buddhism was ever intended to be a religion in the usual sense of the word. For it advocated no form of worship, ceremony, prayer or appeal to supernatural intervention.

Buddhist ethical values develop as a logical consequence of what has just been discussed, and the result is a system of ethics founded neither upon tradition nor upon revelation. Acknowledging that actions are preceded first by thought and motivation, we see that good and evil originate from the mind. Thus, a mind that has realised the Buddhist goals of subduing greed, hatred and egoism while developing love, wisdom and compassion is a mind that will have a natural and spontaneous virtue. The need for arbitrary rules of conduct will be greatly lessened, and one's goodness will be genuine rather than enforced or premeditated.

The great advantage of such an ethical system in the modern world is that it transcends but does not contradict the mores of cultural and national boundaries. At the same time it can be applied in a variety of different cultural circumstances with or without regard to tradition, history or taboo.

Therefore, while Buddhism proceeds from a very different set of premises than most other religions, we note a nearly complete agreement as to the standards of ethical conduct: love, kindness, charity and generosity are universally hailed by all of man's great religions regardless of whether their doctrines are built upon revelation, mysticism, metaphysics or psychological insights. Whether they teach divine creation or cause and effect, they all teach kindness. In addition, Buddhism takes a further step in this direction; that is, it teaches how to achieve these ethical ideals as living realities. It not only teaches to love; by psychological practices it tells how to achieve the genuine feeling that is love. For love and compassion, like all other aspects of this universe, arise through cause and effect.

In our discussion of Buddhism to this point, we see it as a system of psychological principles and practices that an individual can apply to the benefit of his own spiritual advancement and emotional wellbeing. Thus, the prime value of Buddhism in the modern world is that it shows one a way to happiness and peace of mind regardless of political and social environment. However, it would be erroneous to assume that the Buddha's doctrine was social and intra-personal to the exclusion of concern for human relationships and society at large.

The reason for emphasis upon individual development was founded upon the principle that the blind cannot lead the blind; or as the Buddha stated, "one, himself sunk in the mire of greed and delusion, cannot pull another out of that mire." One should first purify oneself to be able to show the way to others. The numerous instances in both ancient and modern times of religious and political atrocities committed by men who sincerely believed that they were serving the causes of justice and righteousness show the wisdom of this premise.

We can only have a better world when we first have better people. Fear, jealousy, egocentrism, hatred and greed are the original causes of human strife, be it petty crime or global war. Education, legislation and arbitration, while useful countermeasures, will not suffice to penetrate to the core of human motivation and alter one's basic ambitions and response patterns. Buddhism is structured to do just this. In fact such is its primary concern.

Personality cannot be separated from society. While the sum total of personalities determines the character and quality of a given society, conversely society influences and formulates the development of personality. This fact was readily acknowledged by the Buddha. He did not advocate social reforms such as we think of today but did deal directly with the social injustices of his time. Perhaps the best example is the caste system. He did not advocate a social revolution to replace this system, but any person who became a Buddhist ceased to have caste identity and thus was no longer subject to caste regulations. He thereby afforded men and women a way to escape from this social injustice, and at the same time he refuted the religious and philosophical rationalizations by which the priests and ruling castes attempted to justify the institution. In similar manner he opposed slavery and elevated the social status of women.

Recognizing that civilizations have flourished under a variety of different political systems and that, because of the universal law of change no society or culture will endure forever, the Buddha did not advocate any particular type of government. When speaking of monarchies, he said the responsibility lay with the king, and the king should cultivate justice, charity, compassion and virtue, both for the prosperity of the nation and as an example for the government ministers and common citizens. A few democratic states existed at the time of the Buddha, and of these he said that they would continue to flourish so long as the citizens could assemble and meet in harmony and would maintain good moral standards.

In the centuries following the Buddha, his followers built hospitals and rest houses in accordance with his teaching of compassion.

The great Indian emperor, Asoka, in the third century BC as a result of his conversion to Buddhism, stopped all wars and conquests, drained swamps, built wells and carried out other acts of public welfare. Other Buddhist rulers have followed this example.

The Buddha declined to preach his doctrine to a starving man until that man had been fed. And of illness he said: "Whosoever would honour me, whosoever would follow me, whosoever would take to my advice, he should wait upon the sick." And to his disciples he said: "Go forth into the world to spread the Teaching for the benefit, welfare, and happiness of all creatures."

Social ethics is but one aspect of the Teaching. Its primary concern is the reduction (and, finally, the elimination) of greed, anger, delusion and suffering. But these primary goals naturally and logically lead to a social ethic and one that operates independently of political, theological or doctrinal ideologies. For it works as follows: as men learn to lessen the greed, hatred and egoism that smoulder in their hearts, and as kindness and compassion gain prominence in human motivations, then will men strive to better the world in whatever way their immediate situation affords. For example, it may be food given to a hungry stranger, or it may be participation in a multi-million dollar campaign against world hunger.

May all beings be well and happy and in peace.

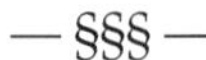

Three Mental Faculties and Guarding the Doors of the Senses

Two Essays

Dr. Elizabeth Ashby

BODHI LEAVES NO. 44

First published: 1969

Three Mental Faculties—Intellect, Intelligence and Intuition

Reprinted from *Sangha*, 1961

In Western Buddhist literature we often find intellect and intuition contrasted with one another, usually to the disadvantage of intellect. This is a very short-sighted view, for both are necessary for the understanding and practice of Dhamma.

The intellect is the reasoning faculty in man. It sees things in their right proportions. It investigates, analyses and discriminates. It accumulates knowledge, and is inclined to forget that "knowledge" isn't "wisdom." Too much stress on intellect produces mental dryness, harsh judgments, and a lack of *mettā* and compassion. Another danger is that investigation may become mere idle speculation. "Speculative views" about the subjects that the Buddha refused to define will lead us into the wilds of sceptical doubt, with all the mental suffering that involves. Another danger is opinionatedness—the canker of clinging to views as in the case of certain Brahmins of old who declared: "This alone is the truth; all else is falsehood!"

Therefore one of the early Zen Patriarchs went so far as to say: "Do not seek after the true; Only cease to cherish opinions." The cherishing of opinions leads to disputes and to vexation, for we wound one another "with the weapon of the tongue."

Intuition is the faculty that perceives truth without having it demonstrated or explained. It feels the truth before the intellect can grasp it and turn it into concepts. Hence intuition is closely allied to the emotions, and this constitutes a danger because the emotions go hand-in-hand with the imagination, and an imagined "truth" may be mistaken for "real truth." This happens because intuition functions on both the mundane and the transcendental plane (*lokuttara*). Our intuitions—our instinctive feelings for and against people or ideas, and our useful "hunches"—do not mean that we already possess Bodhi, the transcendental intuition that "knows according to reality." This mundane intuition can be extremely deceptive, and may lead to all kinds of trouble. It has to be examined in the light of a third mental faculty: intelligence. Intelligence is the ability to make skilful (*kusala*) use of the intellect. Lacking this, both intellect and intuition go astray.

All Buddhist schools recognise the part intuition must play in the attainment of gnosis—that sure certain knowing that "done is what had to be done." The winning of Enlightenment by intellectual means, "the way of the head," is very, very rare, though some of the great disciples are known to have done so.

The Zen school in particular stresses the importance of intuition. A great feature of Zen is to accept life as it comes, and to make the appropriate response. Note, the appropriate or right response. This does not mean acting on the first impulse that comes into one's head. Most human impulses arise from greed, hate or delusion, and it is only the trained disciple who can act both spontaneously and rightly every time. Impulsive action frequently ends in disaster, as in the case of Don Quixote.

A Western writer has said that Don Quixote was "Zen incarnate." This is a sad travesty of the facts as recorded in that glorious fiction. Cervantes has drawn the picture of a very courageous and idealistic gentleman (hidalgo, a man of good family), whose intellect had been vitiated by a prolonged course of sensational fiction. He believed the romances of chivalry to be true histories, and thought it was his destiny to sally forth as a knight-errant, in order to right wrongs and relieve the oppressed. No one doubts his high motives, but as he was completely lacking in judgement he committed innumerable follies, whereby he not only suffered himself, but also brought trouble on other people. He believed that in the practice of his calling a knight-errant was above good and evil. Hence he bilked an inn-keeper and, in order to obtain the supposed "helmet of Mambrino," committed a bare-faced highway robbery.

On another occasion he imagined that a flock of sheep was a hostile army, and dashing into the middle of it, he killed seven of the creatures before the shepherd could beat him off. He was then severely cudgelled, and Sancho Panza, the loyal peasant who served him as squire, was also badly mauled. This unbalanced behaviour was typical of the poor deluded man; when he scented adventure he never waited to ascertain the facts but at once issued an arrogant challenge to the supposed aggressor, with the result that he was at once attacked and beaten up.

The pitiful thing was that the knight really had a very good intellect. Judged by the standards of his time, he was a man of considerable culture; he could read and speak Italian, and also knew some Arabic. He could converse sensibly and even eloquently upon most subjects; it was only when chivalry was mentioned that he "slid off into madness." His monomania was such that he never attributed his misfortunes to his own stupidity, but believed they were the work of a malign enchanter who had a grudge against all knights errant. If anybody questioned the validity of his opinions he fell into a fury, drew his sword, and at once became the centre of an unseemly brawl. This may be "living by Zen" (which is open to doubt); it is certainly shockingly bad Buddhism.

If, as postulated, Don Quixote was "Zen incarnate," why does not the story end with some kind of apotheosis equivalent to satori? Instead the knight—we call him so though even his knighthood was spurious, having been conferred upon him for a joke by a village inn-keeper—is overthrown by a bogus knight-errant, a young man from his own village, a graduate of Salamanca, newly down from the University, who with the connivance of Don Quixote's good friends, the priest and the barber, had gone out to bring the wanderer home The knight creeps back to die of a broken heart, first making a pathetic recantation of his follies.

It is begging the question to say that Cervantes did not know his business. His object was to ridicule the books of chivalry, because they were silly in content and usually bad as literature. He did this supremely well, and incidentally produced one of the most tragic stories ever penned—the ruin of a noble mind.

This long digression is not an attack upon Zen. Zen is so great and so venerable that its position is unassailable. But Don Quixote is a warning against the assumption that spontaneous action is necessarily right action. It is frequently just the reverse.

What practical conclusions can be drawn? First we should remember that the Noble Eightfold Path is a discipline. The second "step" is a combination of right intention and right thought. To achieve this, mental culture is needed. This is the function of the intellect guided by intelligence. "Mental clarity" is one of the dhamma listed as occurring in good (*kusala*) consciousness. It is essential for the practice of the Four Right Efforts, i.e., to recognise unskilled mental states, and not only to "send them to their ceasing," but also to discourage them from arising in the future; then to encourage the arising of healthy mental states, and to strengthen them when they have arisen.

It is a commonplace that intellect can be strengthened by use. Some of its dangers have already been pointed out; another danger is that it enjoys diversity. It is always playing with ideas and forming concepts. It therefore encourages dualism and is obsessed with "the ten thousand things," so that it never sees them in their "suchness." It is the function of intuitive wisdom to actually experience "suchness." According to the Ven. Nyanaponika Thera, the intuition can also be cultivated.[48] A careful and frequent study of this will benefit us all.

— §§§ —

Guarding the Doors of the Senses

Reprinted from *Sangha*, 1961

"He sees a material shape with the eye, and he comprehends the fetter that arises through the eye. He hears a sound with the ear, and he comprehends the fetter that arises through the ear" … and so on for the other four senses—smell, taste, bodily feeling and consciousness. The Pali Canon is full of similar statements, and it behoves us to examine them carefully.

The fetters most likely to arise through the eyes are sense desire and ill-will. We see a rose, a chocolate or a cigarette, and immediately would like to satisfy our craving by reaching out and grasping them. The process seems instantaneous, but it is not really as simple as that. It depends on the 17 thought moments that are involved in any fresh arising of consciousness. For instance, you

48 Nyanaponika, *The Power of Mindfulness,* Wheel No. 121–122.

are walking past a row of shops, not thinking of anything in particular, your consciousness is in the state of *bhavaṅga* (merely the "life continuum"), when a flash of colour impinges on the eye-door. It is sufficiently vivid to disturb the condition of *bhavaṅga*—so you pause and have a look (adverting the mind). You then perceive a scarlet object lying on a fishmonger's slab, it is covered with a kind of armour, has two large claws in front and a thick jointed tail. Your previous experience enables you to name it as a lobster. Then by association of ideas the word "mayonnaise" springs into your mind, and you think "How I'd like a lobster salad for supper instead of bread and cheese!" If a few grains of dust have already been removed from your eyes, there will ensue a kind of debate—"Shall I give way to this sense desire? There is nothing intrinsically wrong about a good meal. Indeed good food builds up what is called morale and is conducive to calm. My poor little ego is all the better for an occasional treat. And I could ask old So-and-so to come in for supper. That would be practising *dāna*. Moreover a willingness to share good things keeps the fetter of avarice in check." And so forth, with a mixture of *kusala* and *akusala* thoughts until the debate is settled one way or the other, whereupon the original impression sinks back into *bhavaṅga* where it lies latent until some fresh association calls it into consciousness again.

For hate arising through the eye you have only to see a wasp settling on the breakfast marmalade. You automatically pick up a knife and crush it, thereby breaking the first precept with a thoroughly *akusala* deed. Minor hates arise when you see some recognised eye-sore, such as a corporation dump defiling the landscape; you at once feel ill-will towards the people who are responsible for the thing. Similarly, the sight of people we dislike strengthens our aversion and builds up ill-will for the future.

Sounds entering the ear-door are not likely to induce greed, though one may be tempted to sit up listening to the radio instead of going to bed or attending to some job. Where sound is concerned, desire is usually due to a pre-craving that impels one to buy a concert ticket or switch on the radio. Many people are so afraid of solitude and silence that they crave for any sort of a sound rather than sit in quietness. But for better-educated people, aversion for sound is the more likely fetter.

The howl of a jet plane can fill the inexperienced meditator with fury. One becomes distracted and breaks out into un-Ariyan speech, cursing the disturber loudly and volubly. A much better plan is to trace the origination of the sound, knowing that having arisen it must inevitably cease. Thus: "The noise is made by a plane piloted by a human being. It came from such-and-such an aerodrome, and was built in a certain factory by government order in response to the re-armament programme. Re-armament is a symptom of the 'Cold War'—[here one must beware of nourishing ill-will for the people who foment war]. War, whether cold or hot, is due to greed, hate and delusion; these are the result of ignorance." By the time one has got back mentally to *avijjā* the offending plane is many miles away and the sound is inaudible. One can then calmly return to the original subject of meditation.

Where minor disturbances are concerned, such as chirping birds or barking dogs, one can follow the Buddha's advice to Bāhiya: "Thus must you train. In the heard there is only what is heard. There is no substantiality in it, no self for you to hate." This method is decidedly helpful, and can be used for putting down irritating talk.

A very present peril that enters through the ear door is gossip. Ninety nine people out of a hundred, whatever they may say to the contrary, thoroughly enjoy gossip. The harm done to the people discussed may be negligible, but the real damage is done to ourselves. We always feel superior to the people discussed and that is the fetter of conceit—a very heavy fetter indeed! It takes a lot of social tact not to listen, or to change the conversation, without being uncivil to one's vis- -vis, but we can at least refrain from adding our own comments.

The fetter that arises through odours and the nose door is very subtle. There is nothing so evocative as a scent. Who can smell, or even hear the words "wood smoke" or "violets," without some emotional repercussion? If the memory is happy, one clings to the past, and probably regrets—"departed joys, departed never to return"—as the old song has it. If the remembered incident is unhappy then the old grief comes to life. Grief (*domanassa*) belongs to the hate group of mental states, and is both wasteful and useless. When Dido asked Aeneas to tell her about the fall of Troy, he replied: "*Infandum, regina, jubes, renovare dolorem.*" It is beyond my capacity to render the drawn-out misery of the Latin vowels, but roughly translated the meaning is: "You ask a shameful thing of me, O Queen, to bring to life an old sorrow."

The Buddha's advice was "Let be the past, let be the future." He never forbade pleasure, provided it was lawful. He said he knew both the satisfaction and the peril that arose through the senses. He stressed the peril because the satisfaction can only be temporary, leading to renewed desire, and so productive of *dukkha*, and fresh becoming. The HERE-NOW is the important place where past kamma is being worked out and fresh kamma originates.

Aversion entering the nose-door is very frequent. It is wise to remove the source of the smell whenever possible for it is usually due to some impurity which, in the interests of cleanliness, ought to be removed. If this is impossible then one should remove one's own "bundle of khandhas," for we are under no obligation to endure remediable ills.

The tongue and tastes may stimulate greed, as when we go on eating after the body's needs are satisfied. This behaviour induces the fetter of sloth and torpor. One type of monk who is hard to instruct is he "who having filled his belly full, thinks only of the ease and comfort of his bed."

Aversion for food can occur when it is badly served or otherwise unappetising, and some people have an inherent dislike of cloves or onions. It is inadvisable to express this dislike when dining in company lest one's host or other guests should be embarrassed.

The body itself constitutes another sense-door. There are two kinds of sensation associated with it; superficial (touch) and deep. The latter depends on joint and muscle movements, and on sensations arising in the viscera; these last are usually unpleasant.

Skin sensation (touch) is very important. Certain textures, such as silk and fur, have a definitely sensuous appeal, and where the opposite sex is concerned, skin texture itself comes into play.

Unpleasant deep sensations may be due to disease or to dietary indiscretions such as that produced by too much cucumber; in which case the appropriate verdict is: "Serves me right!"

Shall we attempt a short-cut to guarding the sense-doors by blocking them entirely? Tie a bandage over our eyes or fill our ears with "honey-sweet wax," as the wily Ulysses stopped the ears of his sailors lest they should hear the song of the sirens and be lured to their destruction? It would be madness to try to cross Oxford Street in this condition—in fact it is a kind of mutilation, and as foolish as the action of Origen who castrated himself so that he would no longer be tempted by "the sins of the flesh." To close the eyes and the ears completely would be to cut out all beauty from our lives. As an aside, it may be remarked that some Buddhists are afraid of beauty. This is a grave mistake, for beauty encourages healthy thoughts and relaxes nervous tension. We can never be aware of absolute beauty. In the Platonic sense, all we know is a beautiful object, whether it be a material shape, a sound or a scent. Provided we do not covet such things, beautiful objects are helpful and inspiring. Indeed, we can get more pleasure from a picture in someone else's house than if it were in one's own. The beauty of a thing seen only occasionally strikes one afresh on each new inspection, but if actually possessed familiarity detracts from its charm.

With regard to pleasures the first principle to be applied is that of the Middle Way: neither over-indulgence nor extreme asceticism. Violent suppression of sense-desire can produce harmful psychological or even physical results in either this or some future life.

Just a few words more about guarding the eye-door. A monk in training is told to keep his eyes on the ground about 12 or 15 feet ahead (the length of the plough-yoke). This enables him to avoid hazards on the path, such as sticks, stones and snakes, but prevents him from seeing desirable objects, like pretty women or rich robes worn by other people. Within the limits of commonsense this technique can be employed in the West; it certainly cuts out the silly game of "window-shopping" so popular with many women!

Where problems of conduct are concerned Buddhism has one infallible answer. This is Right Mindfulness. Mindfulness makes us aware of our mental states whenever fetters arise, and we can then practise the first of four Right Efforts, and send the fetter to its ceasing. This is far from easy. Desires and aversions are so liable to become obsessions and dominate the mind. In such cases the use of a mantram may banish the intruder. *Om mani padme hum* or the great mantra from the Heart Sutra: *Gate, gate, paragate, parasamgate, Bodhi, Svaha*! The invocation with which *pansil* (the Five Precepts) opens—recited in Pali—is a fine mantram. If we take refuge in the Triple Gem we cannot go far astray.

The mind-door (consciousness being the sixth sense) is the most difficult of all to guard. Likewise it is the most important. Consciousness is on the run from morning to night, greedy for any new distraction, however trivial; hence the constant warnings in the suttas about unskilled (*akusala*) thoughts, the encouragement of which causes skilled thoughts to decline. If we attend closely to things which should not be closely attended to, trouble arises. If we constantly occupy our minds with things like lobster salad, roast duck and caviar, we are training ourselves to be gormandisers. This does not mean we should never think of food—it is a very important subject. The cankers, *āsava*, "manias," "outflows," are prone to arise in an ill-nourished or sickly body. In the Far East food is regarded as medicinal—a medicine to prevent disease. For this reason food requires just as much attention as a chemist would give to making up a prescription. Good food is conducive to calm, one of the limbs of enlightenment. Once more the Middle Way is indicated.

Unwise attention is particularly dangerous when thinking about other people. If we keep remembering the faults of somebody we don't like, our aversion strikes deeper and deeper roots until a real hate arises, productive of constant woe. It is just as much a mistake to reflect too much about an attractive person, for unwise reflection can change a friendship into an infatuation leading to unhappy results.

People of the intellectual type have also to be on guard against constant conceptualising. We become obsessed with ideas, possibly quite unworthy ones, and prefer to sit down to write an article for a Buddhist magazine rather than to practise the arising of mindfulness with regard to the prosaic behaviour and unedifying conglomeration of parts that constitute the "own body."

This business of guarding the doors of the senses sounds pretty tough, and it certainly is so. The Buddha himself said: "This Dhamma is deep, difficult to understand," and he never gave the impression that the Eightfold Path was edged with primroses. The loveliness of the Dhamma, "lovely in its beginning, lovely in the middle, and lovely in its ending," is due to a quite different quality that derives from our highest instincts and aspirations. Unless we are prepared to do something about it in the way of mindfulness, we had better stop playing at Buddhism; instead take up some easy-going cult that pretends to expand or exalt what the intelligentsia calls the "human psyche"—the in-dwelling self-conceit present in all of us.

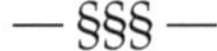

This Self Business and Other Essays

M. O'C. Walshe
Natasha Jackson
Dr. Elizabeth Ashby

Bodhi Leaves No. 45

First published: 1969

This Self Business

by M. O'C. Walshe

From *The Buddhist Path*, Journal of Wat Dhammapadīpa, London. Vol. 2, No. 5

"Do it yourself"—"There is no self"—"Be a lamp (or an island) unto yourself." It is not very surprising that the newcomer to Buddhism (and sometimes even the old stager) gets rather puzzled about this "self" business. Let us therefore attempt to shed a little light on this difficult but important subject.

The best place to begin is at the beginning. The observance of this simple rule makes a lot of things easier, though the fact is not always remembered. The English language possesses several pronouns such as myself, yourself, and so on, which are rendered in Pali by *attā* (in Sanskrit *ātman*). This is the everyday use, which is completely matter-of-fact and unmetaphysical. Some such terms are inevitably used in all languages. They are convenient and conventional, implying nothing whatever about the reality or otherwise of the "entity" they refer to. We merely need to note that in Buddhism such an entity is considered, for the best of reasons, only relatively or conventionally real. In terms of absolute truth there is no such thing, but in terms of relative truth there is. All we have to observe, then, is whether in any given case a statement is made in terms of the relative or the absolute truth. This alone obviates much confusion.

But this distinction, though vital, does not of course remove all difficulties. Let us first take a look at the "self" which does—relatively—exist. We are very familiar with this, our nearest and dearest, and so it comes as something of a shock to learn that it is not "really" real. We may even be quite indignant at such a suggestion. And yet even here there is something rather odd. Many people today do not believe in an immortal soul, or any entity that survives bodily death. But if this "self" does not survive the death of the body, it surely cannot be very real even now. We are not, for the moment, discussing the Buddhist view of rebirth, but merely suggesting that for the non-believer in survival the self must after all be a very peculiar thing.

However, there is at least one important sense in which the relatively real self is taken quite seriously even in Buddhism. If I robbed a bank last week, I can't avoid the consequences by declaring that, as I don't really exist, it wasn't really me, whether in a court of human law or in terms of the law of karma. Neither human nor karmic justice will accept such a plea. In fact in the Buddhist view of things, karma will even catch up with me after death if it has not done so before! So our relative reality, however ultimately illusory, is not without its importance.

At this point it may look suspiciously as if Buddhists were trying to have it both ways. They agree, it appears, with the implication of materialism that there is no permanent or immortal soul, while also apparently agreeing with the Christian idea of post-mortem rewards or retribution. Curiouser and curiouser, as Alice would have said.

Let us see. The relatively real "entity" is in fact a process—a constantly flowing river which, though not one drop of water remains stationary, nevertheless is for us, conventionally and practically, "the same" river. If we prefer the image of an electric current, we can also think of rebirth as the continuing flow of such a current even though successive bulbs are worn out. This flow goes until the fuel that feeds it—craving—has ceased.

One of the various factors that go to make up our "personality" is volition (*cetanā*). It is this which many people identify with the self "I want." Yet this too is just as impersonal as all the rest, which is why we can become aware of conflicting desires within us. The whole of karma is based on this volition factor, so that for the relatively real "me" it is very important. This is the main reason why self-knowledge is so vital. But it should by now be clear that "self-knowledge" in Buddhism does not mean getting to know one's true self (for there is no such thing), but seeing through the spurious self.

People learning to practise mindful self-awareness sometimes ask at this point: "If I am supposed to be observing myself, what is it that does the observing?" In the light of what has been said, this may be quite a puzzle. But the simple answer is actually that one moment of consciousness has for its object a previous moment of consciousness. And by practising this exercise we gradually learn to realise that the process actually is just as described. A point is then eventually reached when, craving being temporarily suspended, the whole thing is seen with utter detachment and thus seen through. This is the beginning of the decisive stage of the cure, the beginning of the path that leads to the cessation of craving and therefore of all sense of frustration and pain.

All things (including our precious "selves") are in truth impersonal (*anattā*) or "void" (*sūnya*) as the Mahāyanists generally prefer to say. Despite certain occasional polemically-tinged suggestions to the contrary, the two expressions are virtually synonymous. And, curiously enough, the realisation of this truth, which looks so negative and perhaps even rather frightening, is bliss ineffable. That, however, is another story.

— §§§ —

The Soul and I

by Natasha Jackson

From *Metta*, Journal of the Buddhist Federation of Australia, September 1968

The doctrine of *anattā* is the most characteristic Buddhist doctrine and also the most difficult to understand, especially for anyone living in a predominantly Christian environment. The influence of a theistic religion, even though it may be given merely lip-service when not openly repudiated, nevertheless has seeped into the "collective unconscious" and in a thousand subtle ways has permeated the whole of our national life and outlook.

To attempt to gain some understanding of *anattā* (Pali, *an*, "without" and *attā*, "soul"), one has first of all to blot out from the mind (if only temporarily) the concept that "everything must have a beginning" and the tendency to equate that beginning with God as creator or prime mover of the universe.

Strangely enough, while many people reject the dogma of a special creation as the work of God in favour of the Darwinian hypothesis of evolution, they still remain very loath to give up the idea of an indestructible, immortal soul, even though they no longer believe it to have been breathed into creatures by an almighty God, recognizing that and similar legends as attempts by primitive people to explain some of the unsolved mysteries.

The Buddha did not speculate about the beginnings of the physical universe which, in his estimation, was a wasteful use of precious time that could be spent otherwise in more practical and profitable ways. He plunged straight into consideration of an observable fact—*aniccā*, which is change, flux, motion, mutability, impermanence. Something arises, is born, develops and grows to maturity, then inevitably decays and finally dies. That is the life-cycle of everything, including man; and it is also true of nations, empires, social systems, worlds and universes.

Hence, the Buddha conceived the idea of a dynamic, constantly changing universe, completely discarding the concept of a static one.

Turning his attention to man, he analysed the human being as made up of five *khandha* or "aggregates." One is the physical body and the other four are mental properties: perception, feelings, the kamma-formations and consciousness. Since all these are in a state of constant flux, changing from moment to moment, and since all are perishable at death, he came to the conclusion that there was nothing in them that could rightly be called a permanent, abiding entity, self, soul or ego.

That, stated briefly, is the *anattā* doctrine.

However, while the empiricist within the Buddha could not admit the possibility of any permanent substance, however subtle or rarefied (such as a soul) within a dynamic universe of constant flux, he also could not accept the proposition that man was nothing more than his physical body, for he considered the mind of man to be of greater importance and more basic than the material shell that housed it. Within that mind was the in-built thirst for life, *tanhā*, a driving force so strong and powerful that it could propel a dying being into existence again and again. Thus, according to Buddhist doctrine, *taṇhā* is the causative link between one life and the next.

Thus, the Buddha saw all life as essentially the same as everything else within the universe, a process of constant change, something like a wave in motion which rises and falls again and again, never the same nor yet quite different, yet remaining within the volume of water that is the ocean.

As to how the doctrine of *anattā* can be reconciled with the further Buddhist doctrine of rebirth, Sir Charles Eliot clarifies it as well as it can be clarified:

> "But in reality, the denial of the *ātman* (Pali *attā*) applies to the living rather than the dead. It means that in a living man there is no permanent, unchangeable entity, but only a series of mental states, and since human beings, although they have no *ātman*, certainly exist in this present life, the absence of the *ātman* is not in itself an obstacle to belief in a similar life after death or before birth. Infancy, youth, age and the state immediately after death may form a series of which the last two are connected as intimately as any other two. The Buddhist teaching is that when men die in whom the desire for another life exists—as it exists in all except saints—then desire, which is really the creator of the world, fashions another being, conditioned by the character and merits of the being which has just come to an end. Life is like fire: its very nature is to burn its fuel. When one body dies, it is as if one piece of fuel were burnt: the vital process passes on and recommences in another and so long as there is desire for life, the provision of fuel fails not."
>
> *Hinduism and Buddhism*, Vol. 1, London, 1921

However, these are only words and with words we can only go along so far and no further. Thoreau conveys something of this thought when he writes:

> "A man sits as many risks as he runs. We must walk consciously only part way towards our goal, and then, leap in the dark to our success."

To grasp the Buddhist doctrines of *anattā* and rebirth, the mind must have sufficient resilience and courage to make a leap in the dark. Some can, others cannot—not at the present stage of their development, anyway. For that matter, a very similar sort of mental leap is required to accept the latest findings of neo-physics, that matter is energy and energy can become matter. This does not make sense—not common sense at any rate, but it works.

— §§§ —

That Tiresome "Self"

by Dr. Elizabeth Ashby

From *Sangha*, October 1960

> Come, let us catch the "I"
> that's always on the wing
> and flittering through the hedge
> of all conditioned things.

Some Buddhist concepts have filtered through to the general public and have been very well received, such as rebirth or "reincarnation" as people usually express it. Somebody gleefully munching lettuce will exclaim "I must have been a rabbit in my last life." But the universality of *dukkha* and the idea of *anattā* repel the western mind. The sequence of thought seems to run like this: "No self—no soul—no immortality." We have most of us grown up with the idea that immortality is a desirable thing; the doctrine of the resurrection promises it. But is it really so much to be desired? Do you remember the Greek myth of Chiron, the wise centaur? He kept a kind of school in a cave where he educated the sons of the local chieftains, teaching them manners and the warlike arts. Hercules, Jason and Theseus were numbered amongst his pupils. Now it happened that Chiron was accidentally wounded by a poisoned arrow. The wound would not heal and caused him great agony; he longed for death, but centaurs are demigods, and as such are immortal. Faced with an eternity of pain the centaur begged a bystander to become immortal in his stead. The request was granted, and Chiron was then able to die. As a reward for his services on earth the gods placed him in the sky where he became the constellation Sagittarius, the Archer, the ninth sign of the Zodiac. We are all in the position of the wounded centaur, for unless we become enlightened we are faced with aeon after aeon of dukkha: that being inseparable from the samsāric round of death and birth.

A potent source of the desire for immortality is the hope that we shall be reunited to our dear ones in heaven. This involves some curious problems. Will our parents be as we knew them in their honoured old age, or in the prime of life? Or as young married people? Likewise, do dead children grow up in heaven, or must they remain children throughout eternity? And what about people who were not so dear? Those worthy beings, Cousin Lil and Uncle Joseph, who lacking either the courage or the capacity to sin, have been wafted into heaven on the wings of blamelessness. On earth they were crashing bores, and if their recognisable personalities persist, the profane mind shrinks from spending eternity in their company. There is also the possibility of meeting our pet enemies and aversions—a real source of dukkha unless we have all become so purged and refined that personal characteristics have been washed out. From which it could be argued that the conventional heaven is not a stage of unmixed bliss.

Personal characteristics, or personality, are nothing more or less than the five aggregates of grasping—body, feeling, perception, habitual tendencies (the saṅkhāras), and consciousness. We can go through them again and again, as though with a fine tooth comb, but we cannot lay in them any separate "self," still less a permanent "soul." The *Poṭṭhapāda Sutta* (DN 9) makes the point that what we call a personality appears perfectly real while it is functioning in any particular life-span, and for convenience sake we must treat it as such. But the personalities that preceded it in the kammic continuum, though they appeared real when they were functioning, have now faded out and become insubstantial. Also the personalities that will succeed it are equally nebulous and in no sense real at the present time. There is a continuity, due to kamma, but no true identity or anything to be called a permanent soul. Apart from five empty heaps there is nothing. The idea of a "self" is just a concept firmly embedded in consciousness, and thriving on our habits of thought.

The feeling of egoity ("I"-ness) is so firmly entrenched in us that the French philosopher Descartes, who flourished in the 17th century, went so far as to say: "I think, therefore I am." But of all the transitory things in the saṃsāric flux, consciousness is the most transient. Our thoughts chase one another with the inconsequence of sheep jumping through a gap in a hedge. There is no abiding "self" in thought to be regarded as stable or permanent. Our personalities that we think of as being identical or homogenous throughout life are nothing of the sort. This is easily demonstrated.

Find an old photograph of yourself at the age of three or four and compare that image with the phenomenon that "you" are now. The difference is remarkable. Between the child and the adult lie 20, 40, or possibly 70 years of varied experience. The childish personality has completely faded out; it is only linked to the adult by the tenuous thread of memory. Our present personalities are still changing, from day to day, almost from minute to minute. Each new contact, every experience modifies them in some way or another. It is impossible to get close enough to the "self" to "put salt on its tail," still less to pin it down like a dead butterfly.

It has been said that our fundamental delusion is "self-importance." This is true, and therefore it is sometimes also said: "Kill out the self." This is psychologically unsound. The more we think of the self, the more fixed becomes the idea of selfhood. There is nothing the ego enjoys so much as occupying the centre of the stage in the full blaze of the lights. It is equally futile to run around thinking "I must be unselfish."

"By oneself is evil done; by oneself is evil left undone." Statements such as this are at first very puzzling to the student. The explanation is simple. The word "self," like the capital "I," is a concise and convenient way of referring to any particular personality and avoids the clumsy circumlocution of always speaking about one's own bundle of khandhas. Provided these terms are used mindfully and in moderation, "I" think we need have no inhibitions about their use. Indeed the capital "I" is sometimes necessary as it shows the reader just how much reliance can be placed on the statement that follows.

It is a strange feeling, when on holiday, to get up with the thought "Today I've nothing to do except enjoy myself." What on earth does one mean by this? We really propose to enjoy the sensations that impinge on us through the doors of the senses. Physical activities, walking, cycling, swimming, the playing of tennis, all give rise to pleasant bodily feeling. Holiday sights—mountains, the majesty of the sea, alpine flowers—produce enjoyment through the eye-door. Holiday sounds, the fluting of curlews on the fells and the cry of gulls on the shore, and the more sophisticated pleasure of the Salzburg Festival reach us through the door of the ear. Sensations through the nose-door are not always so pleasant. Contrasted with the scent of the Corsican marquis and the aromatic fragrance of the Spanish countryside we have the strange and most unwelcome odour of continental "plumbing." Such things serve to remind us that no holiday is perfect: that dukkha underlies all our lawful pleasures.

Perhaps we really enjoy our "selves" when egoity is at its height. This can occur when we have had a bit of worldly success and been praised or feted in consequence. It could also be stimulated by getting gloriously drunk—a most inadvisable proceeding. Some people get a terrific "kick" when faced by imminent danger, as in mountaineering or motor racing. Soldiers, too, have experienced it in the heat of battle. Drugs which induce psychological states, such as soma in ancient India and mescalin at the present day, heighten perception and lead their addicts to believe that the super-conscious has been attained. A similar danger attends the wrong practice of yoga. In essence these are all states of delusion; there is no real self to experience them: nothing except the mock-show of samsāra.

People who fear that anattā means annihilation often take comfort from the idea of "becoming one with the infinite," analogous to the Indian concept of the ātman, a kind of great self, or over-soul as Emerson called it. It was said that the ātman functions in each one of us, and to realise the ātman in our individual selves was to achieve moksha or deliverance. Another interesting doctrine is the "mind-only" idea, put forward in the Laṅkāvatāra Sūtra. This seems to be a vast store-consciousness or sea of unconsciousness in which we live and move and have our being. These views may be sound—I know not—but they are only views, and the Buddha would have nothing to do with "views." He refused to discuss these things, saying that they did not lead to morality, calm or enlightenment. What then is a puzzled student to do? Why, DROP IT, as a Zen master boldly declared. Stop speculating, for it only leads to the jungle of doubt and perplexity with its attendant miseries of worry and flurry. Instead, persevere with the practice of Dhamma, including the cultivation of faith in its aspect of confidence.

Here is a suggestion for dealing with self-importance. Stop fussing about this tiresome "self" and turn the mind outwards to watch and investigate the happenings of everyday life. For instance, if one finds it necessary to suspend one's individual bundle of khandhas from a strap in the underground, the following line of reasoning could be pursued with profit: "This unpleasant bodily situation has arisen because—impelled by some desire or other—"I" chose to travel in the rush hour. It is a conditioned thing and will therefore cease. This will happen (a) if "I" faint or (b) when the train reaches Charing Cross. The discomfort that "I" feel does not matter when compared with the universality of dukkha; it is not important." This method can be applied to emotional states as well as mundane contretemps.

We cannot by a mere act of will get rid of the "self," but we can cultivate the attitude of mind that is willing to let the "self" go. Wise reflection on the three marks of existence, anicca, dukkha and anattā helps to bring this about.

This article is merely a student's attempt to produce some orderly ideal on a subject that is of vital importance. If readers find some of the conclusions only "half-baked" they may be stimulated to finish the "cooking" themselves. Wise reflection helps skilled mental states to arise, and causes unskilled states to decrease.

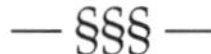

The Way to Happiness

H. L. B. Ellegala

Bodhi Leaves No. 46

First published: 1969

The Way to Happiness

"Even so, Monks, have I seen an ancient road, an ancient track, followed by the Rightly Awakened Ones (Buddhas) of former times. And what is that ancient road? It is the Noble Eightfold Path. Along it have I gone; and going along it, I have fully come to know decay and death, its uprising, its ceasing, and the way leading to the ceasing of decay and death."

So has the Buddha said, and that is just what he, in his infinite compassion for all mankind, wanted every one of us too to see and to know and to tread. This is the Path of deliverance from *saṃsāra* to Nibbāna, and it is made up of eight factors to be developed, eight steps of training to be taken simultaneously, or as many as is possible, and not steps to be taken in numerical sequence. This is the middle way between the opposites of sensual indulgence and extreme asceticism.

The first step is Right Understanding (*sammā diṭṭhi*). It means a knowledge of the Four Noble Truths, the Three Signs of Being (*ti lakkhaṇa*), and the universal Law of Causality. The Master was unequivocal in his utterance on Right Understanding. His long ministry of forty five years was devoted to making people understand Truth, and not urging them to have faith or to believe blindly. In his discourse to the Kālāmas of Kesaputta,[49] he pointed out clearly that no belief, no tradition, no dogma, no authority, should stand in the way of investigation. Yet he made it clear that the Right Understanding with which the Noble Eightfold Path begins has a definite meaning. It does not mean that one may hold views in conflict with the Four Noble Truths.

Then with Right Understanding, the pilgrim starts on his chosen journey that he might have a glance into the realm beyond phenomenal existence (*saṃsāra*) and assure himself that the stupendous struggle to gain it is worth all the ceaseless labours involved.

---

49 *Kālāma Sutta*, Wheel No. 8.

The second step is Right Thought (*sammā saṅkappa*); that is thoughts of renunciation (or selflessness), good will and non-harming (or compassion). The Dhammapada lays strong emphasis on the limitless power of thought, as proclaimed in its opening verse:

> "All that we are is the result
> Of what we have thought.
> It is founded on our thoughts;
> It made up of our thoughts."

Many outstanding scientists and philosophers of today have come to recognise what the ancient seers had known. Sir James Jeans in *The Mysterious Universe* says, "The universe can best be pictured as consisting of pure thought."

The Dhamma teaches that Right Understanding and Right Thought lead to wisdom (*paññā*); wisdom gives us sound reasons why we should be selfless, renunciatory, loving and compassionate. "True wisdom is endowed with these noble qualities: all thoughts of selfish desire, ill-will, hatred and violence are the results of a lack of wisdom in all spheres of life, individual, social or political,"[50] and all loving kindness (*mettā*), compassion (*karunā*), sympathetic joy (*muditā*) and equanimity (*upekkhā*) are the results of great wisdom, Right Thought, Right Effort and Right Mindfulness. The unlimited power of thought is indefinable, and it may truly be said that thought, not faith, can move mountains. "More hath been, and still more can be wrought by thought than this world of ordinary mortals can ever dream of."

Let us then pour out loving thoughts at dawn and dusk daily to our kith and kin, friends and acquaintances, near or far, enemies, known or unknown, and all other living beings that are, and those yet to be, in the four quarters, above, below and all around, and influence them, in however small a way, to be free from suffering and sorrow and to be happy.

This is the Hymn of Universal Love (*mettā*) which anyone anywhere may sing silently and joyously, and see what wonders it is capable of achieving. "If mind (the source of thought) is comprehended, all else is comprehended," says a Mahāyana text (*Ratnamegha Sutta*).[51]

---

50 Walpola Rāhula Thera, *What the Buddha Taught*, p. 49.

51 As quoted by Nyanaponika Maha Thera, in *The Heart of Buddhist Meditation.*

The third step is Right Speech (*sammā vācā*).

> "Though one's speech be a thousand words,
> Vain words all strung together;
> Better a single phrase
> Which calms the one that hears."[52]

The Chinese proverb—"He who knows does not speak and he who speaks does not know"—is pregnant with profound meaning. The fool is garrulous; the wise man is silent. Words are for the many but thoughts are for the few. So the pilgrim avoids gossip, scandal, tale-bearing, and other harmful talk. He is truthful in the spoken as well as in the written word. Gentle and pleasant speech is a reflection of his refined character, and "truth is the speech of inward purity." Distortion of facts and false propaganda are eschewed. In the intense struggle for the realisation of truth, how can you be false to yourself or others?

The Dhammapada admonishes thus on the wrong use of speech:

> "Use not harsh speech when harshly spoken to.
> Men may retort; painful are quarrelings,
> And punishment may follow your harsh words.
>
> If you can keep your tongue from wagging oft,
> Silent as some cracked gong, you have thereby
> Nibbāna won; no brawling is in you."

(vv. 133–134)

The Buddha himself was reviled and falsely accused. But how did he take all that? One day he visited a brahmin's house by invitation for alms-food; on his arrival, to the utter dismay of all those present, the host abused him thoroughly. Narrow-minded brahmins hated him and his teaching.

But the Compassionate One said to the man, "Friend, if you invite people to your house for a feast and on arrival they do not partake of the feast, what will you do?" The foolish man arrogantly replied, "Then we and the others of this household will enjoy the feast." "I decline to enjoy your feast (of abuse)," was the Buddha's gentle rebuke. Later the man became one of his followers.

---

52 Dhammapada, v. 100.

The fourth step is Right Action (*sammā kammanta*). The negative side of it is abstention from killing, stealing, adultery, alcoholic drinks, stupefying drugs, cut-throat competition, baneful exploitation and similar unwholesome activities; these cater to immoral self-gratification. Positively, its role enjoins compassion, honesty, justice, equity, fair-play, purity and sobriety. In terms of the Law of Causality, every volitional action has its reaction, good or bad. The deed affects the doer in compliance with the same law.

Right Action is behaviour that is right for oneself as for others. To return evil for evil is immoral, for hatred is not appeased by hatred but by love. Right Action also means diligence in looking after one's teachers, parents, wife and children and the exercise of hospitality and charity. "True giving (*dāna*) covers far more precious gifts than pats from hand to hand. Money and gold are the least of charity."

There is yet another field for Right Action, the field of public service, which comprises the building of schools and hospitals, running of community centres, homes for the aged, treatment of animals in distress and the like. Life is expressed in terms of causes and effects; let us create good causes, and their effects will look after themselves.

At the behest of the Emperor Asoka whose name is respected throughout the civilised world, education, social service, and even the treatment of sick animals in veterinary hospitals was instituted. This was in keeping with the highest ideal of kingship as laid down by the Buddha. Asoka's rule of over forty years of peace and contentment is unique in the annals of history. Rulers in other countries followed his noble example. To cite only one instance, Empress Komyo of Japan (7th century AC) opened a hospital for lepers and personally washed and bathed leper women in that asylum and brought comfort to the stricken in many other ways.

The Buddha himself set an example in service to the needy, which pious people have emulated throughout the Buddhist world. A monk named Tissa was suffering from a dire disease: his case had advanced so far that nobody would even so much as approach him. When the All-Compassionate One heard of it, he went to the monk's cell and had warm water prepared; he himself bathed and cleaned the ulcers which covered Tissa's body, and washed and dried his soiled clothes. All this done, the exalted Attendant administered spiritual medicine to the dying monk. At the end of the talk, Tissa brightened up, acknowledged his gratitude to his master, then attained sainthood and passed away.

Right Livelihood (*sammā ājīva*) is the fifth step. This is meant to bring out the basic meaning of "live and let live" in actual practice—i.e. in harmony and cooperation with companions. "But in this modern world Right Livelihood can be one of the most difficult rules to follow. So many kinds of work are harmful to society and are unworthy of a true Buddhist. There are the arms trade and the nuclear warfare industries, the alcohol trade, drug peddling, occupations involving the slaughter or vivisection of animals, yellow journalism, dishonest advertising and publicity, and business methods that involve deception, excessive profit and usury. Buddhism is not a narrow-minded religion: it regards human frailties with understanding and sympathy. Yet the sincere Buddhist cannot profess one code of morality and earn his livelihood in an occupation with another, debased code." Right Livelihood precludes trading in arms, poison, liquor, slaves and animals for slaughter. Also repugnant to the spirit of Right Livelihood are hunting and fishing.

Right conduct (*dhammacariyā*) in the means of livelihood is obligatory for all. There is a higher code for monks and nuns but for the lay-people, right conduct is laid down in the Sigālovāda Sutta.[53] It has been written of this code: "The Buddha's doctrine of love and goodwill between man and man is here set forth as a domestic and social ethics with more comprehensive detail than elsewhere, and truly we may say even now of this *vinaya* or code of discipline, so fundamental are the human interests involved, so sane and wide is the wisdom that envisages them that the utterances are as fresh and practically as binding today as they were then at Rājagaha." To this has been added: "Happy would have been the village or the clan on the banks of the Ganges, where the people were full of the kindly spirit of fellow-feeling, the noble spirit of justice which breathes in these simple sayings."[54] Happy should be the people on the banks of the Volga or the Seine, or the

53 See *Everyman's Ethics*, Wheel No. 14

54 *Dialogues of the Buddha*, Part III, p. 148.

Thames or the Mississippi oranywhere else, rural or urban, if only they could imbibe the spirit of this magnificent code of ethics that is the Sigālovāda Sutta.

Right Effort (*sammā-vāyāma*) is the sixth step. This is basic to all others, for without effort no progress is possible. The Buddha went through six years of intense suffering with heroic effort to gain freedom for all. He did not give up hope even when he was almost dying of starvation. His determination was matchless.

Effort in the context of the Eightfold Path is four-fold. The first is the avoiding of anything unwholesome or evil in the mind; the second is the overcoming of evil which has already arisen. When an evil propensity rooted in greed, hate or delusion has arisen in one's mind, then one should switch one's thoughts in the opposite direction—towards the virtues of altruism, love or wisdom. Then the impure thoughts are replaced by pure thoughts. The third is directed towards the developing of good and wholesome tendencies, leading towards enlightenment. The fourth is to maintain the wholesome states already gained, with diligence, until the mind reaches its goal of perfect concentration, leading to mental equilibrium.

We live in an age of tension and flurry. We are being consumed with the three flames of hate, greed and delusion. Commonsense tells us that the real effort on our part should be to develop mental energy for the purification of the mind, so that these three flames might be extinguished. Should we not put out the fire when our house is in flames?

The seventh step is Right Mindfulness (*sammā sati*). What is mind? Who knows it in its entirety except a Fully-Enlightened One, a Buddha? Still we can form some idea of it and its working. Nyanaponika Mahā Thera says: "Particularly does the culmination of human wisdom, the teaching of the Buddha, deal not with something foreign, far, or antiquated but with that which is common to all humanity, which is ever young, and nearer to us than our hands and feet—the human mind.

"In the Buddhist Doctrine, the mind is the starting point, the focal point and also, as the liberated and purified mind of the saint, the culminating point. Mind is the very nearest to us, because through mind alone are we aware of the so-called external world including our own body."[55]

The first two verses of the Dhammapada are far-reaching in their tremendous significance:

> Mind goes before all states, mind is the chief;
> Mind-made are they, and whosoever acts
> With an impure mind, him misery pursues
> As a wagon-wheel follows the oxen's hoof.
>
> Mind goes before all states, mind is the chief;
> Mind-made are they, and whosoever acts
> With a pure mind, him happiness pursues
> As his own shadow ever follows him.

The implications of these two profound verses are shatteringly penetrative. Act well your part with a pure heart, and there lies all happiness.

Nyanaponika Mahā Thera again says, "The Buddha's message, as a doctrine of the mind teaches three things:

—to know the mind—that is so near to us, and yet is so unknown;
—to shape the mind—that is so unwieldy and obstinate, and yet may turn so pliant;
—to free the mind—that is in bondage all over and yet may win freedom here and now."

In order to achieve these three things there is only one way—the development of the Fourfold Mindfulness (*satipaṭṭhāna*) or the Foundations of Mindfulness. The Buddha said, "The only way that leads to the attainment of purity, to the overcoming of sorrow and lamentation, to the ending of pain and grief, to the entering upon the right path and the realisation of Nibbāna is the four foundations of mindfulness." These are (1) contemplation, without attachment to anything mundane, of the body, one's own or another's, as to how it arises and how it passes away, with the realisation in fact of the composition of the body in all its details; (2) contemplation of feelings, agreeable, disagreeable or neutral, their arising

55 *The Heart of Buddhist Meditation*, p. 21.

and passing away, with the realisation in fact of the absence of any entity or ego which experiences such feelings; (3) contemplation of the mind in its arising and passing away; (4) contemplation of mind-objects, namely, of lust, anger, sloth, worry and doubt, and of the ten fetters (*saṃyojana*), of the aggregates or the five groups of existence (*pañca khandha*), of the seven factors of enlightenment (*bojjhaṅga*), of the six sense-bases (*saḷāyatana*), their arising and passing away, and of the Four Noble Truths (*ariya sacca*).

When the state of Right Mindfulness is attained, the pilgrim is master of delight, discontent, fear, anxiety, hunger, thirst, pain and peril, which are submissive to his will. He gains the four absorptions (*jhāna*) which purify the mind and bring happiness here in this world, which one may enjoy at will without difficulty, without effort. There are such pilgrims.

The crowning success in the perfection of Right Mindfulness is the attainment of sainthood or Arahantship, and that may be reached within the space of a few years or even a few months or weeks; it depends on the mental capacity and the alertness and assiduity of the meditator. "Verily, monks, whosoever practises these four foundations of mindfulness in this manner (of meditation as prescribed) for seven years, then one of these two fruits may be expected by him: highest knowledge here and now, or if some remainder of clinging is yet present, the state of Non-returning (the state of purity just before the attainment of Arahantship)."

Then, reducing the period of time taken by the earnest meditator, with the merit of his acquisition of this faculty and the power thus gained, in this life and also in previous lives, the Master comes down from years to months and weeks and says, "O monks, let alone half a month, should any person practise these four foundations of mindfulness in this manner (of meditation as prescribed) for a week, then one of these two fruits may be expected: highest knowledge here and now, or if some remainder of clinging is yet present, the stage of Non-returning."

The foundations of mindfulness are so vital that the All Knowing One has laid the greatest emphasis on them in the *Satipaṭṭhāna Sutta*, a discourse that commands immense devotion and popularity in the Theravāda countries. The *bhāvanā* or meditation it prescribes, namely in-breathing and out-breathing (*ānāpāna-sati*), for gaining insight is a healing balm to all those who are trying to get rid of the self-acquired restlessness of the present day world. "Rare in this world are those who can claim freedom from mental illness even for one moment; rare are those in whom the taint of impurity has been wiped out (arahants)."[56]

Right Mindfulness is the springboard, as it were, from which the Buddhist meditator takes his flight, beyond the bounds of the intellect, into the realm of realisation (*bodhi*) which is equivalent to Nibbāna.

The Buddha has fully explained Right Mindfulness in the *Satipaṭṭhāna Sutta.*[57] Bhikkhu Piyadassi Mahā Thera says of it: "There is no other single discourse in the entire Buddhist Canon that is regarded with so much deference and high esteem by those who follow the original teaching of the Buddha."[58] For many, it is Right Mindfulness that has overcome cold and heat, hunger and thirst, subdued greed and hate, and vanquished death itself.

Right Concentration (*sammā samādhi*) is the eighth and the last step. We are quite familiar with normal concentration. Dr. Edward Conze defines it as the "narrowing of the field of attention in a manner and for a time, determined by the will. The mind is made one-pointed, does not waver, does not scatter itself and it becomes steady like the flame of a lamp in the absence of wind."[59] This is concentration in a general sense; it could be on a purely material and non-spiritual plane.

Here we are concerned with Right Concentration (*samādhi*) which leads to penetrative insight and wisdom (*nāna-dassana*). Modern extrovert civilisation hinders man at every turn in doing the one thing he must do, namely, develop his higher understanding and spiritual well-being. He is preoccupied with the pursuit of fleeting pleasures and is, therefore, never really happy. But the few, the happy few, who yearn to transcend samsāric conditions are ever in love with meditation, the one "instrument" which is capable of conducting them to Nibbāna.

---

56 *Buddhist Meditation*, Piyadassi Thera.

57 MN 10

58 *Buddhist Meditation*, op. cit.

59 op. cit.

A world of people mentally ill at every moment of their lives needs an effective remedy; and the Master Physician, after successful self-treatment, has given a unique prescription which anyone with Right Understanding, Right Effort and Right Mindfulness can apply to himself successfully. What he and many others have done many more can do. That is the systematic practice of *vipassanā bhāvanā*. The nearest equivalent term, as used in the West, is meditation.

"Meditation," writes Conze, "is a European term, which means three different things always clearly distinguished by Buddhists themselves, i.e., mindfulness, concentration and wisdom. The Pali word '*bhāvanā*' means 'becoming more' in self-development, and meditation practices constitute the very essence of the Buddhist approach to life. An intensely practical religion, Buddhism by contrast is inclined to treat doctrinal definitions and historical facts with some degree of unconcern. As prayer is in Christianity, so meditation is the very heart-beat of this religion."[60] But meditation recognises no God as prayer does; it recognises facts, not dogmas.

In meditation, one fixes one's attention steadfastly on one definite object at a time (*citta ekaggatā*), in a wholesome or pure state of consciousness, oblivious of what is going on around, from the sound of a bicycle bell to the roar of an aeroplane. Buddhaghosa in his unique work, *Visuddhi Magga* (Path of Purification) has described forty subjects for meditation (*kammaṭṭhāna*). Nibbāna is not one of them, for Nibbāna cannot be even imagined, much less known, before meditation lifts you to the plane of transcendental insight where you actually experience it.

Buddhist texts tell us how the Blessed One practised meditation and how he instructed his followers to practise it themselves. Many, indeed, were those who gained insight and liberation by means of it.

One might put the question, "Does meditation really do what is so confidently claimed for it?" The answer is plain: "Try it yourself instead of wasting time in verbal quibbling, and worrying yourself with doubt and scepticism." No better proof can be had than personal experience. So why not try it? Apply the same standard of

---

60 *Buddhist Meditation*, op. cit..

test to prayer and see where it will lead you, if you like. The God of theism is "quite useless to all who strive for self-liberation and self-enlightenment,"[61] says Christmas Humphreys.

Ānāpāna-sati (concentration on in-breathing and out-breathing) is important as a practical exercise in *vipassanā bhāvanā* (insight meditation); it is popular in the Theravāda countries and is becoming known also in the West where the Teaching of the Buddha has been welcomed. It can be practised at any time, but preferably at dawn for obvious reasons. A quiet, solitary situation is conducive to good results. The usual posture is the lotus posture, a favourite form with almost all yogins. Seated cross-legged, the left foot placed on the right thigh and the right foot on the left thigh, with straight back, looking neither up nor down, eyes closed or partially closed (some have their eyes open), one starts breathing in and out. Tension and rigidity are harmful; purity of mind, calm and physical comfort are helpful. Those unable to seat themselves in the lotus posture may use a chair or even stretch themselves on a lounge or a sofa. Some practise meditation while walking about in a garden early in the morning, at noon or in the cool of the evening.

In *ānāpāna-sati*, you breathe in and out, and you breathe long or short; in other words, naturally and unforcedly. As you breathe in and out, you count mentally from one up to 10; counting beyond 10 is likely to cause thought to be confused or to go astray; less than 5 is not enough to get you into the "stride." Calm or stillness of mind is very important. Having got as far as 10, you go back to 1, and repeat the exercise about ten times at the early stage and increase gradually up to about thirty. Normally it will take from five to fifteen minutes or even a little longer. Each numeral may be repeated twice, i.e. 1–1, 2–2, 3–3, 4–4, 5–5, 6–6, 7–7, 8–8, 9–9, and 10–10. As you inhale, when the air touches your nose, count 1; and as you exhale, when the air again touches the nose, count 1. There should be no suspension of breath between inhaling and exhaling.

In the early stages, use the counting to prevent attention wandering. As you progress, you will be able to concentrate on in-breathing and out-breathing alone. Counting may go on "until without

61 *Concentration and Meditation*, p. 261.

counting, mindfulness is established."[62] It is only a preliminary requirement, a "dotted line" to guide the novice. Once one has mastered mindfulness and cut off rambling thoughts which are only too eager to clasp external objects, one will know when the counting has to be given up, as sooner or later it must be done.

An instructor in print is not the ideal teacher, yet those who cannot conveniently avail themselves of the help of a competent teacher in the flesh might usefully be guided by the written word. Even here one cannot be too cautious in selecting really good books. But authoritative books are available. Buddhaghosa's *Visuddhi Magga* is pre-eminent. Dr. Conze's opinion of it is: "He (Buddhaghosa, 4th century AC, sage and scholar) has composed one of the greatest spiritual classics of mankind. If I had to choose just one book to take with me on a desert island, this would be my choice." If he had to choose two, the other would most likely be Sir Edwin Arnold's *Light of Asia*. There is an excellent English translation of the former, by the late Ñāṇamoli Mahā Thera, titled *The Path of Purification*. Other helpful books are: the late Nyanatiloka Mahā Thera's *The Word of the Buddha,* (Buddhist Publication Society, Kandy), and a book by his pupil, Nyanaponika Mahā Thera, *The Heart of Buddhist Meditation,* (Rider & Co. London). There is also Soma Mahā Thera's *The Way of Mindfulness* and several other booklets published by the Buddhist Publication Society, Kandy, Ceylon.

Theravada Buddhist scripture has forty subjects for meditation. So the meditator has a choice of what he wishes to meditate upon, and in this sense too the Dhamma is intensely practical (not concerned with incredible dogmas), opening as it does the eyes of its followers to "see things as they really are." Karel Werner, the well-known Czechoslovakian psychologist, says "The Dhamma is the only one of the spiritual messages of the past which can undergo a scientific analysis," and emerge triumphant.

It would be appropriate here to explain the object of meditation once again. In the first place, it is mental health. When one is physically ill, what can one do efficaciously? In the mental realm, the position is worse. Since mind is the source of both good and evil, its sound health is of the highest importance; the good must be

62 Conze, *Buddhist Meditation*, p. 67.

raised to better and best, and the evil reduced to naught. That is the development of morality and spirituality for realising Nibbāna.[63]

Starting from the solid ground of mental well-being, the task of meditation becomes easier—the task of breaking through intellectual limitations and conceptual barriers in order that one may come face to face, as it were, with reality. "To confront absolute truth," says Mr Francis Story, "to comprehend the real order of things in its entirety, one has to transcend the intellect. The intellect selects, narrows the range of cognition and arranges things in its own way, and in so doing imposes the limitations of its nature. We have to break through those conceptual barriers and grasp reality on a different level. That is the great objective of Buddhist meditational practices—they are to develop the higher consciousness that reaches beyond the intellect. That higher consciousness alone is capable of seeing reality face to face."[64]

Some may say, "All these precepts, beautiful and grand, cannot be put into practice in the modern world, in this imperfect world of ours." They want something simpler or nothing at all. They are content with feeding their sense-desires for momentary self-gratification, and sometimes pray to a god or gods for salvation from their self-inflicted suffering. Certain Buddhists pray even to the Buddha for salvation and lesser favours! And what have they ever got in answer? Conscious personal experience, on a strictly empirical basis, will yield proof that such prayers are of no avail. And this man-made world of turmoil: who has made it imperfect but man; and who can make it perfect but man?

Thousands and thousands of men and women have trodden the Way, and some of them have expressed the supreme joy of their lofty experiences in beautiful poetry—namely, the *Thera Gāthā* (Songs of the Brethren) and *Theri Gāthā* (Songs of the Sisters). Silently and steadily, monks and nuns, lay-men and lay-women tread the same Way today; they will never turn back, for they know it is the only Way (*eka magga*), but they do not talk about what they do.

The eight parts of the Path are comprised in the three words: morality (*sīla*), concentration (*samādhi*), and wisdom (*paññā*). The first

63 "Buddhism and World Thought," in *World Buddhism Annual*, 1907.

64 *Dialogues on the Dhamma*, Wheel No. 80/81, p.10.

two parts comprise wisdom, the next three, morality, and the last three, concentration. Since inward purity is a *sine qua-non* for *samādhi*, morality has got to be developed first. Once morality and concentration are developed, only then will wisdom gain perfection. "Two features that distinguished Buddhist ethics were the practical and workable systems devolved for lay people, and the skill with which practices in current belief or ritual were spiritualised and given a moral significance."[65]

Finally, on his deathbed in the Sāla Grove of the Mallas of Kusināgara, the Buddha told the wandering monk Subhadda, "In whatever doctrine or discipline the Noble Eightfold Path is not found, neither in it is to be found a man of true saintliness, whether of the first, or of the second or of the third or of the fourth degree.

But in whatever doctrine or discipline the Noble Eightfold Path is found, in it and in it alone is to be found the man of true saintliness of the first, of the second, of the third and of the fourth degree. Void are the systems of teachers in which the Noble Eightfold Path is not found. May the Brethren follow that Path and gain the perfect life, that the world may not be bereft of arahants" (*Mahā Parinibbāna Sutta*).[66]

This declaration of the Enlightened One effectively disposes of the fallacious view popularly held that in this dark age (*kali yuga*) there can be no arahants—the holy ones. It is also a reminder of the fact that Nibbāna cannot be attained by one who persists in holding wrong views (*micchā-diṭṭhi*).

Appamādena sampādetha—Work out your salvation with diligence.

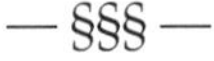

— §§§ —

65 *The Life of Buddha: As Legend and History,* Edward J. Thomas, 1927, p. 175.
66 *Last Days of the Buddha,* Sister Vajirā & Francis Story, Wheel No. 67/69.

Women in Ancient India

C. D. Weerasinghe

Bodhi Leaves No. 47

First published: 1970

WOMEN IN ANCIENT INDIA

1. Mahā Pajāpatī Gotamī

Within a week after the birth of Prince Siddhattha who was to become the Buddha, his mother, Queen Mahā Maya, died, and from his infancy the young prince was tended and cared for by his step-mother Mahā Pajāpatī Gotamī who had become the consort of King Suddhodana, the ruler of the Sakya kingdom.

Mahā Pajāpatī's affection towards Prince Siddhattha was the same as for her own children and she took the greatest care of him. After the death of King Suddhodana she devoted her time to the study of the Buddha's doctrine. Her leisure hours were spent in getting up a suitable robe to be offered to the Buddha.

At the end of the fifth *vassā* period of the Buddha, spent at the Pinnacled Hall at Mahāvana near Vesāli, Mahā Pajāpatī Gotamī brought the robe prepared by her to be presented to the Buddha. But when the robe was offered to him, to her great surprise the Buddha refused to accept it. Repeatedly she offered it to the Buddha, but each time it was refused by him. At this she was deeply grieved. She remembered incidents in Prince Sidddattha's life and how she had taken the place of his mother. Tears filled her eyes at the Buddha's refusal to accept her gift. But yet Mahā Pajāpatī persisted in her offer of the robe.

Seeing the embarrassment of the Queen, the Buddha explained that he would not wish to receive the robe as a personal gift but suggested to her that it should be offered to the Order, the Mahā Sangha, whose members come from everywhere in the four directions. This would be a still greater meritorious act. After this explanation, when the robe was duly offered to the Mahā Sangha, the Buddha accepted it.

Bhikkhunī Sangha

As time passed Mahā Pajāpatī realised more and more the truth of the Buddha's Doctrine, and as her son, Prince Nanda, had entered the Sangha, she too expressed a desire to live a life of renunciation, as a nun. But so far no Order of Nuns (Bhikkhunī Sangha) existed, and therefore she begged permission from the Buddha to admit women to the Sangha. But the Buddha for several reasons refused such permission. Undaunted, however, Mahā Pajāpatī cut off her hair, donned yellow robes and accompanied by several Sakyan ladies, she walked from Kapilavatthu to Vesāli. Travel-worn and weeping she stood outside the porch of the Pinnacled Hall at Mahāvana, where the Buddha was residing, and repeated her pleading to the Venerable Ānanda who had seen her standing at the gate.

The Buddhist texts record how the Venerable Ānanda Thera, greatly moved by this pathetic sight, appealed to the Buddha on behalf of Mahā Pajāpatī and the other Sakyan ladies. Finally the Buddha granted permission to women to enter the Sangha, on certain conditions, which Mahā Pajāpatī gladly accepted. Thus was instituted the Order of Bhikkhunīs.

As time passed, this Order of Bhikkhunīs expanded and produced many noble and saintly members. In the same way that the arahants Sāriputta and Moggallāna were the two chief disciples of the Order of Bhikkhus, similarly the arahant nuns Khemā and Uppalavaṇṇā were made the two chief female disciples of the Bhikkhunī Sangha.

The Order of Nuns founded in response to the pleas of Mahā Pajāpatī Gotami had far-reaching results. Women, who before the advent of the Buddha were placed in very unfavourable circumstances, found this Order of Bhikkhunīs a great blessing.

In this Order of Buddhist Nuns, queens, princesses, daughters of noble families, widows, bereaved mothers, helpless women, ex-courtesans and slaves could meet on common ground, irrespective of rank or caste. Even the lowly ones were thus elevated by the dignity of their religious quest, and they found consolation and peace. Many of those who otherwise would have passed their lives in oblivion, reached the very summit of human achievement—full emancipation in sainthood, as recorded in the moving and sublime stanzas of the *Theri-Gāthā* ("Psalms of the Sisters"), which form a part of the Buddhist Canon.

From that time 2500 years ago, the status of women in India rose considerably. People were made to realise the importance and dignity of woman in society. In the dispensation of the Buddha, women are given their rightful place in the family and in society.

Mahā Pajāpatī Gotami was indeed fortunate. In her worldly life she was the consort of King Suddhodana. She had the privilege of tending Prince Siddhattha when he was young. She was mother of Prince Siddhattha's step-brother, Prince Nanda, who entered the Order and achieved arahantship. She was the cause of the founding of the Order of Bhikkhunīs and not only did she herself achieve arahantship, but made it possible for other women to breathe a free atmosphere in which they could seek emancipation just as men did.

2. Yasodharā

In the life of Prince Siddhattha perhaps no one showed him greater devotion than his consort, Princess Yasodharā. It was by proof of valour and strength that Prince Siddhattha won Yasodharā. But Buddhist stories show that she had been the consort of the Bodhisatta in countless previous births.

Both Prince Siddhattha and Yasodharā were of the same age and their married life was a happy one. They lived in luxury, blissfully unaware of the vicissitudes of life outside the palace. But before long it dawned on Prince Siddhattha's mind that life was by no means as pleasant as it had been made to appear to him and that enjoyments in the royal household were but fleeting pleasures.

Prince Siddhattha severed himself from his beautiful consort, his newly born baby, and the countless pleasures of palace life to seek a way to end the miseries of life. Barefooted and bareheaded, wearing the yellow robes of an ascetic, he walked about in the scorching sun or piercing cold, begging his food. Princess Yasodharā too endured privations, though of a different sort. She bore the pangs of separation without a murmur. It was only after attaining Supreme Enlightenment that the Buddha visited Yasodharā again.

When the Buddha visited Kapilavatthu and came to King Suddhodana's palace, all but Princess Yasodharā came to pay their reverence to him. She thought: "Certainly, if there is any virtue in me, the noble Lord himself will come to my presence. Then I will reverence him."

And when the Buddha entered Yasodharā's chamber in the company of the King and two of his disciples, and sat on the prepared seat, Yasodharā came, clasped his ankles and placing her head on his feet, paid reverence to him. The Buddha had given directions that she should be allowed to salute him as she wished.

King Suddhodana then commented on her great love and said: "Lord, when my daughter heard that you were wearing yellow robes, she also robed herself in yellow. When she heard you were taking only one meal a day, she also did the same. When she heard that you had given up lofty couches, she lay on a low couch. When she heard that you had given up garlands and scents, she also gave them up. When her relatives sent messages to say that they would maintain her, she did not even look at a single one. So virtuous was my daughter."

The Buddha then said: "Not only in this birth, but in a previous birth too, she cared for me." He then related the Candakiṇṇāra Jātaka.

Yasodharā proclaimed to the world her role as perfect consort to the Bodhisatta since the time of the Buddha Dipankara, who foretold what the ascetic Sumedha would become in the future. And it was this ascetic Sumedha who became Gautama Buddha, the Enlightened One of our present age.

According to the *Pūjāvaliya*, Yasodharā, on her 78th year, just before she passed away, said: "I have now reached my 78th year. I have been your inseparable shadow and obedient wife in countless births. Even so, in a few lives some of my actions might appear to have been shortcomings. But these were attributable to the frailties inherent in womankind and for them I beg your pardon now, my Lord!"

She further added: "Yet, however, their effect has been to foster your endeavours towards perfection. And, in this life, with my help, you achieved your objective in a far shorter time than other Bodhisattas."

Then Yasodharā went on to say, "For me too, rebirth is now ended and I shall be no husband's wife again. In keeping with the tradition of the Buddhas of former times, before age and decay afflict me, I must pass away before you. And now I take my leave of you, my Lord."

Yasodharā, the consort of the Bodhisatta, was indeed an ideal partner. In her advice to young wives she described how self-sacrificing she had always been. She said, "I have submitted myself to his wish to be offered as an object of alms, without a murmur. I have for many births slaved for others to release him from difficulties and punishments. I have willingly allowed him to give away our children." This was in reference to the Vessantara Jātaka.

She further added, "I have asked him to give away my jewellery and have abandoned all forms of royal grandeur and comforts when he sought forest life. Then I gathered forest foods, leaving him undisturbed in his meditations. Similarly, the Lord in countless births gave his own life for my sake."

The great devotion of the Bodhisatta's consort, in their many births together, is a lesson to all womankind. Her sacrifices were such that Yasodharā can be classed as a peerless consort.

In her final birth Yasodharā submitted to her husband's Great Renunciation without a complaint. She brought up her son Rāhula well and finally allowed him to follow in the footsteps of the Buddha and enter the Order. When she herself entered the Order of Bhikkhunīs she attained to final emancipation in arahantship.

3. Visākhā

Visākhā, the devout daughter of Dhanañjaya, a millionaire of Sāvatthī, can be classed as an ideal lay woman. Judged by modern standards, Visākha remains an example to all womankind. She was not only intelligent, but was also gifted with all feminine charms. In addition to this, she was fabulously wealthy. She was able to win the love and esteem of Puññavaddhana, the son of another millionaire of Sāvatthī, named Migāra. Her young husband did not hold the same religious views as Visākhā who, quite early, had become a lay follower of the Buddha. But nevertheless, due to Visākhā's tolerance, there was always domestic happiness.

As a young girl she was so intelligent that she was able to grasp the Buddha's teaching when he came, as he often did, to her home on her father's invitation for an alms meal. It is said that when she heard the Dhamma from the Buddha for the first time, she attained to stream-entry (*sotāpatti*), the first stage of sainthood.

According to tradition, Visākhā in the prime of her life possessed not only beauty, but also great physical strength. Even in her youth she excelled both in worldly wisdom and spiritual insight.

The marriage of Puññavaddhana and Visākhā was a great event in the city. On her wedding day, in addition to her large dowry, Visākhā received from her father, as an heirloom, an exquisitely rich ornament, called "Mahālātā Pilandhana" (Great Parure). She also received ten admonitions from her father and it may be said that her following of these admonitions was the secret of her happy home life. The admonitions of Dhanañjaya to his beloved daughter were:

"The indoor fire should not be taken outside the home."
(Troubles at home should not be discussed with outsiders, as such talk tends to increase troubles in the family.)

"The outside fire should not be brought inside."
(The talk of outsiders who speak ill of the family, should not be repeated in the house. Such tale bearing destroys family harmony.)

"Give only to those who give."
(One should lend to those who will return what is given.)

"Do not give to those who do not give."
(One should not lend to those who do not return the articles.)

"Give to him who gives as well as to him who gives not."
(Poor relatives and friends should be helped even if they do not repay the loan.)

"Sit happily."
(She should sit in a becoming way and consider status and seniority. In the presence of her parents-in-law and her husband, she should keep standing.)

"Eat happily."
(She should take food after seeing that seniors and husband are served, and also the servants provided for.)

"Sleep happily."
(Before a wife retires for the night, the needs of the seniors of the

family should be seen to, and she should check that doors are locked and other household duties done.)

"Wait upon the household fire."
(The needs of husband and senior family members in the house should be well attended to as a sacred duty.)

"Honour the household divinities."
(Parents-in-law and the husband should be honoured as the divinities of the home.)

Visākhā's tact and patience made her husband's home an ideal one. Her father-in-law finally became a follower of the Buddha and her husband gave her complete freedom to carry on Buddhist activities.

At Sāvatthī she built the "Eastern Monastery" (Pubbārāma). The Buddha spent six Rainy Seasons in that monastery and delivered several discourses there which were of particular interest to laymen. In the course of time she became one of the most prominent supporters of the Buddha and the Order. She was chosen to settle disputes that arose among the Bhikkhunīs. It is said that some of the rules for Bhikkhunīs were laid down at her suggestion. In that distant age when women were not much esteemed in society, Visākhā, by her obedience and reverence shown to elders, won the respect of all and the prominence given to her in the Buddhist scriptures.

It is true that her great wealth stood her in good stead in helping her to acquire the highest place among women. She used her wealth for hospitality and for assisting her less fortunate sisters as well as in support of the Sangha.

4. Kisāgotamī

When the Buddha was residing in the Jetavana monastery, built by that famous lay supporter of the Sangha, Anāthapiṇḍika, a woman named Kisāgotamī came to him with a very sad tale. She belonged to the Gotama clan and therefore was a relation of Prince Siddhattha who had become the Buddha.

This Kisāgotamī was a remarkably beautiful woman. She had a delicate, tender and frail body. And because she was slender, she was known as Kisa (slender) Gotami. She was well married, her husband being a wealthy merchant. They had a lovely baby boy and were a happy and contented family.

But when the child was about a year old he fell ill, and before any physician could be summoned he died, causing untold grief to the parents. This was indeed a cruel blow to the delicate mother and she would not accept the fact that the child was dead.

Kisāgotamī, in her grief, ran about distraught, clasping the dead child's body to her breast; nor would she heed the sad counsel of those who told her that the dead could not be brought back to life. Kisāgotamī ran up and down the city sobbing and begging those she met to give her child some medicine. Some of the passers-by in the street, seeing this pathetic sight, did not contradict Kisāgotamī's belief that the child could be restored to life. At last, an elderly man understanding the woman's pitiful plight, directed her to the Buddha.

At that time, the Buddha was preaching the Dhamma to a group of eager listeners. To the amazement of all, Kisāgotamī thrust herself forward and placed her dead baby at the Master's feet, imploring him to bring it back to life.

The Buddha patiently listened to her and gazing at her with gentle eyes said, "Sister! There is an infallible medicine with which I can heal your affliction. Fetch me a few mustard seeds from a house in the town. But," the Buddha added, "you must get these mustard seeds from a house where there has never been a death."

The unfortunate woman failed to realise the significance of the words of the Buddha, and, with the hope of restoring her dear son's life, she immediately set out in search of the mustard seeds.

Still hugging her dead child, she went from house to house in search of the life-giving mustard seed. There was the mustard seed all right, and the pitying householders were only too glad to give it to the wretched mother. But when she told them that it had to be from a house that had never known death, they said:

> "Here is the seed, but we have lost our slave!
> Here is the seed, but our good man is dead!
> Here is some seed, but he who sowed it died
> Between the rain-time and the harvesting!"

The Light of Asia

Till late in the evening Kisāgotamī went from house to house in Sāvatthī in search of the mustard seed. But everywhere she heard the same pathetic tale—and at last she came to realise the universality of death. Truth dawned on her and she learnt to accept the fact that death was inevitable for all. Then she knew at last that her child was dead. She left the body at the charnel-field and returned to the presence of the Buddha.

She fell down at the feet of the Master and said: "Now, O Lord, I understand the great lesson you taught me, by asking me to get mustard seed from a house where there had been no death." Then:

"My sister! Thou hast found—the Master said—
Searching for what none finds—that bitter balm
I had to give thee. He thou loved'st slept
Dead on thy bosom yesterday; today
Thou know'st the whole wide world weeps with thy woe."

The Light of Asia

Kisāgotamī realised the truth of the Buddha's words. She learnt that all existing things change and are subject to decay. And, as she learnt this universal truth, she attained the first stage of sainthood. She then entered the Order of Nuns (Bhikkhunī) and quite soon thereafter she attained arahantship.

On that occasion the Buddha preached on the impermanence of all worldly things and declared that the aim of life should be to attain the Deathless State, Nibbāna.

5. Paṭācārā

When the Buddha was residing at the Jetavana Monastery in Sāvatthī, there lived in the neighbourhood a young girl named Paṭācārā. She was endowed with all the possessions of which a woman could be proud: she was exquisitely beautiful; her parents were rich; and she could have won the love of any young man of the country for purposes of marriage.

Nevertheless, Paṭācārā had a clandestine love affair with one of the household servants and as she was aware that her parents would never agree to her unequal marriage with this serf, she eloped with her lover and lived in a jungle den in a far-away forest. As time passed, Paṭācārā was expecting her first baby and she had a very keen desire to visit her parents in Sāvatthī.

But Paṭācārā's husband was afraid to face his former master, as he thought that he would be punished for secretly winning the love of the girl and eloping with her. Paṭācārā, however, was determined to see her parents and when her husband was absent, she stole away from her forest abode. On the way, however, a baby boy was born and yielding to the pleadings of her husband who had followed her, she returned to their hut in the forest.

In the course of time, Paṭācārā was expecting her second child and she felt once again a very strong desire to visit her parents. For the second time she stole away from the hut and was on her way to Sāvatthī, this time accompanied by her first child. Once again her husband followed her, and while in the forest she gave birth to her second child.

On this occasion there was very heavy rain and her husband, wanting to provide a shelter for his spouse and the little children, went in search of some leaves. But, to Paṭācārā's great dismay, he did not return. Paṭācārā was worried and spent a restless night.

On the following morning, she set out in search of her husband, and to her untold sorrow she beheld her husband dead, close to an ant hill. He had been bitten by a snake when he was about to cut leaves. Nevertheless, Paṭācārā continued her journey to her parental home.

On the way, the unfortunate Paṭācārā had to cross a river which was in spate due to the previous night's rain. And as the current was very swift, she left the elder child on the river bank and crossed the river carrying the newly born infant. Reaching the opposite bank she left the infant there and started back to fetch the other child. She was almost mid-way across the river when she spied a hawk hovering over the infant on the bank she had just left. The hawk, thinking that it was a piece of meat, carried the baby away. Paṭācārā cried out in the hope that the hawk would leave the child. But it was of no avail. The elder child, seeing the mother waving her hands in the attempt to drive away the hawk, thought that his mother was calling him and walked into the river, where he was swept away by the current. Thus she had lost her husband and her two little children.

So Paṭācārā continued on her way all alone. But as she approached the place of her parental home, she saw a fire and anxiously inquired what it was. One of the passers-by told her, "Last night, owing to the heavy rain, a house came down and all its occupants were killed. In that funeral pyre the dead are being cremated." It was her parents' house and Paṭācārā realised that her father, mother and brother were all dead.

Under the weight of all these losses she had suffered, her mind's sanity broke down. She ran distraught, and in her mad flight her cloth fell off. People seeing that mad woman running naked threw stones at her, but she continued her flight until she came to the Jetavana Monastery where the Buddha was preaching.

Seeing Paṭācārā's plight the Buddha spoke to her. His kind and compassionate words brought Paṭācārā to her senses and to her great shock she realised that she was naked and covered herself with her hands. One of the assembly passed a garment to her and she covered herself with it.

The Buddha then gave a sermon pointing out that everything in the world changes and is subject to decay. These changes bring great sorrow to the mind and the only way to avoid that sorrow is to end the cycle of births by attaining Nibbāna.

Paṭācārā accepted the words of the Buddha. She entered the Order of Bhikkhunīs and in due course attained arahantship. She was singled out by the Buddha as being foremost among the nuns in her knowledge of the disciplinary rules of the Order. After losing all, Paṭācārā ultimately won to the highest, final deliverance.

— §§§ —

Buddhist Observances and Practices

Piyadassi Thera

Bodhi Leaves No. 48

First published: 1970

Buddhist Observances and Practices

Standpoint

Buddhism is a system of moral, mental and intellectual training proclaimed and laid down by Gotama Buddha. It involves neither an exclusively intellectual or rationalistic way of life nor a way wholly devoted to ritualistic observances, but embraces both the intellectual and emotional aspect of man's life—his head and heart. Looked at from this point of view Buddhism is not, as some hasty critics would conclude, a mere philosophical speculation, a doctrine of metaphysical and logical abstractions bereft of practical value or importance. The Buddhist way of life, the Buddhist method of grasping the highest truth, awakening from ignorance to full knowledge, does not depend on mere academic knowledge or purely intellectual development, but on a doctrine which has its practical counterpart, and it is this happy combination of theory and practice (*ratio atgue usus*) that leads the follower to enlightenment and final deliverance.

The Buddha's attitude towards life is not merely intellectual but practical. It is a realization of that which is good and beneficial. It makes for ethical perfection as well as mental emancipation. This implies a cultivation of good emotions and an abandonment of the bad. The emotional aspect too should be developed though that alone does not lead us to the final goal. Good emotions should always be blended with right understanding. They should go arm in arm.

It is now quite clear that in the interplay of doctrine and discipline *(dhamma-vinaya)* or knowledge and conduct *(vijjā-caraṇa)* the two constitute a single process of growth. "As hand washes hand and foot washes foot so does wisdom cleanse conduct and conduct cleanse wisdom."[67]

67 DN 4.

Rituals, the observance of set forms or rites, have a place in almost all religions. These rituals are more on the emotional side.

However, one has to be careful so as not to overdo these observances; for then one tends to become obsessed with emotions. There is the risk of one becoming a victim of maudlin sentimentalism. One should not go to extremes in anything but should follow the middle path so well extolled by the Buddha.

It should always be borne in mind that the Buddha was not a Creator God, an incarnation of God, a Brahma, or a supernatural being. He was a human being who achieved the highest mental and intellectual attainments open to men. Unaided by any teacher, human or divine, he reached the acme of purity and was perfect in the best qualities of the human nature. He was an embodiment of compassion and wisdom (*karuṇā* and *paññā*) which became the two guiding principles in his dispensation (*sāsana*). Through personal experience he understood the supremacy of man, and attributed all his attainments and achievements to human effort and intelligence. The Buddha never claimed to be a saviour who tried to save "souls" by means of a revealed religion.

No Mediators

It may also be observed that according to Buddhism wrongdoing is not regarded as a "sin," for that word is foreign to the teaching of the Buddha. There is no such thing as "breaking the Buddha's laws," for he was not a law-giver, an arbitrator or potentate who punished the bad and rewarded the good deeds of beings. The doer of the deed is responsible for his own actions; he suffers or enjoys the consequences of deeds, and it is his concern either to do good or to do bad.

Again Buddhist monks are not priests who perform rites or sacrifice. They do not administer and pronounce absolution. A Buddhist monk cannot and does not stand as an intermediary between men and "supernatural" powers for Buddhism teaches that each individual is solely responsible for his own liberation. Hence there is no need to win the favour of a mediating priest. You yourselves should strive on; the Buddhas only show the path.[68] The path is the same ancient path trodden and pointed

68 Dhammapada, v. 276

out by the Enlightened Ones of all ages. The attitude of the Buddha towards his followers is like that of an understanding and compassionate teacher or a physician. Hence there is no praying and petitioning to an external agency for deliverance. This is the Buddhist standpoint.

The Buddha Image

In Buddhism there is what is called *Buddha vandana* or reverencing the Buddha. The Buddha, however, is not in existence to receive the homage of others. Then why pay reverence and obeisance to one who is not in existence? Why do Buddhists go before a Buddha image, a Bodhi tree, a stupa or pagoda or some such object, worship them and pray?

Well, here there is no praying to or worshipping of inanimate objects. Before the image, the Buddhists are only recalling to mind the greatness of their guide and teacher whom the image represents. The highest worship is that paid to the best of men, those great and daring spirits who have, with their wide and penetrating grasp of reality, wiped out ignorance and rooted out defilements from their minds. The men who saw Truth are true helpers, but Buddhists do not pray to them. They only reverence in gratitude and admiration the revealers of truth for having pointed out the path to true happiness and deliverance.

In this act of reverence it is the devotee who gains and benefits. His thoughts, speech and deeds become pure when he thinks of the virtues of the Buddha and concentrates on them; he gains inspiration and moral support to emulate the Master. It is a helpful meditation.

We honour our departed ones. Why do people lay wreaths at a war memorial? Why do they give pride of place on the walls of their homes to pictures of their dear departed parents and other beloved ones? Do they respect the picture or the frame? Certainly not. Their honour and homage is in the name of the dead one. So when a Buddhist approaches a Buddha image which is an object of meditation, and thinks of the teacher in respectful admiration, are we justified in calling that act of reverence useless idolatry?

It must, however, be mentioned that in the case of developed individuals, symbolic worship is hardly necessary. They could visualise the greatness of the Buddha without the aid of a symbol which is necessary and even vital in the case of those who are not advanced in mental development.

However, it is not only the emotional type but even high intellectuals and great thinkers who have gained inspiration from a Buddha image. Jawaharlal Nehru in his autobiography writes:

"At Anuradhapura (in Ceylon), I liked greatly an old seated statue of the Buddha. A year later, when I was in Dehra Dun Gaol, a friend in Ceylon sent me a picture of this statue, and I kept it on my little table in my cell. It became a precious companion for me, and the strong calm features of the Buddha's statue soothed and gave me strength and helped me to overcome many a period of depression."[69]

Count Kayserling in *Travel Diary of a Philosopher* writes: "I know nothing more grand in this world than the figure of the Buddha. It is the perfect embodiment of spirituality in the visible domain."

Offering of Flowers

It is a common sight in Buddhist lands to see the devotees, both young and old, and even the very babes, offering flowers before an image or some such sacred object, lighting an oil lamp or burning incense in the name of the Buddha.

Children take delight in gathering flowers and arranging them in order, before they offer them in the name of the Buddha. While learning to appreciate the aesthetic aspect of things, they also learn to be generous, to let go, and above all to respect the *Buddha,* the Teacher; the *Dhamma,* the Teaching; and the *Sangha,* the Taught.

Now when a Buddhist offers flowers, or lights a lamp, and ponders over the supreme qualities of the Buddha, he is not praying to anyone; these are not rites, rituals or acts of worship. The flowers that soon fade, and the flames that die down speak to him of

---

69 *An Autobiography,* John Lane, The Bodley Head, London, p. 271.

the impermanency (*anicca*) of all conditioned things.[70] The image serves him as an object for concentration, for meditation; he gains inspiration and endeavours to emulate the qualities of the Master. Those who do not understand the significance of this simple offering hastily conclude: "this is idol worship." Nothing could be more untrue.

Buddhist Marriage Ceremonies

There are no marriage ceremonies in Buddhism as we find in other religions. The Buddhist monks are not priests who solemnize marriages. That being so, they do not take part in marriage ceremonies. In Ceylon, those who attach importance to traditional customs, often invite a layman, generally an elderly relative well versed in ceremonies, to perform the marriage ceremony by reciting devotional versos to evoke the blessings of the "Triple Gem," the *Buddha*, the *Dhamma*, the *Sangha*, on the couple to be married.

At some wedding ceremonies a bevy of girls dressed in their national white costume recite together benedictive verses in Pāli, known as the *Jayamaṅgala Gāthā*, which describe some of the outstanding virtues of the Buddha. Often a few days before the actual marriage ceremony, monks are invited to the homes of the bride and the bridegroom for a *dāna* or midday meal. After the offerings, the monks will recite the Suttas, discourses of the Buddha, especially the *Maṅgala Sutta*, a discourse on the Blessings, and one of them will deliver a short sermon by way of exhortation, citing examples of happily married lives recorded in the Buddhist texts. Most popular among these examples is the married life of Nakulapitā and Nakulamātā recounted below.

Some Buddhists prefer to visit a temple or monastery immediately after their wedding ceremony to obtain the blessings of the Buddhist monks, who recite the *parittas* or discourses of protection (see below). The couple also receives a short exhortation dealing with the reciprocal duties of the husband and wife as explained by the Buddha in the *Sigālovāda Sutta*,[71] and so forth.

70 For details on worship, see Wheel No. 18, *Devotion in Buddhism.*

71 DN 31. Translated in Wheel No. 14, *Everyman's Ethics.*

The monks perform all their religious duties with no charge. The laity in turn see to the needs of the monks who really depend on the devout laity for their bare necessities, the fourfold requisites: robes, food, dwelling place end medicine.

Neither wedding ceremonies nor registering of marriages are performed in the Buddhist Vihāras, temples or monasteries, for they are secular activities.

The Story of Nakulapitā & Nakulamātā

Two striking incidents mentioned in the text show how far absolute good faith and pure love between two married couples can go. Nakulapitā and Nakulamātā are a genial couple who lived during the time of the Buddha Gotama. When the Master visited their home, they approached him respectfully, and then Nakulapitā the husband, said: "Lord, I was quite young when I brought home Nakulamātā who was a mere girl. Ever since we were married, Lord, I am not aware of having transgressed against her even in thought, much less in person. Lord, we do wish earnestly to behold each other not only in this very life but also in the life to come."

Then Nakulamātā, the wife, spoke in just the same way. Thereupon said the Buddha: "If both wife and husband wish to behold each other both in this very life and the life to came, if both are matched in faith *(saddhā)*, in virtue (*sīla*), in generosity (*cāga*) and in wisdom *(paññā)*, then do they behold each other in this very life and in the life to come."[72]

The other incident also is recorded in the Aṅguttara Nikāya.[73] Once Nakulapitā was grievously ill. Then his wife, Nakulamātā, came to his bedside, spoke to him tenderly, and made him understand her many virtues, and that he should not entertain any thoughts of anxiety, worry or doubts on her account. She advised him not to undermine his health by such disturbing thoughts.

When Nakulapitā was thus counselled and consoled by his loving Nakulamātā, his sickness subsided. Thus saved by her willing

72 A II 61.
73 A III 295.

hands and loving heart, Nakulapitā, leaning on a staff, visited the Buddha and saluted him. Thereupon the Blessed One, while praising the virtues of Nakulamātā said: "Good man you have greatly gained in having had as your guide and teacher such a wife as Nakulamātā who is so full of compassion toward you and so well-wishing."

It is said that the couple attained sanctity (the paths) together, and that these two were placed by the Buddha as chief of those that win confidence.

Buddhist Funeral Rites

Among the Buddhists, the funeral rites, as in the case of marriage ceremonies, are simple and not elaborate. When a Buddhist passes away, the close relatives will invite the monks to the house of the departed one or to the cemetery to perform the rites. The congregation will first recite the three Refuges *(tisaraṇa)* and the five Precepts (*pañca sīla*). Next, the close relatives (in the case of a parent, the children, if any) will offer white clothes to the monks. Merit thus accrued is shared with the departed one thus:

> *Idaṃ me ñātinaṃ hotu*
> *Sukhitā hontu ñātayo*
>
> Let this (merit) accrue to my relatives
> May they be well and happy!

While reciting the Pali verse they will pour water from a jug into an empty cup till it overflows, an act symbolic of the passing of merit to the departed. The monks will then recite together a special verse in Pāli suitable for the occasion:

> *Aniccā vata saṅkhārā—uppāda vaya dhammino*
> *Uppajjitvā nirujjhanti—tesaṃ vūpasamo sukho*

Impermanent are all component things, They arise and cease, that is their nature; They come into being and pass away, Release from them is bliss supreme.

This is followed by a short sermon emphasizing the impermanency of all conditioned things—how death comes to all, and puts an end to this brief span of life.

On the sixth day after the death, a monk is invited to the house of the deceased after dusk to deliver a sermon. It is customary for the preacher to speak mainly on impermanency and suffering *(anicca* and *dukkha),* the twin realities of existence, and the nature of this drama of life and death. Relatives and friends attend this sermon.

On the following (seventh) day, several monks are invited for the *dāna,* the midday meal, and the merit thereby accrued is shared with the departed one. Most of these performances are repeated at the end of the third month also.

In a non Buddhist country, in the absence of monks the laity themselves could together recite the two verses and share merit with the departed one.

On Occasions of Death

1. *At the Death Bed*

There are sciences and knowledge which are helpful to facilitate the comfortable birth of man, but there is no science which helps man to pass out of this existence with the least discomfort. Buddhism, which stresses the importance of thought, regards the last thought of the dying man as most important in that it helps to condition the nature of his next existence. On several occasions, the Buddha, realizing that a man was about to die, has spoken such appropriate meaningful words as would help the dying man to get into the correct frame of mind.

Even the very sight of a Buddha, or in the absence of the Buddhas and arahants, even a Buddhist monk, or a saint, at times, is a balm to the dying person. The *Dhammapada* Commentary[74] records the following story:

At Sāvatthī, there lived a miserly brahmin whose only son was known by the name of Matthakundali. When the boy was sixteen years of age he suddenly fell ill. His mother was eager to consult a doctor; the mean-hearted father, however, would not send for one lest he might lose his wealth. When the boy was tottering on

74 *Dhammapadaṭṭhakathā,* Vol 1, p. 25.

the verge of death, a physician was called in. But he left the place knowing that the illness was beyond remedy.

The father, who had no doubts about his son's imminent death, pondered: "When my son dies all my friends and relatives will throng to see him, and they will cast eyes on the wealth in my household and consequently I shall fall into difficulty." So he carried the dying child and laid him down on the open terrace.

Knowing the sad plight of Matthakundali, the Buddha visited him. The dying child caught a fading glimpse of the Master, radiant and sparkling with boundless love.

It was a spectacle of grandeur which he had never witnessed before. In his rapture he wished to raise his hands in salutation to the Compassionate One. But this he could not do, for his limbs were benumbed with feebleness. Then, with a heart and mind suffused with awe and reverence, he gazed upon the Master, thus saluting him mentally. The Buddha commented:

"He has done enough," and retraced his steps to Jetavana monastery. As the Blessed One departed the boy died and was reborn in a celestial deva realm, in a good state of existence.

One of the blessings resulting from the practice of *mettā* or loving kindness is that a man never dies with a confused mind (*asammūḷho kālaṃ karoti*).[75] In view of this importance of the last thought of man, the Buddhist practice has arisen of reciting the Satipaṭṭhāna Sutta,[76] the well known discourse on the Foundations of Mindfulness, by the bedside of the dying man. This would help the dying man to entertain a wholesome thought before he breathes his last. Even if he does not understand the import of the words, being a Buddhist who with *saddhā* or confidence has listened over and over again to the melodious recitation of Pāli *gāthā*, he will in every probability be induced to enter into a wholesome state of mind by the mere enjoyment of that melody. Whosoever helps a dying man to enter into the correct frame of mind therefore is rightfully his best friend *(kalyāṇa mitta).*

---

75 *Mettānisaṃsa Sutta,* A V 342.

76 MN 10, DN 22; see Wheel No. 13.

2. *Burial and Cremation*

The reader might like to know the Buddhist practice regarding the disposal of a dead body. Is it a burial or cremation?

In the *Mahā Parinibbāna Sutta*[77] (the discourse on the passing away of the Buddha wherein are recorded in moving detail all the events that occurred during the last months and days of his life), the Venerable Ānanda, the personal attendant of the Buddha, asks this same question: "How are we to deal, Lord, with the remains of the Tathāgata, the Perfect One? The Buddha's answer was that the body should be cremated as in the case of a *cakkavatti rāja*, a universal monarch.

Apart from this statement of the Buddha no mention is made in the text about the disposal of a dead body. There is no uniform practice. Some prefer to cremate and others to bury the bodily remains of a person. However, in the present era with the growing scarcity of available land space, and the rapid increase of population to alarming proportions, cremation is preferable to burial. From a hygienic point of view, too, a cremation is preferable.

Regarding the disposal of the ashes left from the cremation, here, too, there is no uniform practice. The ashes may be kept in an urn or enshrined in a monument erected to the memory of the deceased if that is the wish of the dead person or the survivors.

There has been a practice of erecting stupas enshrining the ashes of the departed Buddha and the arahants. The sight of such can induce a sense of calm by helping one to recall the unblemished lives of these saints. The Buddha himself has mentioned this in the *Maha Parinibbāna Sutta.*

The Value of *Paritta* (*Pirit*)

"Recent research in medicine, in experimental psychology and what is still called parapsychology has thrown some light on the nature of mind and its position in the world. During the last forty years, the conviction has steadily grown among medical men that very many causes of disease, organic as well as functional, are directly caused by mental states. The body becomes ill, because the mind

77 DN 16; see Wheel No. 67/69.

controlling it either secretly wants to make it ill, or else because it is in such a state of agitation that it cannot prevent the body from sickening. Whatever its physical nature, resistance to disease is unquestionably correlated with the psychological condition of the patient."[78] "Mind not only makes us sick. It also cures. An optimistic patient has more chance of getting well than a patient who is worried and unhappy. The recorded instances of faith healing include cases in which even organic diseases were cured almost instantaneously."[79]

In this connection it is interesting to observe the prevalence, in Buddhist lands, of listening to the recital of the Dhamma for protection and deliverance from evil, and for promoting welfare and well-being. The selected discourses for recital are known as paritta suttas. *Paritta* in Pali, *paritrāna* in Sanskrit and *pirit* in Sinhala, mean principally 'protection.' They are used to describe certain suttas or discourses (spoken by the Buddha) that are regarded as affording protection and deliverance from harmful influences. The practice of reciting and listening to the paritta suttas began very early in the history of Buddhism. It is certain that their recital produces mental well-being in those who listen to them with intelligence and are confident in the truth of the Buddha's words. Such mental well-being can help those who are ill to recover, and it can also help to induce the mental attitude that brings happiness, and to overcome its opposite. Originally in India those who listened to paritta sayings of the Buddha understood what was recited and the effect on them was correspondingly great. The Buddha himself had paritta recited for him, and he also requested others to recite paritta for his own disciples when they were ill. This practice is still in vogue in Buddhist lands.

The Buddha and the arahants can concentrate on the paritta suttas without the aid of another. However, when they are ill it is easier for them to listen to what others recite, and thus focus their minds on the Dhamma that the sutta contains than think of the Dhamma themselves. There are occasions, as in the case of illness which

78 For the physical basis of resistance, see *The Nature of Disease* by J. E. R. McDonagh, FRCS.

79 Aldous Huxley, *Ends and Means* (London, 1946), pp. 258–259.

weakens the mind, when hetero-suggestion has been found to be more effective than auto-suggestion.

According to the Dhamma, the mind is so closely linked with the body that mental states affect the body's health and well-being. Some doctors even say that there is no such thing as a purely physical disease. Unless, therefore, these bad mental states are caused by previous evil acts *(akusala kamma-vipāka)*, and so are unalterable, it is possible so to change them that mental health and physical well-being will follow.

The vibratory sounds produced by *paritta* are soothing to the nerves and produce a state of peace of mind and bring harmony to the system.

How can bad influences springing from evil beings be counteracted by the recitation of paritta suttas? Well, they are the result of evil thinking. They can, therefore be destroyed by the good states of mind caused by listening intelligently and confidently to paritta sayings, because of the power of concentration that comes into being through attending wholeheartedly to the truth of the sayings.

Paritta sutta recital is a form of *saccakiriya*, of depending on the truth for protection, justification or attainment. This means complete establishment in the power of truth to gain one's end. The saying: "The power of truth protects the follower of the truth" *(Dhammo have rakkhati dhammacārī)* is the principle behind these sutta recitals. If it is true that virtue protects the virtuous, then a person who listens to these sayings with complete confidence in the Buddha's words which spring from complete enlightenment, will acquire so virtuous a state of mind that he will conquer any evil influence.

The recital of paritta suttas also results in material blessings through the mental states caused by concentration and confidence in listening intelligently to the recital. According to the Buddha, right effort is a necessary factor in overcoming suffering *(viriyena dukkhaṃ acceti)*.[80] Listening to one of these recitals in the proper way can also generate energy for the purpose of doing good, and following the path of wordily progress with diligence.

---

80 Saṃyutta Nikāya I 214.

It is understood that listening to these paritta suttas must produce in the intelligent and confident listener only wholesome states which can cure and prevent illness. There is no better medicine than truth *(Dhamma)* for both mental and physical ills which are the cause of all suffering and misfortune. So the recital of paritta suttas may, when they are listened to rightly, bring into being mental conditions of health necessary for material progress, physical welfare and well-being.

The Book of Paritta or The Book of Protection

It is both interesting and refreshing to note that there is hardly a Buddhist home in Ceylon where this Book of Paritta or Book of Protection is not found. It is given an important place in the Buddhist home. It is even treated with veneration.

Now what does this book contain? It is a collection of twenty-three suttas or discourses almost all delivered by the Buddha and found scattered in the five collections, *Nikāyas,* which form the *Sutta Piṭaka* or the "Basket of Discourses." These suttas found in the Book of Paritta (Protection) are preceded by an enunciation of the Three Refuges *(saraṇagamana);* the Ten Precepts *(dasa sikkhāpadāni);* the questions asked of a novice *(sāmaṇera-pañhā)* also known as the young one's questions *(kumāra-pañhā).* The most popular among these twenty-three suttas are the Good Omen Discourse *(Maṅgala Sutta),* the Jewel Discourse *(Ratana Sutta)* and the Loving kindness or Universal Love Discourse (*Mettā Sutta).*

Among the discourses of the Paritta Book are also included such important suttas as the *Dhammacakkapavattana,* Setting in Motion of the Wheel of Truth (the first sermon of the Buddha delivered at the Deer Park at Isipatane, Benares); *Sacca-vibhaṅga,* the Analysis of the (Four) Truths, and the *Bojjhaṅgas,* the Seven Factors of Enlightenment.[81]

It is customary for monks when they are invited to the homes of the laity on occasions of domestic importance such as birthdays, house-warming, illness and similar events, to recite from the Book of Paritta (protection) the popular suttas mentioned above. On

81 For an account of the *bojjhaṅgas* read *The Seven Factors of Enlightenment,* Piyadassi Thera, Wheel No. 1.

special occasions, monks are invited to recite the paritta suttas not for short periods but right through the night. At the commencement of this recital, the monks (generally about twelve) who have been invited will recite the three popular suttas mentioned above. Thereafter, a pair of monks will commence reciting the remaining suttas for two hours. They will then retire and will be followed by another pair for another two hours. In this manner the recital will last till dawn.

While the recital lasts, there will be found a vessel or jar of water placed on a table before the monks. On this table there is also the Book of Paritta written on talipot (*ola*) leaves, and also a ball of thread which is unloosened and passed on to the monks and the laity who hold the thread while the recital of the three popular suttas goes on. At the close of the recital of the entire book at dawn, the thread is broken into portions and distributed among the laity. The water is also distributed among them. These are meant as symbols of the protective power of the paritta that was recited. They have their psychological effects.

A question may arise whether recitals from the Book of Paritta will in every case result in the protection sought for. In this connection, the same reply given by the Venerable Nāgasena to King Milinda, why the recital of paritta does not in all cases protect onefrom death, is worth remembering. Due to three causes paritta may have no effect: kamma hindrances (*kammāvaraṇena*); hindrances from defilements (*kilesāvaraṇena*); and a lack of faith (*asaddhanatāya*).[82]

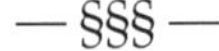

82 *Milinda Pañhā*.

Saṃsāra and The Way of Dispassion

Two Essays

Francis Story

Bodhi Leaves No. 49

First published: 1970

Saṃsāra

In Buddhism *saṃsāra* means literally "revolving in the cycle of rebirth." This cycle of rebirth ranges over the whole of the manifested universe, comprising thirty one abodes of beings with the various forms and degrees of consciousness appropriate to their condition. Technically it is not associated either with *rūpa* (form) or *arūpa* (formlessness) since it includes both conditions. Therefore its material factors are not an essential part of *saṃsāra;* it does not mean either the world, or the physical universe, as those terms are commonly understood. They are terms relating to a part or aspect of *saṃsāra* but are not synonymous with it.

Saṃsāra is a condition; but a "condition" ordinarily implies a "something" which is subject to the condition, and which can assume fresh conditions from time to time. The philosopher Bergson maintained that change is the only reality, and this agrees so closely with the Buddhist view of the spatial and temporal universe that we can take it as our first definition of *saṃsāra*. The only reality of *saṃsāra*, then, is change—the state of impermanence (*anicca*). There is, let us say, a reality of change which corresponds to the relative reality of the universe considered from the standpoint of conventional truth (*sammuti sacca*). On this level we deal with things as they appear to us in association with other things. If we try to isolate any particular object from its surroundings we find that we cannot do so. There is nothing that can be predicted about the object except in relation to other objects or ideas in the context of which it has its existence. If we say, for instance, that the object is square, we are dealing with its shape in relation to other shapes known to us. If we say that it is hard we are comparing its tactile effect with that of other objects which are softer. If we say that it is green we are contrasting its colour with that of other objects which produce a different sensation in our visual consciousness. The whole of our knowledge of the object is, in this sense, subjective. We can never know the object itself, but only its reflection in our own consciousness through the six doors of sensory cognition.

Can we be certain, then, that there is any object in reality? If there is, it must be a thing distinct from our knowledge of it. But we can find no proof of the existence of such a thing. A man who is red-green colour blind will see our green object the same colour as a red one. Now, supposing the green object we are examining is a leaf. In course of time the green leaf withers and becomes red. In the process its shape, texture, colour and other qualities will undergo transformation, yet we call it the same leaf although we cannot find any factor of identity between the red, withered leaf and the green, fresh one. In other words, we cannot find an object called a "leaf" which has changed; all we can discover is the process of change.

This can be applied to all the phenomena of the universe, not excepting human personality. There is the process of change, but no "thing" that changes. This is the Buddhist concept of *anattā;* but it was also noted by Plato, who pointed out that we cannot have any certain knowledge of qualities which are fluctuating and relative, because the thing which possesses those qualities cannot truly be said to be anything at all, since it is always half-way on the road to becoming something else. Plato was compelled to take the Buddhist view that the familiar world must be regarded as a world of becoming, rather than as a world of being, since it never truly is anything at all. He therefore concluded, in complete agreement with Buddhism, so far as he went, that we cannot have certain knowledge of the familiar world which is manifested to us through our sense-experience, precisely because that world is not wholly real. In Buddhism there is no word corresponding to "existence;" the Pali word *bhava* means "becoming," not "being."

Plato was driven to the desperate expedient of splitting his concept of the universe into two aspects, transcendence and immanence. These, in Platonic philosophy, divided the universe into two halves, between which it is impossible to establish any connection. Plato could not define in what way the real was related to the unreal, which is not surprising, since by its very nature the real cannot be related to anything. In the same way, the Vedantic idea of the *paramātman*, the eternal, unchanging soul of things, cannot be in any way connected with the phenomenal attributes of human personality such as body, mind, character, disposition, emotions and other psychic factors. It is clear that if there were any such eternal, unchanging soul, it would bear no relationship whatever to the impermanent, ever-changing human personality. It is therefore vain to imagine that this phenomenal ego possesses a soul-factor which identifies it with the *paramātman*. The phenomenal ego, just like the leaf or any other object of the familiar world, is *anattā*—devoid of any essential being or reality. What we call the "leaf" is a causal process of change, but no "thing" that changes.

"The world is imperfect; it is, indeed, shot through with evil and suffering. Moreover, being filled with change and decay, it cannot, as Plato insists, be wholly real." Thus writes Prof. C. E. M. Joad in his book, *Philosophy* (English Universities Press). Here is the doctrine of *anicca*, *dukkha* and *anattā* coming from one who, on his own statement, had never studied Indian philosophy. Now, *saṃsāra* is known by these three qualities: impermanence, suffering and absence of essential reality. They are qualities, but like the process of change we have been examining, they are qualities without any substratum of a "thing" to possess them. Just as there is change, but nothing that changes, so there are these qualities without any "thing" to support them.

Idealism claims that there is no existence of the phenomenal world whatever, but that it is solely an idea. Materialism maintains that the material world is the only reality, and that mind and consciousness, discrimination and volition are only its by-products. Both theories involve the same contradiction as Plato's doctrine of transcendence and immanence, in that each ignores the gulf it creates between the known world and the world of reality. Materialism cannot be true because we have already seen that there is by definition nothing essentially real in physical phenomena or material substance. Idealism equally cannot be true because it ignores the fact of a common standard of agreement concerning knowledge of the universe. If Berkleyan idealism were true it would mean that each individual lives, like a lunatic, in a world of his own mental creation with his own laws, and there would be no basis of agreement between one man's view of it and that of another. Idealism attempts to overcome this difficulty by holding that the existence of other individuals is itself only an idea; in other words, that when we take leave of our friend and he goes out of our sight and hearing he ceases to exist. But we know that he continues to exist independently of our knowledge of him, because when we next meet him he can tell us all that happened to him in the time between. If he ceased to exist when we parted we should have to assume that we too ceased to exist the moment we were outside his field of cognition; but we know very well that we continued to exist and that our current of experience, like his, carried on in the interim.

Buddhist philosophy avoids these two extremes of idealism and materialism, though it leans, if anything, towards the idealist position. The Buddhist position is anti-substantialist; there is no eternal self-existing matter. Similarly there is no eternal self-existing quiescent substance known as mind, having a prior existence, which is merely stimulated into activity when brought into contact with the sense objects by means of the sense organs. Mind, according to Theravada doctrine, is rather a product brought into being by the interaction of the *indriya* and *visaya* (the psychic faculties and their range of activity). The word *mano* (mind) is derived from the root *ma*, to measure. It therefore signifies the act of calculating, evaluating and judging. Technically it may be rendered "reason"; but it can also mean simply "mind" in the same sense as *citta*. The Mahāyānists, however, who maintain that the whole universe is but the creation of mind, and that nothing exists outside the mind,[83] use in this connection the word *citta*, not *mano*. Occasionally the word *viññāṇa* is used in place of *citta*.

The three principal schools of Buddhist thought from which all the later sections developed were the Sthaviravādins (Theravādins), Madhyamikas and Yogacarins. The first believed in the existence of the external world and its constituent parts, the *dhammas*. The second categorically denied the existence of the world and the *dhammas*, and did not even trouble to classify the *dhammas*. This school came nearest to Berkleyan idealism. The third believed that the universe, though an eject or reflection of the consciousness, has yet a relative existence and that, in fact, the *dhammas* are but stages of the mind's unfolding.

It is this last school which most successfully avoids the pitfalls of the extremes, and which comes most into line with present day knowledge of the universe. The *dhammas*, primary elements of the familiar world, exist independently of our knowledge of them, yet the energy that sustains them through the four stages of arising,

83 McGovern, W.M. 1968.

maturing, decay and disappearance is a mental force, and their existence is only transitory and relative. Thus, the object of the familiar world which we recognise by sense-cognition may not *An Introduction to Mahayana Buddhism.* necessarily bear any relationship to the external series of events which produces the impression in our consciousness; yet, nevertheless, the series of events is actually taking place. There is, in fact, a discrete and logically connected sequence of such events taking place all the time in the spatial-temporal complex of *saṃsāra*. *Sammuti sacca*, relative truth, as opposed to *paramattha sacca*, ultimate truth, has its basis in *avijjā*, or nescience. In the sense of *sammuti sacca* the universe, as the Sthaviravādins claimed, is real; in the sense of *paramattha sacca* it has no existence whatever, and the Madhyamikas are right. To get a full grasp of truth, both these standpoints have to be taken into account, for both are "one" on their own level. Where all are in agreement is that thought and volitional action are the cause of the arising of the *dhammas* both as units and as aggregates. The qualities are present though they may be interpreted differently by individuals, and there is a common level of relative consciousness on which they compose a logical pattern. But neither philosophy nor science can lift human consciousness out of the network of *saṃsāra* to be able to view that pattern as a whole and understand its origin. Buddhism frankly admits that this can only be achieved through meditative insight; it makes no claim that ultimate truth can be discovered by dialectics.

For ages philosophers have disputed among themselves concerning the nature of the universe without coming to any conclusion. The Greeks had philosophy, but did not know what to do with it; their transcendental speculations always remained a rather uncomfortable appendage to their real religion, which was a warm and sensuous love of life itself. The scholiasts of the Middle Ages wrangled about theological points that today only raise a smile. And if it should seem that the Buddhist concept of *sammuti sacca* and *paramattha sacca* is only another way of expressing Plato's idea of transcendence and immanence, carrying with it the same difficulties and objections, the answer is that in Buddhism philosophy is only an intellectual exercise, a game with logical rules played out in the sphere of relative truth. Buddhism shows a higher way towards realisation: the way of direct insight, free from the fetters of conceptual thinking. Buddhist philosophy analyses the components of the phenomenal universe very precisely, and in accordance with methods used by the best minds throughout the ages; but it does not pretend that this method will do anything more than exhibit the transitory, painful and illusory nature of *saṃsāra*. "This," says Buddhist philosophy in effect, "is *saṃsāra*, the round of existences created by ignorance. It is relatively true, but to discover that which is absolutely true, the *asaṅkhata dhammā*, you have to destroy the relativities of thought and speculation, and the only way to do so is by training the mind, tranquilising its restlessness and putting an end to its cravings."

— §§§ —

The Way of Dispassion

Gotama Buddha, the Lord of compassion, incomparable Teacher of gods and men, praised and exalted the holy life of purity, and commended the virtuous disciples who practised self-renunciation. In many ways he showed his mercy to the world, setting forth the noble doctrine of emancipation, so that all beings, hearing his gentle voice, were uplifted and inspired. Himself the greatest exponent of renunciation, who through many births had perfected the ten pāramis of a Bodhisatta, he gave the fruits of his virtue freely and ungrudgingly to the world, and taught the Truth for the welfare of all.

When he descended from the Tusita Heaven into his mother's womb for the last birth, he came into a world sunk in the threefold misery of *lobha, dosa* and *moha*. Then, as now, men harboured in their hearts delusion and hatred; they were led away by wild and inordinate cravings, and under their influence perpetrated deeds of cruelty and violence towards one another. They held in light esteem the claims of others to justice and benevolence, and thought only of their own material advantage. Their minds were aflame with craving, and passion was the arbiter of their lives.

Nowhere could they find happiness, for the satisfaction they sought could never be attained in a life governed by the three characteristics of *anicca, dukkha* and *anattā*. Yet they desperately strove to make their pleasures permanent, thinking that by repeating the momentary sensation over and over again, or by pursuing fresh experiences when the old ones grew stale, they could live perpetually in the enjoyment of the senses.

But rich or poor, strong or feeble, they were subject to the infirmity of the flesh, to sickness, old age and death; and the delights they hankered after, and for the sake of which, they brought ruin upon themselves, became as nothing, swallowed up in the jaws of time, the destroyer of all compounded things.

Then came the Buddha, proclaiming:

> "Passion and hatred arise from the self:
> Evil thought, delight and horror also arise therefrom.
> Arising, they torment (the mind) as boys (torment) a crow."
>
> Sūciloma Sutta (Sn 2.5)

The Enlightened One perceived that the self was the cradle of all the passions, and it could only be by surrender of that false, deceptive ego that peace and tranquillity could enter the mind. Looking with infinite compassion on all sentient beings, he saw them without distinction of good or bad, high or low. All are actuated by the same self-motive, and it is under that primal delusion that beings return again and again to the round of existence, drawn back irresistibly by their attachment, to work out their self-imposed destiny in accordance with their *kamma*.

Foremost among the virtues that tend towards conquest of self the Buddha proclaimed *dāna*, or universal charity. To put the needs of another before one's own is but the first step in the practice of *dāna*: its consummation and final flowering is to realise that there is no individual self—that whatsoever one does to another is done, as it were, to oneself. At that point even self-sacrifice ceases. There being no self, there is no sacrifice—only the all-comprehending benevolence of Buddhahood, that permeates the universe of living creatures with love, above, below and in all quarters. Fear and hatred, deception and greed cannot enter the mind that is released from self (*sakkāya-diṭṭhi*), nor can the darkness of ignorance obscure it. Luminous and serene, the light of the arahant shines forth; even in the flux of impermanence he finds the changeless eternity of Nibbāna.

> "Being untainted by the world, delighting in charity, established in the precepts and virtues, practising renunciation of the world, and obtaining excellent knowledge, may I be replete with strength and power!"
>
> "The Aspiration of Buddharakkhita," *Jinālaṅkāra* 248.

Disinterested charity therefore is essential to spiritual progress, and must be cultivated by whosoever would aspire to the bliss of Nibbāna. It extinguishes the grasping tendencies that are the cause of rebirth and suffering, and makes renunciation a habitual attitude of mind. The Bodhisatta gave his possessions and even life itself for the welfare of others. Such sacrifice can be possible only when it has ceased to be sacrifice as we understand it and has become instead the expression of a complete reorientation in thought. Expounding the principle of the non-self, the Vajracchedikā Sutta says: "And, O Subhūti, the *pāramī* of the highest perfection of endurance (*khanti*) belonging to the Tathāgata, that also is no *pāramī*. And why? Because, O Subhūti, at the time when the king of Kāliṅga cut my flesh from every limb, I had no idea of a self, of a being, of a living being, or of a person; I had neither an idea nor no-idea. And why? Because, O Subhūti, if I at that time had had an idea of a self, I should also have had an idea of malevolence." The Sutta continues concerning *dāna* thus: "A Bodhisatta, after putting aside all ideas (concepts based upon phenomena), should raise his mind to the highest perfect knowledge, he should frame his mind so as not to believe in (depend upon) form, sound, smell, taste or anything that can be touched. For what is believed is not to be depended upon. Therefore the Tathāgata preaches: a gift should not be given by a Bodhisatta who believes in (depends upon) anything; it should not be given by one who believes in form, sound, smell, taste or anything that can be touched."

Here the Yogācārin psychology is clear. It is to the effect that for the complete perfection of *dāna pāramitā* all idea of giver and recipient must be abandoned, as also all belief in the thing given—that is to say, as to its essential reality. The significance becomes transferred entirely to the action (*kamma*): it has no egocentric reference whatever.

The Buddha's Way of Dispassion leads to complete integration of the psychic faculties: it gives the penetrating vision that sees directly into the nature of causality, and beyond it, to the uncaused and uncompounded. That having been attained, no external events, no happenings in the realm of relative reality can give rise to sorrow, resentment or desire. The mind is finally liberated, poised on the wave crest of the ocean of *saṃsāra*, never to be submerged beneath the seething waters.

> "Knowing this body to be as foam and understanding its mirage-like nature, one will escape the tight grip of the King of Death, having destroyed the power of Māra."
>
> Dhammapada

No longer is there friend or foe for him who is thus liberated. Those who ignorantly consider themselves his enemies he enfolds with loving compassion, protecting them from their own evils, striving only to prevent them from harming themselves. Against their malevolence he puts up his dispassion, neutralising their hatred as water neutralizes a corrosive acid, and overcomes them with the weapons of harmlessness and purity.

The state of sublime equanimity is to be reached through understanding the nature of the five-*khandha*-process—that it is impermanent, lasting no longer than an instantaneous flash of light, that it is a mere aggregate of physical form, feelings, perceptions, mental formations and states of consciousness, and that it is without any persisting ego-entity. A continual unfolding of empty phenomena, conditioned by antecedent tendencies, it cannot form any basis for happiness: it can only give rise to new and ever unsatisfied desires. In ignorance we desire pleasure, but our real quest is for the self that enjoys the sensations. Since that self is nowhere to be found we remain unhappy, unable to perpetuate the present moment or anchor it to any firm ground of reality. The essence of the experience eludes us: in the moment of grasping it is gone.

We are urged to relinquish this hopeless effort to find satisfaction in the world of *anicca*, *anattā* and *dukkha*, and instead, to fix the mind steadfastly on the state of *virāga*, dispassionateness. In some texts the word *virāga* is used almost as an equivalent for Nibbāna (*tanhakkhaya virāga nirodha nibbāna*). This *virāga* consists in the extinction of attachment to sense-objects, the giving up of the concept "I" as the performer of actions and the ground of merit and demerit. It differs from suppression of selfhood, in that it cuts deeper than the mere inhibition of desires and reactions by any effort of will. The Tathāgata condemned forceful exertion of will-power in austerities. They are only a different expression of violence—violence directed against the unreal—in place of violence against the equally unreal not-self. The practice of such austerities in an extreme form serves only to divert the current of self-consciousness or to dam it, thus increasing its pressure. The psychological tension mounts, and instead of being extinguished the ego becomes magnified. The hold on self must be relaxed, not tightened, and this it to be brought about gradually and naturally by creating an opposite impulse, a tendency that manifests in disinterested activity for the welfare of others.

Benevolence as taught by the Buddha is an active principle that directs to one goal the purposes of heart and mind. By its cultivation the mind is freed from the *asavas* and the heart is made capable of a love that is universal and dispassionate, without attachment to ideas or objects. The mind of an arahant who has attained this beatitude of selfless, dispassionate benevolence, shines in the darkness of *saṃsāra* clearly and steadily, like the flame of a lamp in a sheltered place; and when the fuel is exhausted, for him there is no rebirth.

Buddhist Ideas in English Poetry

Cyril Moore

Bodhi Leaves No. 50

First published: 1970

Buddhist Ideas in English Poetry

Like as the waves make towards the pebbled shore,
So do our minutes hasten to their end,
Each changing place with that which goes before
In sequent toil all forwards do contend.
Nativity, once in the main of light,
Crawls to maturity, wherewith being crowned,
Crooked eclipses against his glory fight,
And Time that gave, doth now his gift confound.
Time doth transfix the flourish set on youth,
And delves the parallels in beauty's brow,
Feeds on the rarities of nature's truth.
And nothing stands but for his scythe to mow;
And yet to times in hope my verse shall stand
Praising thy worth, despite his cruel hand.

So Shakespeare, England's greatest poet, expressed his idea of *anicca*, the law of change. The sense of change, of passing and death are constantly recurring in English poetry. So is the idea of suffering (*dukkha*) and rarely, very rarely there is a striving after *anattā*, but never is that supreme Buddhist truth realised, for ever since Plato and the late Old Testament prophets, the Churches in the West have firmly held that man possessed a soul.

It is not surprising that the poets who see into the heart of things should see these truths, for did not the Buddha himself say:

"Whether Buddhas appear in the world, or whether Buddhas do not appear, it still remains an immutable fact that all physical and mental constituents of existence are impermanent (*anicca*), are subject to suffering (*dukkha*) and that everything is without an ego (*anattā*)."

But to return to change, of which Shelley said: "Nought can endure but mutability," the former Poet Laureate, John Masefield, has described it cosmically in *The Passing Strange*:

Out of the earth to rest or range
Perpetual in perpetual change,
The unknown passing through the strange.
For all things change, the darkness changes,
The wandering spirits change their ranges,
The corn is gathered to the granges.
The corn is sown again, it grows;
The stars burn out, the darkness goes;
The rhythms change, they do not close.
They change, and we, who pass like foam,
Like dust blown through the streets of Rome,
Change ever too; we have no home.

But change, as the Buddha showed, is accompanied by suffering and poets are more intensely aware of suffering than ordinary people. The universality of suffering has been summed up by Francis Thompson, a Catholic poet:

Nothing begins and nothing ends
That is not paid with moan;
For we were born in others' pain
And perish in our own.

Suffering has never been more poignantly described than by the young lyrical poet, Keats, "gold-dusty from tumbling amid the stars," when, in the ecstasy of that lovely *Ode to a Nightingale*, he remembered the dread disease (TB) which gnawed at his lungs. He then cried out in anguish against:

The weariness, the fever and the fret
Here, where men sit and hear each other groan,
Where palsy shakes a few, sad, last grey hairs.
Where youth grows pale, and spectre-thin, and dies;
Where but to think is to be full of sorrow
And leaden-eyed despair.

"And thus (as the Blessed One said) have you long time undergone suffering, undergone torment, undergone misfortune and filled the grave yards full: verily, long enough to turn away and free yourself from them all." But that deep insight, which saw the cause of all this suffering in the craving and clinging of our own desires, had not been attained by the poets who cried out in bewilderment.

Meanwhile the theologians try to reconcile the problem of pain with their conception of an all-wise and infinitely-loving God. We will leave them with their dilemma.

One poet at least did understand the law of cause and effect which gives rise to *kamma*. William Blake, in the eighteenth century, might have been writing as a Buddhist when he said:

> He who shall hurt the little wren
> Shall never be beloved of men.
> A robin redbreast in a cage
> Puts all heaven in a rage.
> A dog starved at his master's gate
> Predicts the ruin of the state.
> The wild deer wandering here and there
> Keep the human soul from care.

This reminds us that *metta*, or loving kindness, for animals is found very frequently in the English poets. One could quote from James Stevens, particularly his poem *The Snare*, which expresses his deep feeling at the cry of a rabbit caught in a cruel trap, or from Ralph Hodgson or W. H. Davies, the tramp poet, who wrote:

> The shot that kills a hare or bird
> Doth pass through me.

But for real understanding which is the heart of mind, there is nothing better than D. H. Lawrence's poem, *The Snake*, from which this is taken:

> Someone was before me at my water-trough.
> And I, like a second comer, waiting.
> He lifted his head from his drinking as cattle do,
> And looked at me vaguely, as drinking cattle do,
> And flicked his two-forked tongue from his lips and mused
> a moment.
> And stopped and drank a little more,
> Being earth-brown, earth-golden from the burning bowels of
> the earth
> On the day of Sicilian July with Etna smoking.
> And voices in me said. If you were a man
> You would take a stick and break him now, and finish him off.
> But must I confess how I liked him,

How glad I was he had come like a guest in quiet, to drink at my water-trough,
And depart peaceful, pacified, and thankless,
Into the burning bowels of the earth.

The Buddha likened the world to a bubble and a mirage; the same simile is in these lines by William Drummond (1585–1649):

This life, which seems so fair,

Is like a bubble blown up in the air
By sporting children's breath,
Who chase it everywhere
And strive who can most motion it bequeath.
And though it sometimes seem of its own might
Like to an eye of gold to be fixed there,
And firm to hover in that empty height,
That only is because it is so light—
But in that pomp it doth not long appear;
For when 'tis most admired, in a thought,
Because it erst was nought.

In Francis Bacon, too, the bubble analogy occurs, with even stronger emphasis on the unavoidable *dukkha* of life:

The World's a bubble, and the life of man less than a span.
In his conception wretched, from the womb
So to the tomb:
Curst from his cradle, and brought up to years,
With cares and fears.
Who then to frail mortality shall trust,
But limns on water, or but writes in dust.
Yet whilst with sorrow here we live oppressed,
What life is best?
Courts are but only superficial schools
To dandle fools;
The rural parts are turned into a den
Of savage men;
And where's a city from foul vice so free,
But may be term'd the worst of all the three?

Domestic cares afflict the husband's bed,
Or pains his head;

Those that live single, take it for a curse,
Or do things worse;
Some would have children, those that have them moan
Or wish them gone;
What is it then, to have, or have no wife,
But single thralldom, or a double strife?
Our own affections still at home to please is a disease;
To cross the seas to any foreign soil
Peril and toil;
Wars with their noise affright us; when they cease,
We are worse in peace;
What then remains, but that we still should cry
For being born, or, being born, to die?

If Buddhism is pessimistic, as some people persist in asserting, then so is the best of English poetry, and it would be a superficial view, indeed, that presented life in any other colours. To call Buddhism pessimistic is evidence of a shallow mind, and perhaps, an unfeeling heart. All true poetry is born of the tragic sense and a sympathetic participation in the woes of others. The man who says, "But I enjoy life! Life is good!" will never make a poet, although he may make a facile rhymester for birthday cards.

E. Housman has well expressed this anguish of the poet for the pain of others:

The stars have not dealt me the worst they could do.
My pleasures are plenty, my troubles are two.
But oh, my two troubles they reave me of rest,
The brains in my head and the heart in my breast.

He goes on to wish (not quite sincerely, one feels) that he could have the ease of mind enjoyed by those:

That relish their victuals and rest on their bed
With flint in the bosom and guts in the head.

No. The true poet would never exchange the acute sensibility that makes him a poet, for the callousness of one who is untouched by suffering that is not his own, though there might well be times when he thinks he would be thankful to do so.

Could there be any grander assertion of mutability, and of the pitiful delusion of power that afflicts mankind, than this magnificent sonnet of Shelley?

> I met a traveller from an antique land
> Who said: Two vast and trunkless legs of stone
> Stand in the desert. Near them on the sand,
> Half sunk, a shatter'd visage lies, whose frown
> And wrinkled lip and sneer of cold command
> Tell that its sculptor well those passions read
> Which yet survive, stamp'd on these lifeless things,
> The hand that mock'd them and the heart that fed.
> And on the pedestal these words appear:
> 'My name is Ozymandias, king of kings:
> Look on my works, ye Mighty and despair!'
> Nothing beside remains. Round the decay
> Of that colossal wreck, boundless and bare,
> The lone and level sands stretch far away.

While most of the religions of the world lay stress on man's helplessness and assert that it is only by supernatural aid that he can attain release or blessedness, Buddhism claims that each must win salvation for himself. Buddhas can but point the way; each must make for himself an island, must go to himself as a refuge This point of view finds expression in many of the English poets, from Shakespeare's:

> The fault, dear Brutus, lies not in our stars,
> But in ourselves,

to Wordsworth's:

> Here must thou be, O man!
> Strength to thyself; nor helper hast thou here:
> Here keepest thou thy individual state;
> No other can divide with thee this work.

It is only fair to state that later in life, when his vision had dimmed, and his poetry had correspondingly deteriorated, Wordsworth became a thoroughly orthodox Christian.

But Browning, too, felt that the Truth was to be found within man himself, not outside, though here again, in agreement with the eternalism of the Western philosophers, he conceived Truth to be something permanent and unchanging, though imminent in man, waiting only to be realised. This is from *From 'Paracelsus,'* for Browning had studied the works of the alchemist:

> Truth is within ourselves; it takes no rise
> From outward things, whate'er you may believe.
> There is an inmost centre in us all
> Where truth abides in fullness; and around,
> Wall upon wall, the gross flesh hems it in,
> This perfect, clear perception—which is truth.
> A baffling and perverting carnal mesh
> Binds it, and makes all error: and to know
> Rather consists in opening out a way
> Whence the imprisoned splendour may escape,
> Than in effecting entry to a light
> Supposed to be without.

It sounds so plausible when one considers how our view of reality is obstructed and perverted by the *āsava* or biases and intoxicants. Nevertheless, as the Buddha said: "A corporal phenomenon, a feeling, a perception, a mental formation, a consciousness, that is permanent and persistent, eternal and not subject to change; such a thing the wise men in this world do not recognise; and I say, also, there is no such thing."

T. S. Eliot, one of the greatest English poets, had some such experience as Browning, though much more deeply realised, for Eliot had read widely in Vedantic and Buddhist writings. He is very difficult to read and understand, yet here and there his lines are shot through with Buddhist thoughts, like veins of gold in amber—as for example in his play *The Cocktail Party*, which achieved a great success in London and New York. There, in trying to unravel the problems of lives tangled by mind-created illusions of human attachment, the psychiatrist, who is the central character, advises his patients that they must "work out their own salvation with diligence." Three times these last words of the Buddha are repeated in the play. The following excerpt from the latest and one of the most significant poems, *Burnt Norton*, though not strictly Buddhist, shows the profundity of Eliot's thought, which approaches some of the Mahāyāna doctrines. It begins:

The inner freedom from the practical desire,
The release from action and suffering, release from the inner
And the outer compulsion, yet surrounded
By a grace of sense, a white light still and moving,
Erhebung without motion, concentration
Without elimination, both a new world
And the old made explicit, understood
In the completion of its partial ecstasy,
The resolution of its partial horror…

The poets of deepest insight are those who find the way which the Buddha found in his darkest hour. It was when, nearly at the point of death as a result of asceticism and self-torture, prostrate upon the ground and unable to rise, he had a flash of memory from his childhood: "I thought (he said) how when the Sakyan, my father, was ploughing, I sat in the cool shade of the rose-apple tree, remote from sensual desires and ill conditions, and entered upon and abode in the first jhāna, which is accompanied by thoughts directed and sustained; born of solitude; full of zestful ease."

Then he asked himself: "Is this, I wonder, the way to wisdom?" There came the answer: "Yes, this is the way to wisdom." So entering upon that way, Gotama discovered the cessation of suffering, the way to Nibbāna.

Wordsworth seems to have had similar experiences, as did Blake and others. But by reason of the hindrances and delusions of their native culture they were unable to follow the way to its conclusion. It is interesting, however, that Wordsworth too wrote about his experiences as boy in the country:

"I was often unable to think of external things as having external existence, and I communed with all that was as something not apart from but inherent in, my own immaterial nature. Many times, when going to school, have I grasped at a wall or a tree to recall myself from this abyss of idealism to reality."

The state came naturally to him, as no doubt it did to the young Gotama. In *The Prelude*, the greatest philosophical poem in the English language, Wordsworth describes the experience in noble language. He calls it:

That serene and blessed mood
In which the affections greatly lead us on—
Until, the breath of this corporeal frame
And even the motions of our human blood
Almost suspended, we are laid asleep
In body, and become a living soul;
While, with an eye made quiet by the power
Of harmony, and the deep power of joy,
We see into the heart of things.

At the heart of things the Buddha found *anicca*, *dukkha* and *anattā*. But the last of these, the truth that all component things are without permanent entity, or soul, is hidden from those who have the delusion of a permanent soul or ego. It is only by those in whom self has become completely extinguished that this, the unique and most profound truth of Buddhism, can be realised.

There is a hint of *anattā* in Shakespeare, so I will continue, as I began, with a quotation from the greatest English poet. His play *The Tempest* is an epitome of life and self-conquest. Near the end of the play the wise man, Prospero, who has gained the magic power of conjuring up gods and goddesses, fairies and nature spirits, has been causing these wraiths to enact a play. Suddenly, with a wave of his wand, he makes it all disappear. Turning to his astonished audience, he says:

Our revels are now ended. These our actors,
As I foretold you, were all spirits, and
Are melted into air; into thin air.
The cloud-capped towers, the gorgeous palaces,
The solemn temples, the great globe itself,
Yes, all that it inherits, shall dissolve,
And like this insubstantial pageant faded,
Leave not a wrack behind.
We are such stuff
As dreams are made on; and our little life
Is rounded with a sleep.

It seems that Shakespeare did not envisage the possibility of rebirth, but his contemporary, Webster, has a suggestive passage in *The Duchess of Malfi*:

I know death hath ten thousand several doors
For men, to take their
Exits; and 'tis found
They go on such strange geometrical hinges,
You may operate them both ways.

The renaissance of classical learning after centuries of neglect and Church disapproval had introduced Platonic and Pythagorean ideas into European thought, as we find in these lines from Milton's *On the Death of a Fair Infant*:

Were thou that just Maid who once before
Forsook the hated earth, O tell me sooth,
And cam'st again to visit us once more?
Or were thou that sweet smiling Youth?

And again from the philosopher Henry More (1614–1687):

I would sing the pre-existency
Of human souls, and live once o'er again
By recollection and quick memory
All that is passed since first we all began.
But all too shallow be my wits to scan
So deep a point, a mind too dull to clear
So dark a matter.

Coming to later times, we find some even more direct affirmations in the English poets of a belief in a continuity of existence through many lives. *In Visions of the Daughters of Albions*, the mystical poet William Blake wrote:

Tell me where dwell the thoughts forgotten till thou call
them forth?
Tell me where dwell the joys of old? And where the
ancient loves,
And when they will renew again, and the night of
oblivion past,
That I might traverse times and spaces far remote, and bring
Comforts into a present sorrow and a night of pain?

Wordsworth, despite his commitment to Christianity, did not give up his belief in a cycle of rebirths, as a little-known poem of his, containing these lines, *Addressed to an Infant* testify:

Oh, sweet newcomer to the changeful earth,
If, as some darkling seers have boldly guessed,
Thou hadst a being and a human birth,
And wert erewhile by human parents blessed,
Long, long before thy present mother pressed
Thee, helpless stranger, to her fostering breast.

How widespread the interest, if not the belief, in rebirth was among the poets of the eighteenth century is a subject has that long been obscured by neglect, possibly because the idea was not an orthodox Christian one.

We find it expressed by Thomas Moore, the Irish poet:

Though new the frame
Thy soul inhabits now, I've tracked its flame
For many an age, in every chance and change
Of that existence, through whose varied range—
As through a torch-race, where, from hand to hand
The flying youths transmit their shining brand—
From flame to flame the unextinguished soul
Rapidly passes, till it reaches the goal!

But the most decided of all the English poets in this respect was Percy Shelley, who, not being bound to the creed of any church, was free to proclaim his belief in rebirth without reserve or ambiguity:

Worlds on worlds are rolling ever
From creation to decay.
Like the bubbles on a river,
Sparkling, bursting, borne away.
But they are still immortal
Who, through birth's orient portal
And death's dark chasm hurrying to and fro,
Clothe their unceasing flight
In the brief dust and light,
Gathered around their chariots as they go;
New shapes they still may weave,
New gods, new laws receive,
Bright or dim are they, as the robes they last
On death's bare ribs had cast.

Hellas

In all these poetic visions it is the idea of an immortal, transmigrating "soul" that dominates the picture; and while the universal principle of mutability is acknowledged, there is no philosophical attempt to reconcile it with the notion of an unchanging entity. The Buddhist concept of rebirth without a persisting "soul" or ego-principle had to wait for more scientific thinkers to give it recognition. Nevertheless, in the lines of Shelley quoted above there is a distinct affirmation of the law of kamma: "Bright or dim are they, as the robes they last on death's bare ribs had cast." It is a confident assertion of belief in a moral order in the universe, from one who had the courage, in youth, to proclaim himself an atheist.

I hope that the reader may be stimulated by these few extracts to search for himself in the rich treasure-house of English poetry for more evidences of thought which touches upon Buddhism. If he does, he will be greatly rewarded. Truth is glimpsed in many different ways by different people, and the poet is not least among those who can claim insight into the realities of human life.

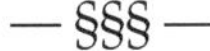

Meditation: The Inward Journey
and
Inner Thoughts and Outward Results

Two Essays

John Andrew Storey

Bodhi Leaves No. 51

First published: 1970

Meditation: The Inward Journey

Introduction

Man has always been an explorer. In earlier times he took to the sea in boats to search for far distant shores. In more recent times with his advanced technology he has turned his eyes to the heavens, and with rockets of unbelievable power has pierced the skies in his search for more distant worlds. Already man has set foot on the Moon, and it is confidently predicted that soon he will visit Mars and other planets. Where all this will end, who can tell? One thing seems certain, that unless man can find sufficient wisdom to match his increasing knowledge it could well end in disaster. With such unthinkable horrors as the nuclear bomb at his disposal he could in a single holocaust destroy himself and all other life on this planet. The acquisition of knowledge leads to cleverness—which is not necessarily a virtue. The practice of meditation leads to wisdom; hence the importance of meditation in the world today.

As I have said, man is by nature an explorer, but as a widely travelled man once wisely remarked "only the inward journey is real." That inward journey is what meditation is all about. It would be folly to imagine that the elementary advice given in this simple primer will take you more than a few steps on that journey, for it is indeed a long and arduous journey that does not end this side of Nibbāna. But even the longest journey must begin with a single step, and I shall be content if this simple primer helps a few people to take those initial steps. Help can be theirs for the more advanced stages, when by mastering these early steps they have proved themselves ready and worthy to receive it.

The reader should take note of a final word of warning and advice. Do not be discouraged if your progress in the art of meditation seems painfully slow. This is no easy task you are on, and quick results should not be looked for. Most worthwhile things take times to achieve, and it is always the hardest won victory that gives the greatest satisfaction. Perseverance is the key-word, and one should always bear in mind the Chinese proverb, that "One should not be afraid of travelling slowly, but only afraid of standing still."

The Art of Meditation

> Irrigators lead the water where they will, fletchers shape the arrow; carpenters bend wood to their will; wise men shape themselves.
>
> Dhammapada

There are many facets to the religious life, and the full religious life is the one that takes them all into account. There is a danger in over-emphasising one aspect, though we are all prone to do this on occasions. Those of us who live in the Western World tend to lay great stress on what we care to believe are the practical aspects of religion. Religion is thought to be of little value unless it is seen to be doing something. One does not despise this. The dictates of compassion cannot be ignored. But there is a danger that in all this busy over-organised activity we may lose sight of the most fundamental thing of all, the development, cultivation, and perfection of oneself. Nor is this a selfish aim, for only as we become masters of ourselves can we truly become the servants of others. The most important thing in all religion life then—in the sense of being the thing we need to do first—is to obtain complete self-mastery, to purify ourselves, to develop the mind and to raise one's level of consciousness. But how is this to be done? Meditation provides the answer. But how does one make a start in mastering the difficult art of meditation?

First of all one must recognize that in meditation—as in all worthwhile things—little is accomplished if one has no real desire to do it and the work is badly done. One's first task then is to try to overcome one's reluctance and to encourage in oneself the desire to meditate. One must also carefully examine one's motives for wanting to master the art of meditation. The increased mental powers which meditation brings are not good or bad in themselves—it all depends upon the use to which they are put. Do we wish to use any new-found powers we may acquire for the good of mankind? It must be remembered too that meditation should not become an excuse for us to neglect our other duties. The time found for it must be taken from our leisure hours.

As in all things one must give due attention to the practical little details. Experience has shown that the best results are obtained when one sticks to a set time and place. A few minutes a day will probably bring better results than half an hour twice a week. The body should be poised and alert, yet relaxed and comfortable. The lotus position—the cross-legged position on the floor—is advised for those who can learn to use it without discomfort, but this is not a matter of fundamental importance. Having taken a comfortable position one must then completely relax oneself, and this is best done by breathing slowly and deeply from the stomach. This relaxes the body while at the same time it helps to stimulate the mind.

Even now one is not ready for meditation, for before one can do that one must develop the necessary powers. A would-be sportsman knows that he will do no good on the field of play until he has first of all tuned up his body and developed his muscles. To this end he will dedicate himself to hours of physical exercise. In the same way it is futile to try to meditate until you have first developed your mental muscles. This is done by learning to concentrate, and all manuals on meditation give lists of exercises in concentration which help to this end. The object of these exercises is to learn how to focus one's entire mind on a given thing and to hold it there for a period of time. In short one must learn to use one's mind like a searchlight and to concentrate its full power on any given point.

One exercise frequently mentioned in text-books is that of concentrating one's full attention on a small physical object. A matchbox or an orange will do. Place the chosen object before you a few feet away and then, when you are completely relaxed, focus the searchlight of your mind upon it. Exclude from your mind all but the object you have chosen for your exercise. See if you can hold this alone in your mind for a whole minute. If you cannot then at least you will have been taught a valuable lesson in humility, for you will have been forced to recognise the gulf which lies between you and even elementary thought control. When you can really carry out this exercise for three whole minutes continuously there will be time enough to move on to the next. There are indeed many exercises which one can use. One can elaborate on the first exercise by concentrating on a matchbox, then after a while closing one's eyes in an effort to picture it in the mind's eye. While looking at it in the mind's eye one should view it from all its different angles, then most difficult of all, try to look at it from all sides at once.

More difficult still one can close one's eye and try to visualise a colour. Take for example the colour blue. With eyes closed, visualise blue, not a blue object but just blue. Then slowly infuse the blue with yellow so that it begins to show as a more greenish blue, not in patches, but simultaneously everywhere. Continue to make it greener and greener until you have a whole world of vivid green. Then just as gradually make your green yellow until your world is a pure and brilliant yellow. Then if you wish, reverse the process back through green to blue. There are, of course, dozens of other exercises I could mention, but I do not wish to duplicate what can be found in any text book on concentration, and with a little imagination one can easily invent one's own. And, of course, it goes without saying that we should make concentration an integral part of our daily life by giving our complete and undivided attention to everything we do.

How easy it is to let the mind wander instead of keeping it fixed on the job in hand, but in striving to curb this tendency we go a long way towards preparing our minds for the practice of meditation. The exercises I have outlined may seem rather trivial and silly, but then so would the 'physical jerks' of the athlete if we did not understand the aim they are meant to serve. Either you can do these exercises or you cannot. If you cannot then you are in no position to despise them. If you can, then by all means pass from them without delay. When some measure of efficiency in concentration has been acquired then one may turn to the practice of meditation, the double purpose of which is to increase one's own enlightenment and to share it with the suffering millions of mankind.

Broadly speaking meditation may be divided into two: lower meditation and higher meditation—or to put it another way, meditation "with the seed" and meditation "without the seed," the "seed" being the subject for meditation. Only those who have considerable experience in the former should attempt the latter, for if it is tried too early, it is apt to produce a negative attitude of mind with a resulting loss of concentration, discouragement and waste of time. Let us then—as this is but a simple primer for beginners—concentrate on lower meditation, i.e., meditation "with the seed."

The choices for the "seed-thought"—the object for meditation—are infinite. One may choose to meditate upon some particular doctrine of religion, or upon some passage of scripture.

One's subject may be a verse or a saying, or something that one has heard in a sermon. You may choose to meditate upon certain facts of life, the immensity of the universe, the complexity of life in all its forms, that everything in existence—oneself included—is in a constant state of flux undergoing ceaseless change.

Or again, the subject may be one of the great virtues. *Mettā*—loving-kindness—provides an excellent subject for meditation. First try to wash from the mind all impurities, lust, hatred and ignorance, and endeavour to suffuse your own being with unbounded love. Then turn your thoughts to a friend and direct the same thoughts of love towards him or her. Then concentrate your feeling upon someone to whom you are indifferent. Next, and most difficult, visualise an enemy or someone you dislike, and even though at first it is difficult to do so without a feeling of hypocrisy, pervade him or her with the warmth of generous and pure affection. Finally, radiate loving kindness to all mankind, then to all forms of life, and so through all of the universe. Nārada Thera's excellent book, *Buddhism in a Nutshell* (Wheel Publication, Special Issue) has a beautiful meditation on the Perfections which for your convenience I include here. It is a meditation I can heartily recommend.

Meditation on the Perfections (*pāramī*)

1. May I be generous and helpful (*dāna*—generosity).
2. May I be well-disciplined and refined in manners. May I be pure and clean in all my dealings. May my thoughts, words and deeds be pure (*sīla*—morality).
3. May I not be selfish and self-possessive but selfless and disinterested. May I be able to sacrifice my pleasure for

the sake of others (*nekkhamma*—renunciation).

4. May I be wise and be able to see things as they truly are. May I see the light of Truth and lead others from darkness to light. May I be enlightened and be able to enlighten others. May I be able to give the benefit of my knowledge to others (*paññā*—wisdom).
5. May I be energetic, vigorous and persevering. May I strive diligently until I achieve my goal. May I be fearless in facing dangers and courageously surmount all obstacles. May I be able to serve others to the best of my ability (*viriya*—energy).
6. May I ever be patient. May I be able to bear and forbear the wrongs of others. May I ever be tolerant and see the good and beautiful in all (*khanti*-patience).
7. May I ever be truthful and honest. May I not hide the truth to be polite. May I never swerve from the path of Truth (*sacca*—truthfulness).
8. May I be firm and resolute and have an iron will. May I be soft as a flower and firm as a rock. May I ever be high-principled (*adhiṭṭhāna*—determination).
9. May I ever be kind, friendly and compassionate. May I be able to regard all as my brothers and sisters and be one with all (*mettā*—loving-kindness).
10. May I be calm, serene, unruffled and peaceful. May I gain a balanced mind. May I have perfect equanimity (*upekkhā*— equanimity).
11. May I serve to be perfect, May I be perfect to serve.

I do not think I need to give any further examples of meditations. Others will suggest themselves to your own mind, and in practice you will find many more.

At the beginning I stated that there are different aspects to the religious life and that many people—particularly in the West—have a great fondness for what they regard as the practical side of religion. Perhaps this is why so many of us have tended to neglect meditation, for to those who have no knowledge or experience of it, it does seem to have little to do with the hard world of reality. Yet in truth, the practice of meditation is of the highest practical value and is a pre-requisite for all real service, for only as we truly become masters of ourselves can we really become the servants of others. The greatest service we can render is that of trying to shed a little light in this world of darkness, a little knowledge in this world of ignorance, a little wisdom in this world of folly.

As the Bhikkhu Buddhadāsa reminds us: "Practising meditation is like sharpening a knife for cutting cleanly, or like polishing a glass so as to see clearly."[84] I would add that it is also like cleaning the windows so that the light that is within you may illumine the path around you that others may see the light and tread more safely the road of life. The light is within thee. Let the light shine. Nor should we overlook the fact that even the act of meditation itself—quite apart from the benefit it brings to ourselves—is an act of service, for like radio stations constantly sending out radio waves we are constantly sending out "thought waves" which in ways unseen and undreamed of raise or lower the moral climate of society around us. A fanciful notion? Perhaps. But who has not at some time or other entered a room and immediately sensed the atmosphere of that room even before a word has been spoken—and even in extreme cases if everyone has already left the room. Sometimes, speaking of such an experience, we say: "The atmosphere was so thick you could have cut it with a knife." Could it not be that in meditation there is an element of "mental telepathy?" If so, the meditation is in part at least a form of "concentrated telepathy" which, when purposefully directed, can convey great benefits to others. In meditation we can join that unseen Brotherhood whose spiritual endeavours help to form a guardian wall about humanity.

I cannot stress too strongly that in this simple primer we have barely scratched the surface of this deep and complex subject. Yet little though it is that we have learned, it is sufficient to make a beginning, and a start upon the road towards enlightenment. Even the acquisition of a little wisdom can work wonders, for as we learn in the Sutta of Wei Lang (Hui Neng):

"Even as the light of a lamp can break up darkness which has been there for a thousand years, so can a spark of wisdom do away with ignorance which has lasted for ages."

The light is there to be found, but so often we are like the man who turns his back to the light and then complains about the shadow

84 Bodhi Leaves No. 33

in front. To those who doubt their ability to succeed there is but one word—TRY. And in meditation, as in all things, there are only two basic rules: BEGIN and CONTINUE.

— §§§ —

Inner Thoughts and Outward Results

> All that we are is the result of what we have thought: it is founded on our thoughts, it is made up of our thoughts. If man speaks or acts with an evil thought, pain follows him, as the wheel follows the foot of the ox that draws the carriage. If a man speaks or acts with a pure thought, happiness follows him, like a shadow that never leaves him.
>
> Dhammapada

It is now generally agreed that man is a member of the animal kingdom, and that like the other animals—to whom he is related—his existence has been brought about by the long processes of evolution. Like other animals man is born as a result of the mating process, he needs food, drink and rest in order to grow and remain healthy, he experiences pain, sickness, and ultimately death. Yet in one important respect man is different from the lower forms of life, for he alone of all the creatures of this planet has the power to think imaginatively, creatively and constructively. A man can think, and his thoughts make him what he is.

The ability to think, the power of thought, is man's greatest gift. It is thought which moulds civilisation and which created many of the things we take for granted. As a tiny seed can produce a beautiful flower, as a small seed can produce a mighty tree, so can thought produce the most wonderful things. Every book ever written, every symphony ever composed, every temple ever built, every scientific discovery ever made, every religious or political system ever created began in the mind of a man as a thought. Religion, philosophy, art, science, politics, and all the things we mean by civilisation begin as a thought. And it was by his power of thought that Siddhattha Gotama became Buddha and gave his Dhamma to the world.

Among the religions of the world it is in Buddhism that the power of thought is given the strongest emphasis. The Dhammapada reminds us that "all that we are is the result of what we have thought," and further reminds us that "the wise man shapes himself." It is of the character-building power of thought in our own lives that I would have us give our main attention.

The creative or destructive power of thought—for it can indeed work both ways—is a great truth that has been known in the East for many centuries. It was the Teaching of the Lord Buddha. In the West we came to the knowledge rather late, but our psychologists now corroborate the ancient truth and tell us that many of our physical and mental ailments are due to our thoughts. So worry, for example, is one of the major causes of ulcers, while fear, anger, hatred, and the constant dwelling on lewd thoughts, all take their toll. The same is true in the moral realm. Evil thoughts, constantly entertained, weaken the character and make one more susceptible to temptation. All evil words and deeds are preceded by evil thoughts, and evil thoughts allowed to remain unchanged will lead eventually to evil words and deeds.

Thoughts then can be either good or bad and can give rise to results that are either harmful or pleasant. It is claimed that some have gained such control over the mental processes that they can suspend thought all together, and for a long period keep their mind a perfect blank. Few of us are likely to achieve this. For most of us thoughts of one sort or another will always be milling around in our heads, and if they are not good thoughts they will inevitably be bad. Since noble and base thoughts cannot co-exist in the mind at the same time, one will always expel the other.

We are not to blame if evil thoughts occasionally enter our minds, but we are at fault if we give them a welcome and allow them to remain there unchecked. As the Eastern proverb has it: "We cannot prevent them from alighting on our heads, but we can prevent them from building their nests there." A keen gardener will root out a weed as soon as it appears in his garden lest it should take hold and eventually destroy his good plants. We should act with the same urgency with evil thoughts, for they too will quickly take root and destroy the noblest flowerings of our minds. The surest way of keeping evil thoughts at bay is to discipline our minds to think constantly of that which is beautiful and true and good. When the mind is full of that which is good, the evil will seek for an entry in vain.

The Dhammapada warns the wise man to guard his thoughts, for they are, it says, "difficult to perceive, very artful, and they rush wherever they list. Thoughts well guarded bring happiness." The Dhammapada further says:

"Let no man think lightly of evil, saying in his heart: 'It will not come nigh unto me.' Even by the falling of water drops, a water-pot is filled; the fool becomes full of evil, even if he gathers it little by little.

"Let no man think lightly of good, saying in his heart: 'It will not come nigh unto me.' Even by the falling of water drops, a water-pot is filled; the wise man becomes full of good, even if he gathers it little by little."

Slowly, like a jar beneath a dripping cave, we accumulate vice or virtue. The choice is ours. The choice is important, for, "If a man speaks or acts with an evil thought, pain follows him, as the wheel follows the foot of the ox that draws the carriage ... If a man speaks or acts with a pure thought, happiness follows him, like a shadow that never leaves him."

We are thinking beings, and out of our thoughts we can create wondrous things. But more important than any work of art, more important than any majestic building, more important than any feat of engineering is that of shaping our selves. And we can do just that as we direct our thoughts towards pure and noble ends, knowing that by our thoughts—which in turn govern our words and deeds—we are preparing for ourselves a harvest of joy or sorrow.

— §§§ —

Mindfulness—An All-Time Necessity

C. F. Knight

and

A Businessman's Dhamma

Reg McAuliffe

Bodhi Leaves No. 52

First published: 1970

Mindfulness—An All-Time Necessity

by C. F. Knight

From *Metta*, November 1967

Amongst the various attempts to define Buddhism is one that describes it as a system of mental discipline, or mind-training. Probably this is more accurate than most others, for whether we describe it as a philosophy, a religion, or a way of life, having regard to its goal—Nirvana—assuredly we find that "taming the mind" is the key to final liberation.

The importance of mindfulness, or mental discipline, cannot be over-stressed. "All that we are is the result of what we have thought," says the Dhammapada. To give those words their full significance is to realize that in that pithy phrase is contained a full statement of the doctrine of kamma. From our thoughts flow words and deeds of a kammic nature, the result of which (*kamma-vipāka*) is that all we are "is founded on our thoughts, is made up of our thoughts." As our past thoughts laid the foundation for our present condition, so our present thoughts are further accentuating or modifying that condition.

In the Mahā Satipaṭṭhānā Suttanta of the Dīgha Nikāya, the Buddha emphasises the importance of mindfulness. In opening the lengthy discourse he says:

"The one and only path leading to the purification of beings, to the passing far beyond grief and lamentation, to the dying out of ill and misery, to the attainment of right method, to the realization of Nirvana is that of the fourfold setting up of mindfulness."

In closing his discourse he further stresses its importance by saying:

"Whoso shall practise these four applications of mindfulness for seven years, nay, for six, five, four, three, two or one year only, or even for six, five, four, three, two or one month, or for a fortnight, or even seven days in him one of two kinds of fruition may be looked for: either in this life arahantship, or if there be yet residuum for rebirth, the state of him who returns no more. It was on account of this that was said which was said (at the beginning)."

The long variable range of time from seven years to seven days is a clear indication that while the setting up of mindfulness is the "one and only path," it is still but a "path," and not the goal. For some it may be longer than for others, according to their pertinacity and the insight acquired, and the hindrances and fetters to be overcome. It is mindfulness that enables us to become conscious of our shortcomings, but it does not eliminate them. That requires possession of the seven factors of enlightenment of which mindfulness is but one in addition to a search for the truth, energy, joy, serenity, rapture and equanimity. Furthermore, the capacity for all factors will quite naturally vary from person to person. Still, the setting up of mindfulness is an all important prerequisite—"the one and only path."

Such then is the necessity for the application of mindfulness insofar as our own spiritual progress is concerned in its most narrow and personal aspect. But it has a much wider application also. Mindfulness at a minimum is consciousness of actuality, awareness, or the grasp of facts independent of insight or intuition. Mindfulness in its broader sense invests every activity, through association of ideas, with a recollection, or calling to mind, of other facts or reactions. For example, mindfulness of a simple nature may be practised as we go about our daily tasks, observing in a specific way our actions, our immediate environment, the people we meet or pass, and so on. On a higher level, the offerings at the shrine and the repetition of the sacred formulas as we participate in our religious observances partake of a sacramental nature as mindfulness associates them with the object of our devotions. Again, in an even more simple form, it is mindfulness and the association of ideas that keep us from injury, from burning in the presence of fire, and on a higher level, it should make us conscious of the suffering created by the use of fire on other unfortunate beings as in warfare as waged today. As mindfulness protects us from pain and injury, it should also make us unwilling to inflict pain and injury on others. Mindfulness as applied to our personal lives is a necessity if we truly strive for perfection, and it should have a wider application in the appreciation of our relationship to our fellow beings. If we can "put ourselves in the other fellow's shoes," we can develop understanding and compassion in our dealings with him, and this is greatly to be desired today.

Before making mindfulness applicable to our wider contacts, our public life and its relationships, let us consider and understand them as they apply to us intimately in our own private lives. To engender love of our neighbour, compassion for him, and extend our help towards him, we must first be possessed of a loving nature ourselves; we must have before we can give. There are those who are more or less willing to assist in many ways others who are on a somewhat similar material, social, or spiritual level. Their sympathy and compassion, their generosity, is confined as it were to a horizontal plane, like a pebble dropped into a pool creating expanding ripples on its surface. They give where they can expect to receive in return. They seek for consolation from those whom they consider "will understand them." Other strata of society are either beneath their notice, or regarded with envy as being "better off" and not in need of help or compassion. True *mettā* and *karunā*—love in its widest sense, and compassion—should be like a gong struck in a silent room, from which the sound-waves are global in nature and penetrate to all six directions. To accomplish this, we must first discipline ourselves, and in order to do this we must understand our own make-up of foibles, eccentricities, short-comings, aspirations and ambitions, so mindfulness becomes a necessity and "the only path."

Let us return to the discourse under consideration for guidance. The early portion of this discourse is introspective—know thyself—and is concerned with (1) the body, in physical structure and activities, (2) feelings, in their sensory meaning, and with regard to their instability, and (3) thoughts, with their ethical and kammic content. The latter portion of the-discourse leads on to mindfulness of ideas, culminating in the perception of the Four Noble Truths, and living within the framework of the Fourth Truth—the Eightfold Way that leads to the "purification of beings, to passing far beyond grief and lamentation, to the dying out of ill and misery, to the attainment of right method, to the realization of Nirvana."

In considering the body mindfully we find it to be in a continual state of arising and passing away. We become aware of its movements and postures; aware of its need of clothing and sustenance, and how we supply these needs; aware of its component parts and their functions; and aware of its final disintegration—then we can say: "There is body."

So too with feelings, as to whether they are pleasant, unpleasant, or neutral; whether they are of a physical nature or of a spiritual nature. We are fully conscious of our reactions to the stimuli affecting our feelings, recognising and classifying the cause and our reaction to it, until we can say: "There are feelings."

Then we mindfully consider our thoughts fathered by our feelings. These cover our conscious life, our intelligent perception of action and reaction. We, at times, speak of our feelings being "hurt," but do we ever mindfully reason as to why they are "hurt?" Probably we expected praise, or a gift that did not eventuate or thanks for services given. Or, maybe, we were censured or blamed unexpectedly. If we are mindful we will realize that the indifference, ingratitude, ill-will or lack of generosity that "hurt" our feelings belongs to another, and that vanity, covetousness, self-righteousness, etc, has been an error on our part.

That mindfulness of our thoughts is important we have already mentioned. It is in this realm that kammic volitions arise with their inevitable results to be experienced at some time in the future, in this life or another.

It is mindfulness that will enable us to recognise the three roots of evil arising from basic ignorance. Greed, hatred, and delusion are born of our thoughts due to an ignorance of their potentiality to reflect on our own lives the very results we are projecting towards others.

It is delusion which in turn gives rise to fear, superstition and intolerance on one hand, and on the other attachment, lust for sensual pleasures, craving and clinging.

It is from hatred that anger, malice and strife arise together with pride, resentment and revenge.

Greed is the source from which arises selfishness, avarice, covetousness, and the lack of generosity.

These evils—greed, hatred, and delusion—first arise to consciousness as the thoughts of our own mind, and later find expression as words and deeds. If we are mindful, it becomes most obvious that in the end we ourselves are the ones who suffer most from their arising.

This mindful self-analysis of our thoughts will enable us to subdue the unwholesome inclinations arising in the mind before they find irrevocable expression in words and deeds. In a like manner we should be just as conscious of wholesome thoughts and inclinations, and foster them. Also we should be conscious of the absence of wholesome thoughts and encourage their arising. Remember: "All that we are is founded on our thoughts, made up of our thoughts." But, do not fall into the famous error of Descartes who declared: "I am thinking, so I exist" (*cogito, ergo sum*). What he should have said on that evidence was: "I am thinking, so there are thoughts."

If the setting up of mindfulness has been successful so far, we know our body for what it is; we know feelings for what they are; we know thoughts with their fateful implications. Now we start to be mindful of the ideas that arise, the mental or psychological phenomena that are outside of the realm of sensory perception and reaction. If progress is to be made, first we must recognise and be mindful of any deterrents. Undue attachment to sensuous desire may gain admittance through any of the sense-doors, and mindfulness is the guardian of the gates. So too in respect to laziness and indifference, undue anxiety, worry and doubt. These should be promptly recognized and overcome or eliminated, while mindfulness itself should be a conscious factor in our determined search for truth, pursued with energy and joyous serenity and equanimity.

This brings us to the mindful recognition of the Four Noble Truths, the first of which is the all-pervasiveness of what is known in Buddhist circles as *dukkha*, a Pali word incapable of direct translation owing to the wide application of its meaning. The usual translations into "ill," or "suffering," are inadequate, unsatisfactory, and misleading, giving rise to the popular criticism of Buddhism as being pessimistic. *Dukkha* does include "suffering" "pain" "sorrow" and "misery," it is true, but it embraces a much wider scope of unease. It is defined as the ever-arising of new forms of existence;

as growing old, with old age's complements of decrepitude, hoaryness, the wrinkled state, the shrinkage of life's span, and the collapse of the sense faculties; as the laying down of the body in death; as the states of woe, heartache, and grief; as the visitation of calamity or illness; as the act and state of mourning, lamenting and deploring; as bodily and mental ill and pain; as the states of dejection and despondency and despair; as not getting what has been wished for.

Elsewhere in the scriptures it is further mentioned that *dukkha* is being separated from those we love and the things we are attached to; it is also being forced into contact with those we dislike, and having to bear with things which revolt us. Summed up, *dukkha* may be said to be all that amounts to disease in life. All the sorrows, the disappointments, the frustrations, and failures of our most cherished schemes are *dukkha*, but one cannot go into all these facets and details each time we wish to speak of the First Noble Truth, so we either use the imperfect and unsatisfactory translations or, better still, the untranslated Pali word—*dukkha*—rather than give an inadequate and wrong idea of it.

This is but one aspect of life as we know it. The Buddha did not eliminate happiness for either the layman or the monk. But happiness itself is based on an understanding of *dukkha*, its arising and its cessation. It is based on our individuality—our physical form, our feelings, our perceptions, our dispositions, and our mental activities as opposed to emotional volition.

The mindful absorption of the First Noble Truth may lend itself to the idea of pessimism if we fail to proceed to the subsequent Truths of its arising, its cessation and the Way leading to its cessation. These, while rebutting the idea of pessimism, are not on the other hand optimistic: they do not do away with the universality of *dukkha*, but they do lead to an understanding of why *dukkha* prevails and permeates our lives. By knowing it, realizing its cause, and treading the Way to its final abolition, we are enabled to transcend the effect of *dukkha*, even to attaining the final goal of never returning to suffer again.

Now applying mindfulness to the arising of *dukkha* we can trace its rise to craving in one form or another, for this or that satisfaction that is so unstable and fleeting. It may be craving for the material things of this world, indulgence of the senses in sensual satisfaction, craving for fame and recognition, craving for the continued relationships of family life, craving for permanence in a world of constant change. Whatever form craving takes, it arises through the senses, through the imagination, or through the memory of past experiences, and only mindfulness will recognise the insidious growth of craving.

The cessation of *dukkha* is to the mindful person the elimination of that craving which gives rise to *dukkha*. At times we are faced with those who tell us any pleasure is an attachment and a source of craving, that it is wrong to like music, to admire a sunset, to enjoy one's food, to appreciate odours, or to become attached to other beings. If this were so, then quite rightly Buddhism could be labelled as being pessimistic. But the Buddha and his disciples could admire the beauty of a tropic moonlight night. The Buddha could look back on Vesāli and its beauty with nostalgia as he saw it for the last time. He praised those who cared for their children, and taught that the support of parents, the cherishing of wife and children, and the helping of relatives was of the highest merit. This applied to his monks as well as to laymen. He taught that brotherly love—association with the wise—was one of the highest blessings. The enjoyment of the good things of life was not condemned by the Buddha, although the acquisition of wealth added responsibilities in regard to its use. It is when craving for things not attained, or for the permanency of those which are attained, creeps in that *dukkha* becomes apparent.

Who has not suffered the loss of a loved one? Perhaps this is the most easy demonstration of attachment, craving, and subsequent *dukkha*. The reciprocal love that exists in a family is natural and virtuous in itself. From that untainted source grows the craving for an unbroken continuance of it. When death intervenes, as eventually it must, *dukkha* finds expression in the sense of loss and the grief that inevitably follows. If we realize that the most pleasant of relationships, the most desirable of experiences, the most fortunate of circumstances, are impermanent and unstable, then we can enjoy them while they last, and part from them with happy memories of the past, rather than with grief and sorrow as to the future.

And so we come to the Way that leads to the cessation of *dukkha*. It is also the Way that will enable us to give to others, to be mindful of their needs and, moreover, mindful of our obligations concerning them.

This Fourth Noble Truth has its eight sections, or steps, as they are often called. They cover a two-fold set of obligations for one who has set out on the holy life. The first is the further development of his own characteristics on the spiritual plane, and the other is his duty to his fellow men. There is another division usually used in dividing the eight steps, based on the development of ethics, concentration and wisdom. However, as we set out to show our obligation to others, for our purpose we will deal with them on the basis of us and others.

In regard to ourselves the first step is the acquisition of knowledge. By this is inferred a knowledge of the three Truths we have just examined—the mindful realization of the universality of *dukkha*, its arising and its cessation. If we are going to be helpful and carry our beliefs into practice for the welfare of others it is obviously necessary that we must have an understanding of the cause and nature of the distress that is so evident in the world of today. This is called Right View.

Then we must be possessed of an aim or aspiration beneficial to others. We need and must have the aspiration toward renunciation in so far as ourselves are concerned—a detachment from selfish desires and ambitions and a willingness to make sacrifices for the good and welfare of others. There must also be the aspiration towards kindness and benevolence in our attitude to others. This is called Right Aspiration.

Our speech needs careful watching for this is so often the source of engendering anger and hatred in others. Lying, slandering, abusive terms, and derogatory statements in regard to others can but have the reaction of repulsion on their part, and lead on to active dislike or aggressive action as a result. To refrain from such speech is called Right Speech.

Speech leads to action as we have just mentioned. If our speech is right speech, our actions will be so influenced that the aspiration towards kindliness and benevolence becomes almost automatic.

The incitement to acts of violence, the taking of life, stealing, or committing carnal offences against our fellowmen cannot arise unless preceded by wrong aspiration and wrong thoughts. To refrain from such behaviour is called Right Action.

The next step is one that is, I think, unique among the injunctions laid upon the devotees of any religion—Right Livelihood. Certainly, the Christian is advised not only to avoid evil, but also the appearance of evil, or what might be assumed to be evil by the critics. Right Livelihood is not only to refrain from actions which in themselves involve direct and immediate harm to others, but also to refrain from depending for means of a livelihood on such a trade or following as will indirectly harm others. The occupations of hunters, butchers, fishers, and the makers of arms, are some of the proscribed occupations. This raises a most difficult point for one who would fulfil all the requirements of the Eightfold Way in the world of today. In a day and time when the world population was so much less, and the opportunities for choosing a trade or following were greater, it may have been possible to avoid occupations which directly or indirectly involved a threat of harm to others. But today, under modern conditions, it is virtually impossible for any individual to avoid being in some way indirectly involved in the harm of others.

This injunction has been rationalized in some cases by, for instance, employing other religionists as butchers, by driving cattle over a national boundary and then importing the products of the slaughterhouse. Again, during a period of war, a sincere conscientious objector may refuse to be inducted into the army, but he cannot earn a living in any trade or profession without paying taxes to sustain the war effort of his country. Under these circumstances there is no choice, but if there be a choice, for instance, if one can work as a carpenter, and though a slaughter man can earn more than the carpenter, it would be wrong to change to this means of livelihood just for the sake of the extra money to be earned. Difficult indeed is it to avoid harm to others for the layman, and it is obvious that a mass invasion of the Sangha is out of the question!

So we come to what is really a key to all the Steps of the Way—the cultivation of effort. In this essay we are primarily concerned with mindfulness, rather than a general exposition of Buddhist doctrines, and, most of all, the application of mindfulness in relation to our fellow men. But it is not possible to separate any one aspect of the Buddha's teachings and isolate it from all others. In dealing with the Eightfold Way at some length, we are only as it were setting out the personal prerequisites that will enable us to give of our best. It will require great effort on our part to fulfil the perfecting of right thought, speech, action, and livelihood, even though we have right knowledge and aspiration.

It also does require effort to take an interest in the welfare of others. The general tendency of today is to let others do our thinking for us and then drift along with the crowd, indifferent as to where we are heading, or on whose toes we are treading. It takes mindful effort to concern ourselves with people we scarcely know or whom we have never met. We read of a flood in the East, of an earthquake in the West, of the genocide of a nation in the North, or suffering of civilian population caught between the cross-fire of armies in the South, but they are only items of news—they do not affect us. We are not mindful of the tragedies involved for those who suffer. One of the epithets assigned to the Buddha was "The Awakened One," and because of his Awakening the floodgates of his compassion were opened to embrace all living creatures. For the most part we could be described as "The Asleep" in regard to our relationships with our fellow-men, and compassion is indeed a rare and seldom met characteristic today. We need to be mindful of our lack in this regard, and overcome the deficiency.

The seventh component factor of the Way is this very mindfulness with which we have been dealing. If subjectively mindfulness is present we should be aware of it, cultivate it, and develop it. If our mental training has been even partially efficient there is a more or less conscious control of our mind. The subjective existence or absence of mindfulness should be noted and mental action taken to develop existing mindfulness, or to bring mindfulness into existence. The whole purpose of Buddhist mind-training is for the adept to be the master of his mind, and by that discipline and mastery perfect his life to his own liberation and the benefit of others. Much interest today surrounds the hallucinatory drug LSD. Repeatedly we are asked for our opinion as to its effectiveness in gaining "enlightenment," or as an aid to meditation. The key to the answer is already inherent in its scientific classification.

It is technically described as a "hallucinatory drug," and its use can only produce hallucinations. This is just the opposite of the purpose of Buddhist mind-training, or the objectives of meditation, and can only bring evil effects to the addict. It is a gateway to delusion, which is one of the three roots of evil the true Buddhist seeks to overcome. It is also one of the forbidden things of the fifth precept, which proscribes the taking of intoxicants and harmful drugs.

The eighth step is the development of mental concentration up to the degree of the meditative absorption, which is not pertinent to our present consideration of mindfulness in regard to our relationship and obligations to others.

Now, if we have developed any such mindfulness, not only have we to some extent become masters of our own mind, but there has been an awakening of our understanding of the problems that we as individuals and the world of today are facing. It is such mental training that enables one to set aside the propaganda of nationalism or expediency, and penetrate to the root cause of the unrest and distress that is so prevalent. Many today are acutely conscious of the immediate circumstances that are causing their distress, and of these some are rebelling against them, whether they be famine, armed conflict, racial discrimination, the uncertainty of the future, poverty, or just sheer boredom from a surfeit of ease and luxury, but few there are who can penetrate to the basic causes for the existing conditions.

Earlier we referred to the function of mindfulness in recognising the three roots of evil—greed, hatred, and delusion—and on a world basis these apply just as equally as on a personal basis, so also does craving as a source of widespread *dukkha*, for world politics and national interests are but the sum total of the characteristics of the individuals holding the powers of government, and moulding the destinies of nations. In view of this it becomes obvious that we must first develop and train our minds, and then use them, if we are going to be of any real service to our fellow men. We must eradicate greed, with its selfishness, copiousness, and lack of generosity; we must eliminate hatred, with its anger, malice, strife, racial prejudices, resentment and revenge; we must wipe away the clouds of delusion that give rise to fear and intolerance, craving for sensual pleasures, and a continuance of the status quo.

In their place we must develop unselfishness and generosity, loving-kindness, tolerance and understanding, patience, and equanimity, and so fit us for the task of changing national and international conditions to a sum total of these beneficent characteristics.

Such is our aim and aspiration as Buddhists. The culmination will depend on the effort put forth as mindfulness reveals the cause and cure of *dukkha*.

— §§§ —

A Businessmans's Dhamma

by Reg McAuliffe

We may begin with two statements which many of us know to be based on experience:

1. The Dhamma, to the extent to which we have applied it in our ordinary life, works. It may reasonably be inferred that the part still to be applied will also work.
2. In the presence of mindfulness, *dukkha* is inoperative. Even when mindfulness is imperfect, *dukkha* loses much of its sting.

Our topic is "Business Man's Dhamma" rather than the Dhamma in ordinary life. Business life, as I see it, has the benevolent and malevolent aspects with which we are familiar. In its benevolent aspect it may provide an interesting and rewarding way of satisfying human needs and in its malevolent aspect it sometimes is as red in tooth and claw as nature herself. How mindful must one be to remain detached in such surroundings?

Would it not be better to practise the Dhamma in one's spare time in the hope that it might have some beneficial effect on one's business life, but otherwise carry on business as before? The answer I get is that there is no choice: the path has been chosen and must be trodden. Clearly one cannot say that one will tread the path consistently and without faltering right to the goal. One can only tread it in each moment which constitutes the present.

I am extremely grateful to a member of the Buddhist Society for valuable advice which he gave me at the Summer School a few years ago. In substance, his advice was to start in a very simple way on very simple activities. One can be mindful from the time of getting up in the morning, through one's morning meditation until the time of getting into the car to drive to the office. Then it all stops. We get the familiar frustration from traffic hold-ups and from cars cutting in and, to make matters worse, our attention is diverted by thoughts about the job, by imaginary situations and imaginary meetings. Given mindfulness, however, car-driving can be restful, relatively safe and, if not a form of meditation, at least a revealing exercise.

In taking up this advice I found it relatively easy, after some practice, to observe the road about 70 to 100 yards ahead in a general and relaxed sort of way, without bothering to focus on anything in particular. In this condition, one's angle of vision is wider, with no noticeable loss of clarity, and one adjusts oneself to the general flow of traffic and notices deviations from it without apparent effort. Given mere attentiveness, it is almost as if the car drives itself: gears change as they should and the brakes come on at the proper time. The experience and the proof were good enough for me.

Driving back from the office is of the same pattern. Ordinarily one would continue conversations started in the office and wrestle with problems out of time and place. Given mindfulness, such irrelevances do not arise as distractions, but only as external phenomena, barely emerging.

So much for getting to and from the office. There remains the eight to ten hours each day of the mental push-pull which forms a large part of business activity. Clearly, mindfulness can be maintained in a simple mental activity, in the same way as it can in a simple physical activity, such as sawing a log of wood. But how can we apply mindfulness to complex situations in which a problem has to be resolved urgently in the place of some factors which are either unknown or imperfectly evaluated? How can mindfulness be applied when an urgent job has to be dropped half-way because some more urgent work has suddenly arisen? What happens when someone starts a course of action which will cut right across the policy decision which one is following? What about a case in which one is calm and mindful and, perhaps because of one's calmness, the workload piles up? Is mindfulness possible or even appropriate in such circumstances?

I do not know the answer to all of these questions. I can only say that such experience as I have had over the past few years in applying mindfulness to business situations shows that it is possible and progressively successful. In my case, the initial step was the hardest, which perhaps is justification enough for starting on simple activities. Moreover, again in my personal experience, when mindfulness is functioning as it should, it is effortless.

In applying mindfulness to business activities, I came upon a number of things which I call "discoveries." Perhaps these things are merely statements of the obvious.

The first discovery was that Dhamma is life and business life is part of it. The alternative was seen to be absurd and the absurdity could be demonstrated, if that were necessary, by trying to pour a quart into a pint pot. This discovery brought about a re-orientation to the job.

Having previously seen that "things" more deeply considered appear as functions, and functions more deeply considered change to a nameless something, I then stumbled upon the second "discovery" which was that complex things are merely simple things arranged in a special way and moving in a certain pattern in a certain direction. There are many cases in which one can deal with simple things one after the other when it would have been impossible to deal with the apparent complex of which they are the constituents.

The third "discovery" was concerned with some of the characteristics of change. It came to me that change was concerned with motion, either in the rate of flow or in the direction of flow. There could not be a change from motion to stopping (because no stopping could be observed), but there could be and often is a reversal in the direction of the main stream of events. Now it appeared that *dukkha* arose at the point of change (if there were personal resistance to it), and vanished if there were adaptation to the new flow, and increased if there were not.

The fourth "discovery" was to me the most surprising of all, namely that there had been no discovery but merely an expression, in imperfect terms, of what had always been known.

I do not know whether these things are true in any real sense. They are true in the sense that they have worked in my case and seem to stem naturally from my present state of development, however low that may be. Once out of the primary school, the results of lessons may be expressed in more appropriate language.

On reflection, "uncovering" may be a better word than "discovery." When one takes off the eiderdown from the bed, one is not surprised to see the bed uncovered. Perhaps our own protective layers are removed less frequently which, in a way, is the only surprising thing about it.

Why Buddhism? Why Theravada? Theravada, Mahayana, Hinayana

M. O'C. Walshe

Bodhi Leaves No. 53

First published: 1971

Why Buddhism?

From *The Buddhist Path*, July 1967

There is a periodical called *'Which?'* which provides guidance to the shopper as to the best bargains among the various branded wares in the market—from cars to contraceptives, from sausages to sewing-machines. Nowadays people will shop around for anything, even a religion or a philosophy of life. There is plenty of choice: Christianity in 57 varieties, Communism, Humanism, Spiritualism, Alcoholism, Drugism, Beatleism, not to mention those steady favourites Don't-knowism and Couldn't-care-lessism. Since every ism usually has several schisms, the selection is practically unlimited. Catholicism with a capital C has given place to Catholicism with a small c. The din is appalling as the siren strains of the Admen compete with the manic screams of the Madmen—and sometimes the two are hard to tell apart. Among the wares on offer is something called Buddhism. This too comes in several brands including Instant Zen.

All these things must be seen for what they are: manifestations of *dukkha.* We find life unbearable, and so we drug ourselves—with spirits, sex, LSD, speed or even horror films. We go off into reveries and fantasies of all kinds. We are willing to face anything and everything in life but ourselves. The short answer to the question "Why Buddhism?" is simply this: because it was Gotama Buddha who taught men how to come to terms with the nasty mess inside their own minds. That is really the only problem we have.

Youth, we are told today, is in revolt. The younger generation faced with the atom bomb and all the horrors of respectable society bequeathed by its elders is not going to pray. It has decided to "drop out." This is just one of those half-truths and quarter-truths we all put up, and is no more valid than any one of the other excuses put up by people of all ages. Of course the world is in a mess, but it always has been, because man is unenlightened.

Of course it is not true to say with some that our present-day troubles are due to decline of religion, just like that. But the crisis in the churches adds to the general moral confusion, and Rome burns while the Pope ponders the pill. If Christianity suffers from a fatal credibility gap, the thoughts of Mao and Kosygin seem scarcely more relevant, while the loudly proclaimed optimism of the Humanists begins to sound suspiciously like what it really is: a desperate whistling in the dark. Besides, our so-called "scientific humanists" are extraordinarily "selective" in their facts. For there is a whole dimension to life beyond the reach of computers of any conceivable kind. Mind is more wonderful than matter, and far less understood. As the facts of extra-sensory perception, "spiritual" healing and the rest become more and more generally known, the total inadequacy of conventional science to explain the world becomes almost as glaringly obvious as is that of conventional religion.

And this is where Buddhism comes in. Biologists as well as bishops need to do their homework better here. We have one reason—and a very good and proper reason—for preferring Buddhist to Western schools of thought: it provides more adequate and credible explanations of the world we live in and of man's existential dilemma. Yet this, though true and admirable, is by no means enough. For Buddhism, taken purely intellectually, does not do the patient much real good. Buddhism is not something to believe but something to do. It is a do-it-yourself religion, although, as has been pointed out by one bhikkhu, this means "Do it yourself and not "Do it your SELF'.

The Dhamma is described in the following terms: *Svākkhāto Bhagavatā Dhammo, sandiṭṭhiko, akāliko, ehipassiko, opanayiko, paccattaṃ veditabbo viññūhī ti*. This means: "Well proclaimed is the Dhamma of the Blessed One, to be seen for oneself, timeless, inviting inspection, leading onwards (to Nibbāna), to be realised by the wise, each one for himself."

Every word of this characterisation merits the most careful consideration. Thus *sandiṭṭhiko*, "to be seen for oneself," implies the Right View (*sammā diṭṭhi*) which is the first step of the Path: a view unclouded by greed, hate and delusion. *Akāliko*, "timeless," denotes that the Dhamma is not in time, is not affected by time, and also that its effect is immediate. And its message is as much for this age as for any other. The idea of seeing is again expressed in the term *ehipassiko,* derived from the imperative "come and see." The doctrine is open to inspection and examination. We are not being offered a pig in a poke. *Opanayiko* means "leading onwards" (to the goal).

Finally this Dhamma is something to be realised or experienced (*veditabbo*) by the wise (*viññūhi*), each for himself (*paccattaṃ*). By treading the Path we can come to know, of our own experience, the truth of the Buddha's teaching. None can say fairer than that.

There are other, and good, spiritual paths which can bring those who tread them to much happiness. Whether they lead him right out of *saṃsāra,* to the Beyond of Suffering, is a different matter which we shall not consider here. Within the Buddhist field too there are different schools of thought. The claim of Theravada Buddhism as taught in the Pali Canon rests on the directness of its approach and its penetration to the very heart of reality.

The West is still preoccupied with the old conflict of science and religion and whether these can be reconciled, or whether indeed science leaves any room for religion at all. In the terms of this conflict Buddhism cannot be identified with either science or religion as conventionally conceived, though if we define religion as "a way of salvation" then obviously Buddhism is a religion. But it is better viewed as the true scientific basis underlying all religions. If that is so, then while other paths may lead to the same goal, they are detours. Buddhism, and Theravada Buddhism in particular, is the direct way.

Why Theravada?

From *The Buddhist Path,* September 1967

The Theravada, or Teaching of the Elders, is the form of Buddhism based on the Pali Canon, as taught in Sri Lanka, Burma, Thailand, Cambodia and Laos, and its claim is that it represents the original teaching of the Buddha in its purity. There may be—indeed there are—arguments about this, but it is difficult to resist the conclusion that in the Pali Canon we have, to all appearances, the only authentic record of what Gotama the Buddha actually said. And if the

Pali language in which his words are preserved is not quite identical with his own language of discourse—as most, but not quite all, Western scholars seem to agree—there is certainly no reason at all to suppose that he spoke Sanskrit, still less any other of the languages of the various Mahayana canons.

More important is the fact that we have here a system of practice which leads directly to the goal: the world's finest mental therapy.

For that is what Buddhism is. The Buddha diagnosed our ills and prescribed the cure. Here in the West we sometimes describe the Theravada as Basic Buddhism. This is fair enough; though the term can be interpreted in more than one way. It can be taken to mean that here we have all the fundamentals, all that is really necessary, so that whatever is additionally taught in other schools is ultimately superfluous; or it can be taken to mean that this must be learnt and mastered first before one goes on to the "higher flights" of Mahayana, etc.

The former supposition represents the Theravada standpoint, properly speaking. Its validity will not be argued here. What about the latter view? The implications of this view are actually rather interesting and may prove disconcerting to some. Let us examine the resultant situation, for which purpose a little historical knowledge is necessary.

Mahayanists in general, apart from some scholars in quite modern times, have normally had virtually no direct knowledge of the Theravada tradition. What they refer to as "Hinayana" is in fact a scholastic tradition by no means totally identical with Theravada, and Mahayana polemics have therefore little or no relevance to this, being simply concerned with flogging the long-since dead horse of the Sarvāstivāda.

The strength of the Mahayana (if one can generalize about such a vast range of proliferating traditions) lies in its recognition of the provisional nature of certain truths enunciated in the "basic" scriptures. Its corresponding weakness, even in the East, lies in a frequent failure to appreciate that these provisional truths must first be thoroughly mastered before they are discarded. While it is useless to carry a raft after you have crossed the stream, it is premature to throw it away before you get to the water.

It was perhaps unfortunate for some Oriental countries that they received Buddhism in a purely Mahayana form, which must inevitably make it extremely difficult to get started. For Western Buddhists to ignore the opportunity to lay a firm foundation by training in the Theravada way is folly.

But we can go further. Granted that one is interested in Mahayana, how far then should one first proceed on the Theravada path? The answer must surely be: until the moment of crossing the stream or—to use a canonical variant of the metaphor—the moment of "entering the stream." This is the moment at which for the first time the profundity of the Dhamma is truly intuited and the fictitious nature of "self" is clearly perceived. After this there is no turning back, no relapsing into "states of woe," though the way ahead may still be long and possibly arduous. He who has reached this point is no longer a "worldling" (*puthujjana*), and ultimate Enlightenment is assured. It is really only at this stage that one can with certainty judge the relevance of this or that "higher" doctrine. But the prospects which appear beyond this point will not be considered here; they are in the true sense esoteric.

"Stream-entry" is not an unattainable goal, though obviously it requires perseverance—and humility. And its attainment or otherwise can be objectively measured. Self-deception in this respect is possible; deception of the teacher is not. When the insight of the Path has been truly gained, the possibility of infallibly discriminating right doctrine will for the first time be given. Likewise the true meaning of "non-discrimination" will be grasped. The "faculties" of faith, energy, mindfulness, concentration and wisdom will at this stage be so developed that they can no longer be overthrown by their opposites. From "faculties" they will have become "powers."

Ancient Oriental polemics have produced—in the name, incidentally, of "non-discrimination"—a spurious dichotomy between Hinayana, or "lesser vehicle," and Mahayana, or "greater vehicle," and the Theravada teaching has been arbitrarily and illegitimately equated in modern times with the "Hinayana." Let us drop these terms, which merely reflect long-defunct controversies.

THERAVADA, MAHAYANA, HINAYANA

From *Sangha*, March 1970

Theravada, the form of Buddhism based on the Pali scriptures which prevails in Sri Lanka, Burma and Thailand, is sometimes referred to as "Basic Buddhism". This can be interpreted, according to taste, in various ways. We would claim that it represents the original teaching of Gotama the Buddha, free from later additions or modifications. Others would regard it as merely the "groundwork" on which higher metaphysical superstructures can be erected. There are several of these superstructures in different Mahayana schools. Let us look at this situation.

The term Mahayana, meaning "great vehicle" (or career), was coined in contrast to another term, Hinayana, meaning "lesser vehicle" (or career), and Hinayana is the label commonly applied by Mahayanists to the Theravada. Strictly speaking, this is incorrect, as the Theravada school was probably scarcely known to the early Mahayanists who coined the term. What they had in mind were certain other ancient schools, more particularly the Sarvāstivāda, whose views differed comparatively little from the Theravada. But these schools have died out, and Oriental Theravadins now often accept the label Hinayana themselves. However, we shall not argue about labels. We can, if we like, refer (without implying any value-judgment) to the Narrow Path and the Expanded Path.

Our claim for the Narrow Path of Theravada would be that in the Pali scriptures we find a way that works—that leads to the goal of Nibbāna (or Nirvana in the Sanskrit form favoured by Mahayanists)—and that those scriptures contain all the essential features of the original doctrine proclaimed by the Buddha for the purpose of attaining that goal. There may be, here and there in the Pali scriptures, some passages which derive from later developments, but there is no evidence that non-Pali sources contain anything vital that is missing from those scriptures.

If this is so, then in the Pali Canon we have all we need for the attainment of Nirvana (let us, in this article, use the well-known Sanskrit form of this word). Such being the case, it would seem unnecessary to look any further afield. To say this is not, of course, to argue that Mahayanists cannot attain Enlightenment. Because the Mahayana scriptures contain things not included in the Pali Canon, this does not mean they are wrong, or useless. All teachings in the form of doctrinal formulations or prescribed practices are—and here all Buddhists of whatever school would agree in principle—fundamentally nothing but *upāyas* or "skilled devices." Any method that gets us moving on the right path is justified. The Truth lies beyond words and theories, and whatever we can say about it is only relatively correct or provisional—a finger pointing at the moon. Some of the "skilled devices" of the Mahayana schools may seem unnecessary to one type of mind, and yet be very helpful to another.

Historically, in very general terms, Buddhism spread in the form of the "Narrow Path" to the south and south-east of India. It was taken in the form of the "Expanded Path" to the countries to the north and north-east. When, in modern times, it was introduced to the West, this was at first mainly in the "Narrow" form, chiefly in the first place from Sri Lanka. Only considerably later were different forms of the "Expanded Path" imported, mainly from Tibet in the form of Tantrayāna (often more or less diluted, or reinterpreted, by Theosophy), and rather later again from Japan in the form of Zen. These are the only three paths (out of various possible ones) which have any considerable following in Western countries. It may be noted in passing that in Japan itself, the "Pure Land" school of Shin has far more followers than Zen, not to mention some of the "neo-Buddhist" schools which often have only tenuous links with the original or even the "Expanded" teaching. Incidentally, Japan also has the Shingon teaching which has much in common with the Tantricism of Tibet, and yet has aroused little interest in the West. Could it be because Shingon lacks the sexual symbolism of Tibetan Tantra? Perish the thought!

Doctrines apart, there is one thing that accounts in large measure for the preference some people have for the "Expanded Path": it tends to be more colourful and—apparently—more immediately emotionally satisfying than Theravada. It makes the kind of appeal which, in Christianity, Roman Catholicism makes in contrast to some of the more dour Protestant sects. Theravada is seen as dry and "doctrinaire"—nor does it give a clear picture of the goal. It has been compared by one writer to a truncated cane, like a mountain whose lower slopes are visible but whose peak is shrouded in mist. Zen might seem like the peak of Fuji-San rising clear into the sky, its lower slopes invisible. Yet somehow, if one can only get into the right state of mind, one would find oneself instantaneously transported to the top! (Actually, one is there already…) To the Western follower of Tibetan Buddhism, perhaps, the even loftier peak of Everest might appear out of the mists, and transport would be forthcoming in wondrous wise if one managed to cope with certain mystic rituals... These descriptions are, of course, libellous. They merely indicate how the three paths may appear to the "ignorant worldling" who contemplated trying one of them.

To such a worldling, the path of Theravada may seem too much like hard work, and the goal itself may appear far too uncertain. The other paths seem to offer both more exciting and, at the same time, perhaps easier possibilities. But after all, it is of nature of "skilled devices" that they are not what they seem. They are in fact "educational toys," as a famous Mahayana parable puts it. A father induced his children to leave a burning house by showing them the most fascinating toys outside.

Let us not indulge, then, in polemics. And let us remember that, when Mahayana scriptures speak in superior tones, as they often do, about the adherents of the "Lesser Vehicle," they are referring not to the existing Theravada but to the long-extinct Sarvāstivādins and others who may, in fact, have deserved at least some of their strictures, and who probably perished as a result in the deserts of scholasticism—the likely outcome of too much speculation and too little meditation.

The Mahayana schools have a wide range of scriptures, scarcely any of which claim historical "authenticity" in the mundane sense. They presuppose some supplementary higher revelation. While this may at one level be regarded as pious fiction, we must realise that these writings are, after all, the work of advanced spiritual teachers and the result of profound meditation. If they are fiction, it is only in the sense of "skilled devices," not vulgar fraud! Their claim is—and whether true or not, it is a serious claim—that they represent more profound aspects of truth than those revealed in the "Hinayana" scriptures, which they transcend but do not abrogate. A Christian writer called one such work "The New Testament of Higher Buddhism," and though we may not accept the claim, this gives a rough idea of the intention.

The main Mahayanist innovation is the exaltation of the bodhisattva ideal above that of the arahant. Coupled with this is the proclamation of wisdom and compassion as the "twin pillars" of the Mahayana. But before considering this further, let us briefly look at the Theravada scheme of things. Enlightenment is to be gained by treading the Noble Eightfold Path, which comprises three sections: wisdom, morality and meditation (or mind-training). A measure of mundane wisdom is necessary before one can even begin to tread the path, but the final fruition of supramundane wisdom can only come when the ethical and meditative sections of the path have been perfected. Thus the goal can in a sense be termed the "wisdom gone beyond" or, in Sanskrit, Prajñāpāramitā. This is, of course, the name given to a voluminous class of Mahayana sutras. Now, while it might be rash to equate the two "wisdoms" too hastily, it would be equally rash to distinguish sharply between them. We at least will not attempt to do so.

An article in *The Buddhist Path* some time ago discussed the bodhisattva (or rather "bodhisatta") ideal from the Theravada standpoint. In Theravada, the term Bodhisatta is applied, especially in the Jātakas, to Gotama before his Enlightenment—he had to perfect various qualities before he was able to become a Buddha. It is also suggested that the original Sanskrit form of the word was not *bodhisattva* or "enlightenment-being" but *bodhisakta* or "one intent on enlightenment." Either derivation of the Pali is possible, but it goes to show that the current Sanskrit may be based on a misconception.

In any case, the Mahayanist argument is that the ideal of gaining enlightenment for oneself is selfish, and that the bodhisattva who seeks to save all beings represents a higher ideal than the arahant. But since an arahant is by definition "self-less," this scarcely holds water. However, we have to consider the possibility that at the time when this view became prominent there may have been many spurious "arahants" whose "enlightenment" was merely self-delusion. Such people have been seen in the West, too, in this day and age.

And the authors of the Prajñāpāramitā scriptures never tired of reminding would-be bodhisattvas that though they were pledged to "save all beings," there were in reality no beings to save! It is perhaps fair comment, based on some experience in the West, to say that spurious "arahants," who generally keep themselves to themselves, are likely to be less of a nuisance than spurious "bodhisattvas" who go round preaching strange doctrines of their own, and who are anyway using their outward activities as an excuse for not "looking within" where the real trouble lies!

And the trouble, of course, with both, is conceit. Far too many Western people (certainly more than one might have believed possible) have snapped up a few "Buddhist" phrases (generally at second-hand). Then, perhaps having had some "experience" which they have misunderstood, they have jumped to the conclusion that they are "enlightened" or nearly so. Whether they then believe themselves to be arahants or bodhisattvas is of little importance. On the other hand, it is another matter whether there are any genuine arahants or bodhisattvas about in the West today. Who knows? In any case, such people would never recognise them... Incidentally, Zen, which is technically Mahayana school, seems a bit mistrustful of bodhisattvas. It aims at self-help, and Hui-neng declared that we should take the bodhisattva vow to "liberate all beings" in our own minds!

Let us return to "Basic Buddhism." The third section of the Path consists of three steps: right effort, right mindfulness and right concentration. That some effort is needed is surely obvious, though some "Zenful" characters in the West have been heard to deny it. They should try just one week in a Zen monastery! Right mindfulness has been declared by the Buddha to be the "one and only way" to liberation. It is the way of *vipassanā*—insight-wisdom. And how else could wisdom be gained but by "mindfulness and clear awareness"? Right concentration includes various things, among them the four Brahmavihāras: the development of loving-kindness, compassion, sympathetic joy and equanimity. So by practising these two steps of the Path we can develop the "twin pillars" of the Mahayana: wisdom and compassion. Perhaps it scarcely matters whether we set out to become an arahant or a bodhisattva. But suppose a bodhisattva, by practising too much mindfulness, became an arahant by mistake… That would be terrible. Or would it?

— §§§ —

Rebirth

John Andrew Storey

Bodhi Leaves No. 54

First published: 1971

Rebirth

Introduction

There has been a prevailing tendency in science to take a wholly materialistic view of life and the universe. This has perhaps been a natural reaction against the superstitions of past ages which have often masqueraded as religious truth. Happily this extreme reaction is now less apparent than it was, and there now seems to be among scientists a more open-minded approach to life and its phenomena. Parapsychological phenomena, which only a decade ago were not considered to be worthy of serious attention, are now being studied with considerable interest. We hear that Russia has a programme to develop telepathy as a tool in its space work. Similar research is said to be taking place in America, as are also investigations into such phenomena as ESP (extra-sensory-perception), pre-cognition and clairvoyance. One of the greatest scientists of our age, Nobel Laureate Erwin Schr dinger, has said that the problem of "mind" is "the most important problem with which science has yet to deal." Sir John Eccles—perhaps the world's most eminent neuro-physiologist—has shown how much recent trends in science have changed, for he now sees the brain as a detector and amplifier of mental influences. He assures us the brain is "just such a machine as a ghost or mind could operate."

In this new climate it is not surprising that there is a growing interest in rebirth—though in the West the phenomenon is usually called reincarnation. The Canadian-born psychiatrist, Dr. Ian Stevenson—now living and working in America—has been one of the foremost workers in this field, and the evidence he has made available is very impressive.

The aim of this essay is to review the evidence and examine the arguments for rebirth in an attempt to make a modest contribution to our understanding of the doctrine. We shall see first that the doctrine is very ancient and very widespread. We shall see that it reflects the natural order which from our observations we know to be cyclical. We shall have a brief look at the evidence from the claimed memories of former lives. We shall try to determine the nature of that which is reborn. And finally we shall examine one of the ways by which the process of rebirth may take place. In this way I hope to make our survey comprehensive so that our evaluation can be truly scientific.

Ancient and Universal

The doctrine of rebirth is very ancient, and also very widespread. It appears in various writings in the sixth century BC though the doctrine itself probably goes back well beyond that. It is a belief accepted by millions of people and, contrary to popular opinion, is not confined to Buddhism and Hinduism. Nor is it confined to the East, for it has many champions in the Western world. A recently published book entitled *Reincarnation in World Thought* (edited by Head and Cranston 1967) lists over four hundred great thinkers of the Western world who have been quoted in favour of the doctrine. In ancient times it had the support of such thinkers as Plato, Plotinus and Pythagoras. In more recent times philosophers like Schopenhauer, Goethe, Hume, Voltaire, T. H. Huxley and Ralph Waldo Emerson have approved it, and to their names we may add the names of great writers like Tolstoy, Thoreau, Browning, Longfellow, Rossetti, Kipling, Tennyson, Masefield and Whitman; musicians like Bruno Walier, Leopold Stokowsky, Sir Henry Wood and Yehudi Menuhin; statesmen like Benjamin Franklin and Lloyd George; and industrialists like Henry Ford. The list is endless and it would be impossible to quote from them all. We will let John Masefield, the late Poet Laureate of England, be their spokesman. In a poem appropriately called *My Creed* he writes:

> I hold that when a person dies
> His soul returns again to earth;
> Arrayed in some new flesh-disguise,
> Another mother gives him birth.
> With sturdier limbs and brighter brain
> The old soul takes the road again.

The language which Masefield has used to express his ideals may not be that which a well informed Buddhist would chose, as we shall see later, but his sentiments are the same and his words express the beliefs of many Westerners. It goes without saying that almost all the great thinkers of the East have believed in rebirth, a fact which even the adversaries of the doctrine find impossible to dispute.

The Natural Law

The fact that almost all the greatest thinkers of the world have accepted rebirth does not of course in itself prove the doctrine to be true. Though it is well to listen to what the wise ones have said, we must not let our respect for them completely colour our judgment. Notwithstanding the support the doctrine has received from the great ones we must, for our own satisfaction, yet ask if it is reasonable and if it does appear to fit into the facts of life as we see them. The answer to both of these questions should, I believe, be "yes."

In the world of nature everything is a ceaseless round of birth, growth, decay and death, and birth again. We have the cycle of the seasons and the cycle of day and night, work and sleep. It would be strange indeed if in the whole of nature man alone was the exception to the cyclic rule. As Nietzsche has said: "Everything goeth, everything returneth. Everything dieth, everything blossometh forth again. So, how could I not be ardent for … the ring of return?" Voltaire expressed the same sentiments when he wrote: "It is no more surprising to be born twice than once: everything in nature is resurrection."

The theory of evolution which has so gripped the imagination in the last hundred years also seems to me to corroborate the doctrine of rebirth. The two in fact would seem to be complementary and rebirth may even throw some light into the way in which evolution works. It is difficult to see how there can be any progress, at any rate as far as spiritual things are concerned, if each person coming into the world is a completely "new soul" starting from scratch. The old battle cry of the evolutionists and optimists "Onward and upward forever and ever" will have little hope of fruition if each person coming into the world has to learn the lessons of love and brotherhood from the beginning. Could it not be that the difference between the ignorant and selfish and the wise and holy is that the latter have lived their earlier lives more wisely than the former?

Is it not also possible that some day all will follow where the wise and holy have trod? Certainly we cannot dismiss the possibility. As Thomas H. Huxley has said: "Like the doctrine of evolution itself, that of rebirth has its roots in the world of reality. None but very hasty thinkers will reject it on the ground of inherent absurdity."

Another important lesson we learn from nature is that "that which we reap must always be of like character to the seed that was sown." This is true not only of the physical order but of the moral order as well. It is by accepting that "Whatsoever a man soweth, that shall he also reap" that we are able to understand the apparent inequalities and injustices of life. Science, no less than religion, teaches us that every effect has its cause. The whole universe, our own lives included, is governed by this law of action-reaction, or cause and effect. What we sow, we must in due course reap, and we are the creators of our own heaven or hell.

The great geniuses of the world should also be seen in this light, particularly those infant prodigies who display extraordinary abilities at an unusually early age. There have been many such cases. The most famous perhaps—at any rate in the Western world—is that of Mozart who composed a sonata when he was four and an opera when he was seven. In 1951 the London Evening Standard gave an interesting account of a little girl called Danielle Salamon who could play the piano before she could talk, and who by the time she was four had already composed several pieces of music and written the scores in a book. These cases are by no means unique; there are many others like them. During the summer of 1967 a BBC television news bulletin gave an account of a three-year-old boy in Korea who is already attending a university where he is doing a course in advanced mathematics, and he is already the author of several books. It certainly looks as though Plato was right when he asserted in his famous *Theory of Reminiscence* that "knowledge easily acquired is that which the enduring self had in an earlier life, so that it flows back easily."

Memories from Former Lives

As we have just seen in the previous section those things which come easily to us are in all probability the very things that we worked at diligently in earlier lives. It is at this point however that many people raise an objection which may be summarized thus: "If we have lived before, why have we no recollections of our previous lives?" As we shall see later there is no such thing as an "immortal self" to be reborn, but if for the moment we may take the question at its face value we may perhaps best answer it by saying that, since we begin each life with a new physical brain, the memories of former lives do not therefore normally register in the conscious mind. As we shall see shortly, there have been many exceptions, but in general, although the physical brain seems to have an important part to play in the retention of memory—in a way which we do not as yet understand, memories of actual events and places would ordinarily perish with the brain. Mahātma Gandhi was probably right when he said: "It is nature's kindness that we do not remember past births. Life would be a burden if we carried such a tremendous load of memories." We should perhaps be grateful that we don't have to recall the sins and follies of previous existences. But are we not in fact being too narrow in our definition of memory? Character is a form of memory, as are innate abilities and likes and dislikes. And as to the ability to recall actual events we must admit that we can only remember a small fraction of all that happens to us in this present life, and little, if anything, of what happened to us in the early years. Yet no one would deny that he was once a three year old simply because he has no recollection of being three. And if the psychologists are to be believed, these forgotten years of early infancy were the most decisive in determining our personality. In such a way is it not possible that the whole of our present character has been determined by the experiences of earlier lives, even though those experiences have been blotted from the memory or buried deep in the subconscious?

But as I have already indicated, it is not all that uncommon for people to claim recollections of former lives. Many hundreds of such cases have been investigated and proved beyond any reasonable doubt. Sometimes such recollections take the form of remembering places not previously visited in the present life. A well-known incident of this kind is recorded in the life of the English poet Shelley. Walking in a part of the country which he had never before visited, he suddenly said to a companion: "Over that hill, there is a windmill." As they breasted the hill and saw the windmill, Shelley fainted with emotion. Even more striking is the account of an

American couple on a world cruise who stopped at Bombay. Walking around the city, they both found themselves extraordinarily familiar with parts of it so that they had no need of a guide and could tell each other in advance of coming to a place, say around a corner, what they would see. They tested this knowledge by going to a particular quarter they thought they remembered and looking for a house and a banyan tree they remembered standing in the garden of the house. When they reached the place where they expected to find the house and tree, they did not see them. But a policeman happened to be nearby, and they asked him if the house and tree had formerly stood there. He confirmed that there had at one time been a house and a tree as the couple described them. He added an additional piece of information. The house had belonged to a family named Bhan. This couple had, for some reason unknown to them, liked the name Bhan and had given this name as first name to their son.

More important as evidence for rebirth are the many recorded cases of people who have actually recalled previous lives. Dr. Ian Stevenson the eminent Canadian psychiatrist—now living and working in America—has investigated many such claims, and his published findings in *The Evidence for Survival from Claimed Memories of Former Incarnations* and *Twenty Cases Suggestive of Reincarnation* make impressive reading. Also of great value has been the research of Francis Story and some of his findings are published in his *The Case for Rebirth*, Wheel No. 12/13. From the many cases around the world that have been investigated I will give just two examples, one from Asia and the other from Europe. Shanti Devi, a girl living in Delhi (born 1926) began from the age of three to recall and state details of a former life in the town of Muttra, about eighty miles away. She stated that her name had been Lugdi, that she had been born in 1902, was a Choban by caste and had married a cloth merchant named Kedar Nath Chaubey. She said that she had given birth to a son and had died ten days later. As Shanti Devi continued to make such statements, her family finally made inquiries when she was nine years old to see if such a person as her claimed husband actually existed in Muttra. There was such a person, and he sent a relative to the girl's house and afterwards came unannounced himself. She immediately identified both of these persons. The following year, after it had been established by an investigating committee that she had never left Delhi, she visited Muttra where she instantly recognised places and people and found her way around with perfect ease. Many statements which she made about her previous life were verified.

Our second case concerns an English woman, Annie Baker, who under hypnosis spoke perfect French, although she had never studied the language or been to France. She spoke of the death of Marie Antoinette as if it had just happened. She gave her own name as Marielle Pacasse and that of her husband as Jules. She stated that her home was in the Rue de St. Pierre near the Notre Dame. Subsequent investigation revealed that although there is now no Rue de St. Pierre, there was one a hundred and seventy years ago. The name Marielle, now very rare, was much in vogue in 1794. Rebirth would seem to offer the best explanation of the link which exists between a Frenchwoman of the eighteenth century and the present-day Annie Baker.

These few cases I have outlined provide just a small sample of the hundreds of similar cases which have been thoroughly investigated and verified. Scholarly research along scientific lines is continuing on this subject—conducted by men of the calibre of Dr. Ian Stevenson and Francis Story—which may one day prove beyond any reasonable doubt that rebirth is a fact, just as much a law of science as is the law of gravity.

What Survives?

On the evidence we have seen so far it seems reasonable to suppose that rebirth does in fact take place. We now have to ask ourselves what it is that is reborn and what are the processes by which rebirth takes place. We shall look at the process of rebirth later on, but it is to the nature of that which is reborn that we must now turn.

Let it be said at once that the traditional concept of the soul as held by most European Christians is not one that we need to espouse in order to believe in rebirth. The idea that there is in man a spiritual or "ethereal double" which is able to survive the death of the body and to maintain itself as a changeless, separate entity does not seem to me to be feasible. What we have to look for is not a "soul" which stays recognisably the same for an eternity, but a principle or entity which is forever evolving—a constantly changing "stream of consciousness," to borrow a phrase from William James. The Buddhist scholar Ven. Walpola Rāhula perfectly expresses the idea I have in mind. He writes: "If there is no permanent, unchanging entity or substance like self or soul, what is it that can re-exist or be reborn after death? Before we go on to consider life after death, let us consider what this life is, and how it continues now. What we call life is ... a combination of physical and mental energies. These are constantly changing; they do not remain the same for two consecutive moments. Every moment they are born and they die. Thus, even now during this lifetime, every moment we are born and die, but we continue. If we can understand that in this life we can continue without a permanent, unchanging substance like self or soul, why can't we understand that those forces themselves can continue without a self or soul behind them after the non-functioning of the body? When this physical body is no more capable of functioning, energies do not die with it, but continue to take some other shape or form, which we call another life. ... As there is no permanent unchanging substance, nothing passes from one moment to the next. So quite obviously, nothing permanent or unchanging can pass or transmigrate from one life to the next. It is a series that continues unbroken but changes every moment. The series is, really speaking, nothing but movement. ... A child grows up to be a man of sixty. Certainly the man of sixty is not the same as the child of sixty years ago, nor is he another person. Similarly, a person who dies here and is reborn elsewhere is neither the same person, nor another. It is the continuity of the same series." As science penetrates more and more to the heart of things, as matter is reduced to smaller and smaller particles, so does it become obvious that what we are left with is not "material" at all, but a system of electronic waves, vibrations, or patterns of energy-concentration. As Arthur Koestler has said in his *The Ghost in the Machine*: "Matter is no longer a unitary concept; the hierarchy of macroscopic, molecular, atomic and subatomic levels trails away without hitting rock-bottom, until matter dissolves into patterns of energy-concentration, and then perhaps into tensions in space." If one accepts—as I think one must—the truth of Koestler's statement, then there are surely no rational grounds for rejecting the idea that there is in man an organized energy-concentration which in a computer-like fashion stores the "personality-data"—the attributes, talents and characteristics—of the "individual." And if one further accepts the proof of science that energy is indestructible, then one cannot logically deny the possibility that this "energy-concentration" can survive the destruction of the physical brain to continue on his ever evolving pilgrimage in the process of which it may operate through many bodies.

The Process Explained

There only now remains the question as to the processes by which rebirth takes place. It seems to me that radio provides a useful analogy of what in fact may happen. It is not beyond the realms of reason to suppose that the energy-concentration—that which the West traditionally calls the "mind" or "soul"—is given out at the moment of death. In much the same way as a radio signal is given out by a transmitter, and that this signal carries with it the "personality-data" of the "individual" which is eventually picked up and "de-coded" by a suitable "receiver," i.e. the newly formed or developing brain of an unborn child. And it may also be that just as a radio signal can only be picked up by the right kind of receiver adjusted to the right wavelength, so a deceased individual's "radio signal" can only be picked up by a brain which is uniquely suited to receive it. At first acquaintance this idea may sound rather fanciful, but it has received support from Sir Julian Huxley, internationally esteemed scientist, philosopher, and self-confessed agnostic. In his contribution to a book of essays called *Where are the Dead?* he makes the following comments: "there is nothing against a permanently surviving spirit individuality being in some way given off at death, as a definite wireless message is given off by a sending apparatus working in a particular way. But it must be remembered that the wireless message only becomes a message again when it comes in contact with a new, material structure—the receiver. So with our possible spirit-emanation. It would never think or feel unless again 'embodied' in some way. Our personalities are so based on body that it is really impossible to think of survival without a body of sorts. I can think of something being given off which would bear the same relation to men and women as a wireless message to the transmitting apparatus; but in that case 'the dead' would, so far as one can see, be nothing but disturbances of different patterns wandering through the universe until they came back to actuality of consciousness by making contact with something which could work as a receiving apparatus for mind." Francis Story comments in much the same way when he says: "It is only necessary to conceive

> ... an energy-potential flowing out of the mind of a being at the moment of death, and carrying with it the karmic characteristics of that being, just as the seed of a plant carries with it the botanical characteristic of its type, and a mental picture is formed that corresponds roughly to what actually takes place."

Conclusion

In our brief survey we have looked at the doctrine of rebirth from several different points of view. We have seen that it is a very ancient doctrine which has been accepted by most of the greatest thinkers the world has known—including many from Europe and America. We have observed that in nature, birth, death and rebirth is the law, as also is the fact that that which we sow, we must in due course reap. We have seen no reason why man should be an exception to the universal rule, and such phenomena as infant prodigies seem to confirm that what is true for the rest of nature is true of man. More striking still is the evidence from the claimed memories of former lives, examples of which we examined. We have studied the nature of that which is reborn, and by analogy have tried to understand how the process works.

Acknowledgments

Acknowledgments are made to the journals *The Middle Way* and *Psychical Studies* in which extracts from this work have appeared, and to Mrs. Mary Peto who has also printed part of this work for private distribution.

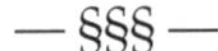

The Scientific Approach to Buddhism

and

The Appeal of Buddhism

Two Essays

Francis Story
(Anāgārika Sugatānanda)

Bodhi Leaves No. 55

First published: 1971

The Scientific Approach to Buddhism

from *The Light of the Dhamma,* Vol. 1:4 (1953)

The eminent scientist, Bertrand Russell, has summed up the position of present-day philosophical thought as follows: "Assuming physics to be broadly speaking true, can we know it to be true, and if the answer is to be in the affirmative, does this involve knowledge of other truths besides those of physics? We might find that, if the world is such as physics says it is, no organism could know it to be such; or that, if an organism can know it to be such, it must know some things other than physics, more particularly certain principles of probable inference" (*Physics and Experience,* Cambridge University Press).

That position requires a little preliminary explanation. In the days when science was believed to hold the key to all the secrets of the universe, the materialistic interpretation of life held undisputed sway. The scientist, it was thought, had only to turn the key—in other words, open up the atom for investigation—and the basic principle of all material phenomena would be exposed. All life and thought-processes were believed to have a material origin and foundation, and there was no room for the supernatural concepts of religion. Everything was a mechanical process of cause and effect, with nothing beyond.

The evidence of physics, so far as it went, was overwhelming; it was supported by the findings of astronomy, psychology and Darwinian evolution. Scientists believed that they understood the nature of atomic processes so well that, if the relative position, direction and force of all atomic units in the universe at any given moment were known, every future event in space and time could be accurately predicted. It was only a question of obtaining the data.

In course of time the key was turned; the construction of the atom was analysed, but it was found to resolve itself into energy, a process of transmutation from one form of radiation into another, a continual cycle of arising and passing away of electronic particles.

With the discovery of quantum mechanics, another modification entered into the accepted scheme of rigid causality. It was found that although the law of predictability held true of large numbers of atomic particles it was not valid for individual atoms. The law of deterministic causality was not absolute; it could only be applied statistically or quantitatively where large groups of atoms were being dealt with. This new concept opened the way for what is called the "uncertainty principle."

From a philosophic viewpoint, which is, strictly speaking, no concern of the pure scientist who is only engaged in the investigation of phenomena, not its implications, this "uncertainty principle" made room for the idea of free-will, which had necessarily been absent from the idea of an universe entirely determined by causal principles that admitted of no variation.

With the changeover from a static to a dynamic concept of matter, the scientist did not alter his materialistic theory because science by its nature has to assume the substance or reality of the material with which it is working; but a radical change took place in the attitude towards knowledge itself. Man, and the working of his mind, is a part of the universe, and his examination of its phenomena is like a person looking into the working of his own brain. He is looking at that with which he is himself identified; he cannot get outside and view it objectively. The picture of the universe presented through his senses is quite different from the picture given by physics; where his senses tell him there is solidity, form and substance, physics tells him there is nothing but a collocation of forces in a perpetual state of flux, of momentary arising and decay; and, moreover, that "solid" forms are really nothing but *events* in the space-time continuum, and that the so-called material object is itself mostly space. There is no such thing as a "solid" as we understand the term; it is merely a convention of speech based upon the deceptive data provided by the senses.

Our senses, however, are the only possible means of contact with events outside ourselves, and the data of physics, similarly, have to reach us through these senses. So the problem arises, can we ever be certain that the picture presented by physics is a true one?

This picture, it must be remembered, is a purely theoretical one; it is a matter largely of mathematical formulae, from which the mind has to make up whatever imaginative approximation it can. The universe of physics is an entirely mental concept; we cannot make up any picture of the space-time manifold of Einstein, so we have to rely upon the evidence of mathematics, which reveals a new dimension entirely outside the range of our normal experience. But the physicist has come to distrust even the working of his own mind, since it is itself a part of this quite illusory fabrication; and so he has been forced to ask himself the revolutionary question, "If physics is true, is it possible for us to know that it is true?" The whole subject-object relationship is thus brought into question. When the mind registers the impression which we call "seeing an object," can we be certain that the object seen really exists outside ourselves, or that there is any event taking place in space-time that bears the slightest resemblance to what we think we see? Science can give us no assurance on this point.

The scientific view of the phenomenal universe has reached this stage, and does not seem capable of going beyond it. To view the picture in its completeness, a mind is required that is not itself involved in the phenomenal process, a transcendental mind that is outside the realm of causality and the subject-object relationship. It must "know some things other than physics."

So far, science has helped us, in its own way, to understand the Buddhist principles of *anicca, dukkha* and *anattā*, for the account it gives of the universe is completely in accord with Buddhist philosophy. The process of universal flux and the inherent substancelessness of matter is a fundamental of Buddhism. More than that, the process has actually been observed in the course of Buddhist meditation; the atomic constituents have been seen and felt, and the *dukkha* of their arising and passing away has made itself known to the mind which has stopped identifying the process with what we call "self," the illusion of *sakkāya diṭṭhi.* The supramundane knowledge of Buddhism begins where science leaves us, but because Buddhism is based upon direct perception of ultimate truth, it is only natural that the discoveries of science should confirm it as they are doing today.

The whole process of the deceptive arising and passing way of phenomena may be comprehended in the word *maya*. This word is usually translated as "illusion" but that is not entirely correct. The sphere of *maya* is that of *relative reality;* that is, it is real on its own level, but not real in any absolute sense. To the consciousness functioning on the same level, or at the same vibrational frequency, a solid is a solid exactly as it appears through the five doors of the senses. But to a consciousness operating on a different level, the solid would be seen in a different way; it would appear as physics tells us it is, a collection of atomic particles in continual movement. The "solid" object would be seen as predominantly space, with the atomic constituents widely separated, like the stars in the night sky, and only held in place by the electronic forces of attraction and repulsion, in just the same way that the planetary systems of the universe are held together. From another level it would be seen simply as the operation of a law, and from yet another plane of consciousness it would be found to be non-existent; there could be only the void, or *asaṅkhata-dhamma*. That plane would be outside the sphere of causality, a state unthinkable to the ordinary mind, which depends upon events in space-time for its consciousness, and we may consider it to be equivalent to the ultimate state of Nibbāna, in which there is neither coming-to-be nor passing away. The space-time continuum of phenomenal perception would be transcended and the timeless, unconditioned state would then be reached.

These ascending levels of consciousness in which the solid object is seen in different aspects, each one more immaterial than the one proceeding it, may be likened to the four *brahma-vihāras*, where the consciousness is freed from the illusion of gross matter, and perceives instead the law that governs it, coming to know ultimately that "matter" is only the expression of that law, appearing in different aspects on the various planes of cognition. To the *kāmāvacara citta* (sense-sphere consciousness), form, or *rūpa*, appears solid and on that level it is what it appears; but to the consciousness which sees it in the light of Dhamma the law of cause and effect becomes apparent, and in the place of *rūpa* the three characteristics of becoming, *anicca, dukkha, anattā* (impermanence, suffering, not-self), are recognised.

There are indications that man has reached the end of his development on the intellectual plane; he has come to rock-bottom in the analysis of physical phenomena, yet still its ultimate secret eludes him. There is more beyond, which mind is not capable of exploring, because the circle of causality in which it moves has been completed. The next state of development must lie in a different dimension. Enough has happened to bring about a complete re-orientation of all our ideas concerning man and his place in the cosmic pattern, and this represents a great advance on both the animistic and materialist views that prevailed formerly. Like everything else, reason revolves in a circle, bounded by the limitations of conceptual thinking, and the point around which it rotates is the difficulty of distinguishing the process that is being examined from the "self" that is examining it. This is the fundamental obstacle, *sakkāya-diṭṭhi* (personality-belief), because in reality there is no "self" apart from the process. In the modern view there is no such thing as "I;" the word is merely a grammatical convention. Everything we know now about the process of thought can be expressed without the use of the word. We have this also on the authority of Bertrand Russell and others. The discoveries of physics have their counterpart in psychology. In analysing the mental processes a great deal of concealed activity has been brought to light, and definite causal relationships have been traced between the conscious and unconscious strata of the mind. The unconscious, in which is stored the accumulated experience of the individual, supplies the tendencies that motivate the conscious activities. Thus it may be identified with the *bhavaṅga*, or life-continuum, which takes the place of any connecting entity between one phase of consciousness and the next. Professor William James was the first psychologist to formulate the theory of point-moments of consciousness. He demonstrated that these point-moments come into being and pass away again in rapid succession, thus giving the impression of a continuous entity, whereas they are, in reality only infinitesimal units of a series, each existing for a fraction of a split-second, and then passing away to make room for its successor. They are, in fact, like the thousands of static pictures on a reel of film, which, when run through a projector, produce the illusion of a single moving picture. Furthermore, we are only conscious of each one in the moment of its passing away; for this reason they are sometimes called death spots, and the resultant consciousness is dependent upon memory.

These point-moments arise in obedience to the law of causality, each having its causal genesis in the one preceding it, but there is no other connection between them. Everywhere in psychology we come upon these causal processes and the continual state of flux in thoughts, mental impressions and cognition, but nowhere can we detect any permanent entity linking the succession of events together. Again, as in physics, we find only causal relationships, and the Abhidhamma analysis holds good throughout.

Freud went so far as to maintain that every overt act of the conscious mind is instigated by an antecedent cause and no thought can arise spontaneously. This he demonstrated in his *Psychopathology of Everyday Life*. When the cause could not be found in the conscious mind he sought it in the unconscious. His researches led him to the theory that most so-called accidents were the result of a subconscious wish—that they were in fact, engineered by the subconscious mind for reasons of its own. The theory has been disputed by later investigators, but Freud collected a formidable mass of evidence in support of it.

From the Buddhist point of view it appears to be at least a partial truth. In as much as the unconscious stratum of the mind carries the tendencies and predispositions of the individual, which are his accumulated *kammic* influences, it is the activity of that portion of the mind which determines the experiences and events of his life. It is not that the unconscious mind wills the events, because it has the nature only of *bhavaṅga*, a current directed by past habitual thoughts, and lacks the quality of volition, which is a characteristic of the conscious mind; but events such as "accidents" are certainly determined by the unconscious mind in the discharge of its mechanical function of projecting those situations that constitute the individual's experience, in accordance with his *kamma. "Mano pubbaṅgamā dhammā; manoseṭṭhā, manomayā*—all phenomena arise from mind; mind is the chief, they are all mind-made." Freud's error was merely that he mistook a partially-understood causal process in the subconscious mind for an act of volition. That is why his theory has never been completely proved, despite the high percentage of successes in his experiments. It is another instance of science approaching Buddhism, but lacking the key that will unlock the last door.

The materialist affirms that mind and mental conditions have a material basis; the idealist, on the contrary, claims that matter exists only by virtue of mind. The evidence adduced by the materialist is that the mind is only a product of the brain, which is a material substance. Physical objects existing in space are contacted through the nerve-channels leading from eye, ear, nose, tongue and skin-surface. The resulting sensation depends upon the existence of the brain, a complex material nerve-centre with its own particular function of collecting and correlating the data thus received. If the brain is damaged it operates imperfectly; if it is destroyed it ceases to function altogether. The mind, then, is considered to be a causal process depending entirely on material factors.

The reasonableness of this point of view cannot be denied, but it does not account for all the facts. If the process is strictly a mechanical one, determined by physical causes which can be traced back to a material origin and obeying a rigid causal law, there is no room for the exercise of free-will. Evolution then becomes a predestined automatic process in which there is no freedom of choice between possible alternatives. Yet even biological evolution demands such a choice, since the production of specialised types is usually attributed to natural selection. Those types, such as the mastodon, brontosaurus, pterodactyl and other extinct species, which made a choice of development that suited them to a particular environment, disappeared when that environment changed; they had over-specialised and could not readapt themselves. There is nothing automatic about the evolution of species; it is conducted on a system of trial and error, and shows at least as many failures as successes. There are some who consider that man himself must be numbered among the failures, since he shows a tendency towards self-destruction, due to the fact that his spiritual evolution has not kept abreast of his increasing mastery of physical forces. H. G. Wells, who saw in the Buddhist King Asoka the highest development of civilised rulership over two thousand years ago, was firmly convinced that, far from progressing, man as a spiritual being had deteriorated since that time, and would ultimately destroy himself.

The idea of a steady progress in evolution has been discarded by science, and present theories are more in accordance with what we know of evolution as it applies to the individual. That evolution requires freedom of choice between the alternatives of right and wrong actions. There is progress or regression, according to whether the kamma tends towards good or bad, and the entire concept of kamma is based upon free-will. It is not, as it is sometimes misinterpreted, a fatalistic doctrine. Previous kamma determines the experiences and situations that have to be faced in life, but it is the characteristic tendencies of the individual, which are the product of accumulated acts of volition, that determine how he will deal with those situations when they arise. There is no such thing as an accident in natural law, but the "uncertainty principle" which we discovered in physics allows for the operation of unknown causes, as in the unpredictable behaviour of individual atoms. In the case of an individual, for instance, it may be possible to predict fairly accurately how the person will behave in a given situation when his characteristic tendencies are known, but we cannot guarantee absolute certainty. An honest man may, under pressure of circumstances, or because of some latent *kammic* tendency, act dishonestly, or a brave man become a coward, and vice versa. This explains the inconsistencies and frequent contradictions of human nature; we can never be absolutely certain that the person we think we know so well will always act strictly "in character." Personality is a fluid structure, altering momentarily, and only guided by certain broad principles which represent the *saṅkhāra*-accumulated tendencies or habit-formations.

Concerning these habit-formations, it may be said that Buddhism is the only system that gives them their due place of importance in the scheme of personal evolution. It is by habit-formations that we are told to eliminate bad tendencies and promote the good ones, thus moulding our own psychology through accumulated acts of strenuous effort, as indicated by the fourfold Right Effort, which is one of the thirty-seven principles of *bodhi*. Now, habit-formation and the association of ideas are closely linked, as modern psychology has proved. In his experiments on conditioned reflexes, Pavlov established the relationship between associated ideas and physical reactions. The dogs he used in his researches were taught to associate the sound of a bell, or some other noise, with the idea of food. When they heard that particular sound, the dog showed the same reactions as though they were seeing or smelling food. Their mouths watered, and they gave other signs of pleasure which proved that the sound and the idea of food had become firmly associated in their minds. The mind of a dog is a very simple thing compared with that of a human being, which makes it easier to trace its sequence of events and their physical consequences. It works almost entirely on this system of conditioned reflexes. The reasoning faculty is rudimentary; and as we descend in the scale of living organisms we find that they become more and more instinctive or mechanical. A termite, for instance, is little more than a mechanical unit controlled by a mind outside itself. Recent experiments with colonies of termites have shown that the directive is the queen-termite, and that the termite-nest must be considered as a single animal, with its brain and nerve-centre situated in the queen. If the queen is destroyed, the termites become confused, running frantically in all directions, and the orderly system of the nest is utterly broken up. The individual termite, therefore, is not a complete organism in itself, but only a part of the whole. They are, as it were, limbs of the main body, detached from it, but functioning in all ways like the limbs of a single animal. It is believed that they are directed by a kind of radar emitted by the queen-termite. When the queen is killed or injured it is as though the brain of the animal were damaged; the limbs move without co-ordination like those of a man who is insane. But the brain of the organism, the queen-termite, is a strictly limited mechanism; it performs the functions required of it for the survival of the termite-nest, according to inherent tendencies transmitted from one generation of queens to another. Within the limits of its requirements it is a perfect organism, but it has no possibility of further development. Why is this? We can only assume that, having reached its limited evolutionary objective, it no longer has to exercise any choice between possible alternatives; it has surrendered the faculty of free-will and has become a set automaton. It represents one of the levels of consciousness dominated entirely by kamma, in which the results of previous conditions are worked out without any opportunity for using them to advantage, and may be considered the type of consciousness characteristic of all the four *apaya* planes (worlds of misery) in varying degrees. The question is dealt with in the section on the classification of individuals (*puggala-bhedo*) in the *Abhidhammattha-saṅgaha* (Ch. IV).

There is an approximation to this automatic type of consciousness to be found even in some human beings, and the termite may be taken as a warning to those who sacrifice their independence of thought to become slaves to authority and tradition; they give themselves a termite-consciousness, and if they re-manifest as termites, it is their own choice. To deliver oneself up to authoritarianism is an easy and comfortable way out of the hazard and pain of having to make an independent choice. But man is a free agent, and to be born a human being is a tremendous responsibility. Having earned that responsibility we should not lightly throw it away. By showing us exactly where we stand in relation to the universe around and within us, Buddhism gives us a clear insight into the divine potentialities of our nature; it is the most emphatic assertion of man's freedom to choose his own destiny.

The Western philosopher of today is bewildered by the confusion into which his speculations have led him. He sees a universe of amoral forces with no fixed centre, a changing phantasmagoria in which all is shadow but no substance, and he is obsessed by the futility of what he sees. His intellectual position has been fairly defined as one of "heroic despair." Discovering no ground for belief in moral values he has come to question whether they have any absolute meaning or whether they are, after all, only products of mankind's collective imagination. Life, for him, has become "a tale told by an idiot; full of sound and fury, signifying nothing." Abstract ideas, such as those of justice, benevolence, wisdom and truth, seem to him only relative qualities, dictated by circumstances and differing from age to age. So ethical standards tend to give way to the demands of expediency.

Only Buddhism can provide the missing element of higher knowledge—the "something other than physics"—which causes all the other elements to fall into place and form a complete and intelligible picture. Seeing the world as the Buddha taught us to see it, we can weigh its values according to the highest standards known to us. And in the process of weighing and assessing, Buddhism encourages us to analyse all the factors of experience, not to hedge ourselves about with dogmas, or cling to preconceived ideas. The Buddha himself was the first religious teacher in this world-cycle to apply strictly scientific methods to the analysis of our own being and the cosmic phenomena in which we are entangled, and his voice speaks to us as clearly today as ever it did 2500 years ago. It speaks to us, not only through his teaching preserved over the centuries, but through the discoveries of modern science also. The teachings, as we have them, may contain something added by later interpreters, but the central truths the Buddha taught are sufficient in themselves to give us the vital clue that has eluded present-day thinkers. When we add their discoveries to the doctrines of Buddhism we find that the whole makes a complete pattern, so far as our rational minds are capable of appreciating it. The remainder we must find for ourselves on the higher planes of Buddhist *jhāna*.

At present it may look as though man has only searched out the secrets of the universe in order to destroy himself with the power he has acquired; and of that there is certainly a danger. But I believe that a change in outlook is beginning to dawn, and that science itself, having destroyed the basis of much wrong thinking, is drawing us ever nearer to the realisation of the truth proclaimed by the Enlightened One. This is what I mean by "the scientific approach to Buddhism;" without being aware of it, the modern scientist and philosopher are being propelled irresistibly in the direction of Buddhism. Their uncertainties and doubts are spiritual "growing pains;" but a time will come quickly when they will realise that, although they have had to reject everything on which their ordinary religious and moral beliefs are founded, there is a higher religion—one based upon systematic investigation and the sincere search for truth—which will restore their lost faith in the universal principles of justice, truth and compassion. Those who now believe that man has come to the end of his tether will then see the opening up of vistas into the future that they only dimly suspect, and will recognise, beyond it all, the final goal of complete emancipation from the fetters of ignorance and delusion.

— §§§ —

The Appeal of Buddhism

In the *Buddhist Forum* of Radio Ceylon on June 1st 1958, four self-converted Buddhists were asked to speak on the subject of "What appeals to me most in Buddhism." The following is the reply given by Anāgārika Sugatānanda (Francis Story).

From *The Light of the Dhamma*, Vol. 4 (1958)

It was many years ago that I became a Buddhist and I was quite young, between 14 and 16, but I remember that it was first of all the two facts of rebirth and *kamma* which convinced me of the truth of the Dhamma. I say "facts" because even among many non-Buddhists rebirth is now well on the way to being a proven truth, and once it is accepted the reality of *kamma* must be accepted with it. In the first place, these two doctrines explain everything in life which is otherwise inexplicable. They explain the seeming injustices with which life abounds, and which no earthly power can remedy. They explain, too, the apparent futility and lack of a satisfactory pattern in the individual human life which, taken as one life out of a measureless eternity is obviously quite pointless, full of unresolved problems and incomplete designs. Take, for instance, a recent and much publicised example of what appears to be a cruel freak of chance—the tragically brief life of a child, Red Skelton's son, whom neither human science nor divine mercy could save. There are, and always have been, countless millions of such cases, besides the untold numbers of blind, deaf and dumb, deformed, mentally deficient and diseased human beings whose pitiful condition is not due to any fault of theirs in this present life, nor to any remediable defect in the organisation of human society.

Materialists may say what they will, but we now know enough of the limitations of science to realise that it will never be able entirely to abolish these evils. At the same time we can no longer derive comfort from religions that science has discredited. While we know that material progress will never succeed in abolishing suffering, it is equally futile to suppose that some special compensation for unmerited misfortune awaits the victims in a future life irrespective of any moral issues that are involved.

The sense of justice, which was very strong in me, demanded a reason for these things and an intelligible purpose behind them. I could not accept the theory that there is a "divine justice" which is different from human concepts of justice, for both the word and the idea can only mean what we take them to mean by human standards. If conditions are not just in the human sense they are not just at all: there cannot be two different meanings to the word. The "justice of God" is an invention of theologians, the last refuge of unreason.

But right at the beginning Buddhism gave me the justice and the purpose which I had been seeking. I found them both in the doctrine of *kamma* and rebirth. Through them I was at last able to understand the otherwise senseless agglomeration of misery, futility and blind insensate cruelty which forms most of the picture human life presents to a thinking person. Those who know something about the subject may say, "Yes, but Buddhism is not alone in teaching kamma and rebirth; Hinduism has it also." That is true; but Buddhism is alone in presenting rebirth as a scientific principle. When I say "scientific" I mean that it is a principle which is in accordance with other universal laws which can be understood scientifically and even investigated by scientific methods. The principle of change and serial continuity is one that runs throughout nature; all scientific principles are based on it. In Buddhism it is the principle of *anattā* which lifts the concept of rebirth from the level of primitive animism to one on which it becomes acceptable to the scientifically-trained mind. *Anattā* means "non-soul", "non-ego" and "non-self;" it is the denial of any abiding or constant and unchanging element in the life-process. Buddhism does not point to a "soul" that transmigrates; it points to a continuum of cause and effect that is exactly analogous to the processes of physics. The personality of one life is the result of the actions of the preceding current of existences, in precisely the same way that any physical phenomenon at any given moment is the end-result of an infinite series of events of the same order that have led up to it.

When I came to understand this thoroughly, which I did by pondering the profound doctrine of *paṭicca-samuppāda* (dependent origination), I realised that the Buddha-dhamma is a complete revelation of a dynamic cosmic order. It is complete scientifically because it accounts not only for human life but for the life of all sentient beings from lowest to highest; and complete morally because it includes all these forms of life in the one moral order. Nothing is left out; nothing is unaccounted for in this all-embracing system. If we should find sentient beings on other planets in the remotest of the galactic systems, we should find them subject to the same laws of being as ourselves. They might be physically quite different from any form of life on this earth, their bodies composed of different chemical combinations, and they might be far superior to ourselves or far below us, yet still they must consist of the same five *khandha* aggregates, because these are the basic elements of all sentient existence. They must also come into being as the result of past *kamma,* and pass away again just as we do. *Anicca, dukkha* and *anattā* are universal principles; and this being so, the Four Noble Truths must also be valid wherever life exists. There is no need for a special creation or a special plan of salvation for the inhabitants of this planet or any other. Buddhism teaches a cosmic law that obtains everywhere; hence the same moral law of spiritual evolution must prevail everywhere. Cosmic law and moral order in Buddhism are related to one another as they are not in any other religious system.

Another fact which struck me forcibly right at the beginning is that Buddhism does not condemn anybody to eternal hell just because he happens not to be a Buddhist. If a being goes to the regions of torment after death it is because his bad deeds have sent him there, not because he happens to believe in the wrong set of dogmas. The idea that anyone should be eternally damned simply because he does not go to a certain church and subscribe to its particular creed is repugnant to every right-thinking person. Moral retribution is a necessity, but this vicious doctrine of damnation for not believing in a certain god and the particular myths surrounding him has nothing whatever to do with ethical principles. It is itself supremely immoral. It has probably been the cause of more harm in the world than any other single factor in history.

Furthermore, Buddhism does not postulate eternal punishment for temporal sins—that is, for misdeeds committed within the limiting framework of time. The Dhamma teaches that whatever suffering a man may bring upon himself is commensurate with the gravity of the evil action—neither more nor less. He may suffer through several lives because of some very heavy *akusala kamma* (evil action), but sometime that suffering must come to an end when the evil that has been generated has spent itself. The atrocious idea that a being may be made to suffer throughout eternity for the sins committed in one short lifetime does not exist in Buddhism. Neither does the equally unjust doctrine that he may wash out all his sins by formal acts of contrition or by faith in some one particular deity out of all the gods man has invented.

In Buddhism also, there is no personal judge who condemns, but only the working of an impersonal law that is like the law of gravitation. And this point is supremely important, because any judge in the act of judging would have to outrage either justice or mercy. He could not satisfy the demands of both at the same time. If he were inexorably just he could not be called merciful: if he were merciful to sinners he could not be absolutely just. The two qualities are utterly incompatible. Buddhism shows that the natural law is just. It is for man to be merciful, and by the cultivation of *mettā, karuṇā, muditā* and *upekkhā* to make himself divine.

Lastly, the truth that rebirth and suffering are brought about by ignorance and craving conjointly is a conclusion that is fully supported by all we know concerning the life-urge as it works through human and animal psychology and in the processes of biological evolution. It supplies the missing factor which science needs to complete its picture of the evolution of living organisms. The motivating force behind the struggle for existence, for survival and development, is just this force of craving which the Buddha found to be at the root of *saṃsāric* rebirth. Because it is conjoined with ignorance it is a blind, groping force, yet it is this force which has been responsible for the development of complex organisms from simple beginnings. It is also the cause of the incessant round of rebirths in which beings alternately rise and fall in the scale of spiritual evolution.

Realising the nature of this twofold bondage of ignorance and craving we are fully justified in the rational faith that, as the Supreme Buddha taught, our ultimate release, the attainment of the eternal, unchanging state of *Nibbāna,* is something that we can reach by eliminating all the factors of rebirth that are rooted in these two fundamental defects. *Nibbāna,* which the Buddha described as *asaṅkhata*—the unconditioned, *ajara*—the ageless, *dhuva*—the permanent and *amata*—the deathless, is the reality that lies outside the realms of the conditioned and illusory *saṃsāra,* and it may be reached only by extinguishing the fires of *lobha, dosa* and *moha*—greed, hatred and delusion.

So we see that *saddhā,* or faith, in Buddhism is firmly based on reason and experience. Ignorance is blind, but Buddhist faith has its eyes wide open and fixed upon reality. The Dhamma is *ehipassiko*—that which invites all to come and see for themselves. The Buddha was the only religious teacher who invited reasoned, critical analysis of his doctrine. The proof of its truth—and hence the conclusive proof of the Buddha's enlightenment as well—is to be found in the doctrine itself. Like any scientific discovery it can be tested empirically. Everyone can test and verify it for himself, both by reason and by direct insight. The Buddhist is given a charter of intellectual liberty.

These are just a few of the features which appealed to me when I first started studying Buddhism in my quest for truth. There were many others which followed later; they came in due course as my own understanding and practice of the Dhamma made them manifest to me. As one investigates the Dhamma, new vistas are constantly opening up before one's vision; new aspects of the truth are continually unfolding and fresh beauties are being disclosed. When so much of moral beauty can be discerned by merely intellectual appreciation of the Dhamma, I leave it to you who are listening to imagine for yourselves the revelations that come with the practice of *vipassanā* or direct insight. There can be nothing in the entire range of human experience with which it may be compared.

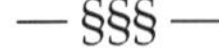

Three Buddhist Tales

Various Authors

Bodhi Leaves No. 56

First published: 1971

The Old Weaver

From the Tibetan *Tang'an*, retold by Dr. H. Hecker
Wissen und Wandel XV, 1

In the country of Tibet there once lived an old weaver who had many sons. Day-in and day-out he worked away at his weaving-loom and never once gave a thought to the meaning of his life, nor to life in general. Even though he was concerned only with superficialities, now and then it did occur to him that he could see no end of his labour. Every day he began his work afresh, and everyday he carried on spinning. During the course of his life he had grown quite rich, and to his many sons he had given wives of good families, so that his clan flourished with many children and grandchildren.

One day the weaver's beloved wife died, and when at the age of eighty-nine he became too feeble to prepare his own food, his many daughters-in-law prepared his meals in turn. When in his frailty the old man came tottering along to his children's homes, other people (as well as his children and their servants) used to laugh at him and ridicule him as the rich old man to whom all his money was no longer of any use. Then his daughters-in-law felt it unpleasant and troublesome when the old man called at their houses; it spoiled their joy of life and harmed the family's good reputation. At last they decided to build a small hut of reeds in one of their gardens for the old weaver, where he could live quietly, while they continued to send him his meals in turn. They all found this solution quite reasonable, and soon the old man moved into his little hut in the garden of his eldest son.

Not long after this, a monk came to the son's house and was received with rich alms-food as well as an invitation to spend the night. The monk replied that his vows did not allow him to spend the night with lay-people in the house, but that he could stay in the garden. When the old weaver saw the lights of the lamps coming into the garden, he came out of his little hut to inquire who had arrived, and the visitor told him that he was a Buddhist monk.

When the monk in return asked the old man who he was, the weaver told him: "O venerable sir, I am the father of all these many children here, whom I brought up and fed and for whom I selected suitable wives. Once I was the owner and master of all these large properties, but now I am laughed at by my family, and my daughters-in-law are ashamed of my old-age and frailty. They have hidden me away in this garden where they may not see me, and I live here quite alone." While he spoke thus the old man's tears flowed.

The monk felt great pity for him and said: "If you are weeping so bitterly about this minor misfortune, how much more will you moan and lament if you fall into an unhappy rebirth. All your life you have been concerned only with superficial and material things, and you have not laid up the more precious treasures of the mind. You are paying for that bitterly now, and after death you will turn around for a long time in the cycle of rebirths. Your present unhappiness is due to your own actions, and yet you unjustly blame your children."

The old man sighed: "O yea, venerable sir, alas, you are quite right. When I was young and had the chance to purify my mind, I failed to do so; and now that I am old and need so much to feel a little satisfaction and joy, I am unable to work for it. O, what I need is a remedy against old-age and death!"

The monk replied: "I know that remedy; I can get it for you."

The old man was startled, and when he asked for instruction the monk advised him to develop meditation on the transiency of all sensuous existence and on its unsatisfactory and void nature. The old man listened very carefully and soon grasped the meaning of it, so that although his teacher left on the following morning he was able to apply himself diligently thereafter in the meditations that had been explained to him. All of the time that hitherto he had spent in sleeping and dreaming and bewailing his fate, he now used to his advantage. He no longer felt bitter and sad when his daughters-in-law dropped the hint that he was nothing but a useless old man whom they all had to feed. He accepted their words quietly and forgave them in his heart. For twelve years he devoted himself to meditation in the garden hut and accumulated a store of virtue and merit that was incomparably larger than his wealth in money and property; but because to his daughters-in-law these spiritual things were quite foreign, they failed to notice any change in him.

One day the families of the old man celebrated a great festival, and only late at night did one of his daughters-in-law remember that they had not taken any food to him. Feeling great remorse, she went into the garden with some food, and was very surprised to find the little hut ablaze with light. Wondering what it could be, she approached, and through the window saw a group of fifteen deities, shining in celestial glory, waiting upon the old man with great respect. Seeing this, she at once ran back to the house to fetch the others, but from what she told them they only gathered that the old man must be dead. When they all came to the garden and saw the deities they were very frightened and quickly turned back to the house, where they discussed the matter and came to the conclusion that it must have been ghosts.

Next morning, however, when they again went into the garden, they found to their surprise that the old man was quite hale and hearty, and that his features glowed and radiated an inner serenity. He did not tell them of his inner experiences since he lacked the ability to instruct others, but from now on many people who had heard of that wondrous happening came to see him, for even just the sight of him was enough to move and benefit them all. He became known as the "Guru Tantri," and many of his visitors were encouraged to return again to their religion and were later reborn in heavenly worlds. The old man, who had once appeared quite useless and a burden to everyone, thus became the spiritual guide of the whole district. At the age of more than a hundred years the old weaver finally passed away, and his family, together with the whole township mourned him for many days.

— §§§ —

Of Dogs and Men

As told by James Allen in *Die Illusion des Ich* (*Buddhistische Warte* I. i)

(Re-translation from the German)

Once there were several dogs who all had the desire to become humans. They met in conclave to deliberate on whether there were any methods whereby they could be reborn as humans and become men. They discussed man's enormous superiority over themselves, his great beauty, his erect walk, his wondrous freedom, his powerful influence, his "eternal" life and his "eternal" youthfulness ("because," they said, "while we get old and die, man does not change"). The great dignity and wisdom of man were also mentioned. Finally, when they had all discussed their various views and opinions, one dog who had kept silent and who was more sagacious and noble than the others, rose to speak.

"All these speculations are in vain," he said, "so long as we continue to live and behave like dogs. If we wish to become humans we must begin by honestly wishing to cease being dogs. As little as we can become men while still preserving the bodily shape of dogs, so also we cannot expect to be humans while still clinging to our dog-like natures. First we must give up our animal habits and pleasures, and renounce all those tendencies that make us what we are now—namely, dogs; then we must cultivate those higher trends that make men to be real human beings. If we diligently strive to make progress, then the best in us will be gradually transformed into a higher nature. We shall become men only by ceasing to be dogs. This can never happen if we continue to be anxiously concerned about our existence as dogs, obstinately cling to all the lusts and pleasures of our dog-like nature, nor if we recoil from the thought that we must stop carrying on being dogs. This is a method which I have found, not by speculation, but by experience. I have practised these things that I have spoken about myself, and having practised these things that I have spoken about myself, and having understood what the nature of human beings is, I shall no longer be reborn as a dog."

After this speech there was much noise and confusion among the assembled dogs, for they all said that what they had heard was tantamount to an entire extinction of dog-selfhood and of the very nature of dog-hood. They argued that this very life consisted of just this distinct and clearly-marked dog-personality, and that their immortality depended upon the survival of this very personality. Thus the teachings to which they had now listened, namely that the only way to acquire a human nature was by the cessation of their dog-nature—that these teachings must be false as they were in conflict with their ideas of an eternal and abiding personal self-hood (which for them was the very foundation of all existence and endeavour).

"Yes," they said, "even though we wish for the higher state of human beings, it is absurd and contrary to our nature to stop being dogs. We can accept only such a teaching as true that leads us to manhood while allowing us to preserve our dog-personalities."

Thus it is also with us humans who, although we seek after truth and aspire to a higher and nobler state, still continue to recoil from changing even a little part of our personalities, to say nothing about the final sacrifice of self. We wish to preserve our feverish craving and our petty self-centred natures because we believe in an eternal survival of our personalities and are frightened to lose them. Yet it is only because of this illusion of self-hood that the endless process of birth and death continues. Even the teacher of Christendom has said: "He who wishes to preserve his life must lose it."

— §§§ —

This Mother and This Son

From *The Udumbara: Tales of Buddhist Japan*
by Kosho Yamamoto, CIIB Press, Tokyo

I

In the prefecture of Nara, in the south-western corner of Yamato Plain, there is a village called Taima. Here, in 942 AD, the venerable master Genshin was born.

His father was Urabe-Masachika. He died when Genshin was only seven years old. It was on the wish of his father that Genshin became a priest.

Already as a boy, Genshin was very clever. Once a priest was so struck by the boy's sharp wit that he went to his mother and begged her to entrust the boy to him so that he could take him to Mount Hiei, the then headquarters of Japanese Buddhism, and there to put him under the care of Priest Ryogen. His mother was glad because it was a good opportunity to make good the wish of her late husband whose last will it had been that the boy should be brought up as a priest.

II

On parting the mother gave the boy a new set of clothes. She also gave him a copy of the *Amidakyo*, telling him that this was a token from his father. Then she said that she would send for him when he had grown up to be a truly holy man, and that otherwise, this was their last meeting.

The boy was taken to Mount Hiei and was put under the care of Ryogen. He was then thirteen years old. Ryogen saw that the boy was no ordinary person and he did his best to help him in his Buddhist studies. Ryogen gave him a priestly name and henceforth the boy was called "Genshin," "gen" being part of Ryogen's name.

In the days of Emperor Murakami, in the tenth year of Tensyaku, young Genshin gave in the presence of the Mikado a lecture on Shosañjodokyo, a translation of the *Amidakyo* under a different title. His learning and eloquence were so wonderful that the Emperor gave him a roll of silken cloth as a token of appreciation.

Glad at this rare honour, the boy sent this imperial gift to his mother, thinking that she would be very glad. And how would she not be glad when no word had come from the boy since he left home three years ago? But she was no ordinary woman to be taken in by anything glaring. She sent the silken cloth back to him, along with a letter, which read:

"To the venerable Genshin,

Since you went up to Mount Hiei, glad thoughts have ever been visiting me. And I thought you were growing up as a holy man. But woe is it that you have been closely associating yourself with the imperial quarters, that you have been going up in status, that the colours of your robe have been changing, that you have been giving lectures to the Mikado, receiving thereby presents and becoming a priest busy with worldly fame and gain …

All these are not acts of one who has renounced the world, and you are sure to repeat lives again and again. One ought to remember that one is blessed with the rarest of the teachings and thus can be saved of an after-life. But I regret that you are drowned in material fame. This is the silliest thing, an act most regrettable. To take anything like that as honour is nothing but base delusion. What worth is there in it to be well known by the people of this world of dreams? Do your best and ever, with an unending effort, awake in Bodhi! …

And are you not one who has shaven off your hair, who has put on the black robe, and left home, abandoning all, so as to live as a sage in the mountains? …

And what do you mean to do with the robe that has been given to you? Even sages whose speech is set aright and whose deeds are in accord with their speech, are said to burn in hell if they cherished possessions. There is nothing in it to lead one to the Pure Land, but to the Three Evil Realms. And nothing goes beyond this. As I have no mind to glance at it, I return this to the honoured priest.

Your Mother"

Then Genshin awoke from his dreams. He retired deep into Yokawa on Mount Hiei, to the Shuryogon-in Temple, there to escape from worldly life and earnestly seek the Way. He is said to have read the Tripiṭaka five times in his life. He became the most honoured, the most learned and virtuous of the whole Hiei Mountain.

III

At the age of forty-two, when news came that his mother was on her death-bed, he for the first time went back to his native place and saw his mother. His first question was:

"Can you say the *Nembutsu*, dear mother?"

"Thank you! … Please do not forget the *Nembutsu* … But my physical strength is gone and I cannot say it."

Thus the mother and her son met after thirty years, though they lived not far from each other.

The venerable Genshin told her all about the virtues of Nembutsu and the adornments of the Pure Land. Her room was swept and cleaned, and washed with perfumed water. The statue of Amita Buddha was set up. He changed his mother's clothing. He then sat and recited the Nembutsu, beating the *kei*, a metal drum used in Buddhist music which gives a sound similar to a cymbal. His mother passed peacefully away, saying the Nembutsu some three hundred times.

Genshin said:

"It was my mother who made me perfect in practice; and it was I who had enabled my mother to attain the end well. This mother and this son, each becoming a Teacher of the Way! This could but be the happy fruit of past karma."

In the 2nd year of Eikan, i.e. 984, in the month of November, Genshin took up his pen and began to write his famous *Ojoyoshu* and finished it in the next year.

Editor's Note: Genshin (942–1017), though ordained in the Tendai school, became one of the great masters of the Pure Land School. His book *Ojoyoshu* (3 vols.), a comprehensive summary of the Pure Land (Jodo) faith, had also a great influence on Japanese literature and art, and became the turning point in Honen's life.

The Story of the Mahinda, Saṅghamittā and the Sri Mahā-Bodhi

Piyadassi Thera

Bodhi Leaves No. 57

First published: 1966

Preface

"Go forth, my brethren, for the gain of many, for the welfare of many, out of compassion for the world." In these words the Buddha gave a message to the first sixty arahants, and through them, to the Sangha for all time. This mandate was fully carried out for centuries, and in obedience to it, the Arahant Mahinda came to Lanka. On being asked by King Tissa who they were, the Arahant replied "Samaṇas are we, oh King, disciples of the King of Truth. Out of compassion for thee have we come from Jambudīpa." The message he brought was the message of the Buddha-dhamma, the way to the attainment of happiness here and now and in the hereafter; from happiness which is transient, to the "highest happiness," the incomparable security of "Nibbāna."

Mahinda's work was twofold; one was to teach the "way to happiness" and the other was the organisation of a national Sangha, which was to maintain by practice and by teaching, the message of the Dhamma. In his first discourse, he most appropriately taught the essence of the Dhamma. In this celebrated discourse of "The Elephant Footprint," he pointed out that the Dhamma must not be merely accepted, but verified each one by himself. It is not enough to reason that as the elephant's footprint exceeds in size those of other animals so the Buddha-dhamma is greater than of any other teaching. One must follow up the elephant's footprint and see the lordly creature face to face. Even so must a follower of the Buddha-dhamma travel in the footsteps of the Buddha until he sees face to face, and realises the Truth of his Teaching. In this way Mahinda set forth the Dhamma, "in the spirit and in letter," as the Buddha had stated in his great message. The Buddha-dhamma is for all, and progress in the Way is gradual in keeping with the potentialities and capacities of the wayfarer. There are some who "leave home" and dedicate their whole lives to the practice of the Dhamma. These are the true Sangha. But to the mass of mankind the Buddha showed a way to happiness here and now, and in the hereafter. In reply to Dīghajānu's question: "Master we are men of the world who support wife and child. How can we attain happiness here and in the hereafter?", the Buddha replied that for happiness here one must practise "four efforts." One must do one's work, whether in the king's service, or in agriculture, trade, commerce, arts and crafts, with zeal and earnestness. Next, one must guard what one has earned by rightful means, from fire and flood, thieves etc. Next one must see that one's expenditure does not exceed one's income (*samājīvakatta*), and finally, one must cultivate good friends. But this is not all. Economic well-being is no doubt essential for happiness here. For happiness hereafter the moral life is also essential. One must practise *sīla*, one must practise goodwill and service of one's fellow men. Finally, one must step by step, train oneself to attain that wisdom which will someday, somewhere, help one to take the road that leads to the undying happiness and security of Nibbāna (*paramaṃ sukhaṃ*).

In these and other ways, the message that Mahinda brought, transformed the life of the people. It held out as a "Mahā Maṅgala," a "great blessing," the life of a good layman; "to support father, mother, to cherish wife and child; to follow a peaceful calling; this is a great blessing." The great commentator Buddhaghosa remarks that a "peaceful calling" includes "social service." He uses this very word and instances of *anākulā ca kammantā* are doing social service, planting gardens and groves, making bridges etc. History records the vast development of agriculture, irrigation works, arts and crafts in ancient Buddhist Sri Lanka. Rice was exported to South India and cotton goods, gold and silver filigree work and Buddha images to ancient China. In the field of social welfare work, we read of a "medical service" with *raj vedhals,* royal hospitals, *bhesajja sāla*, dispensaries, and homes for the old and infirm, the orphan, the lame and the blind. The Buddha-dhamma created the Sinhala literature and the fine arts which were the artistic expressions of the Buddha's way of life.

The Arahant Therī Saṅghamittā, true spiritual successor of Pajāpatī Gotamī, Bhaddakaccānā (Yasodharā), Dhammadinnā, and thousands of other arahant therīs came to Lanka to help women who had the moral fibre and spiritual urge to live the holy life of the "homeless." The Sinhala bhikkhunīs did not live lives of cloistered virtue. They too served society by maintaining maternity homes etc. Chinese records show that Sinhala therīs went to China to establish the order of bhikkhunīs there.

To the two noble brother and sister, the Sinhala Buddhists owe an immense debt of gratitude. We too must not forget the message they brought and for which they spent their lives here. Their earthly remains too are with us. Our forefathers walked by the light of the Dhamma. Let us hope that we and those who come after us will do likewise. The lamp that Mahinda and Saṅghamittā lit centuries ago in Lanka should not be allowed to flicker or go out.

S. F. De Silva
(Former Director of Education and Ambassador
for Sri Lanka in China)

— §§§ —

The Story of the Mahinda, Saṅghamittā and the Sri Mahā-Bodhi

Namo Tassa Bhagavato Arahato Sammā Sambuddhassa

To the Buddhists of Sri Lanka, each and every full moon day *(pasalosvak poya)* of the year has a definite significance. Of these the most holy and the most significant is the Vesākha (Vesak) full moon, because it is connected with three events in the life of the Buddha—the birth, enlightenment and the final passing away *(parinibbāna).* Vesākha, therefore, is a triple anniversary most sacred to the Buddhists all over the world.

However, full moon days like *poson* (June) and *unduvap* (December) have a special significance to the Buddhists of Sri Lanka only. The reasons are well known to them and that is why they celebrate with whole-hearted devotion these full moon days.

To the Buddhists of Sri Lanka, *unduvap* full moon day is a day of sacred memories in view of its unforgettable association with an emperor's daughter, a noble woman of great self-sacrifice and deep religious fervour, who came to this island and dedicated her life for the weal and happiness of the people, especially the womenfolk of Laṅkā.

She is none other than the arahant Therī, Saṅghamittā, the daughter of Emperor Asoka of India, and the sister of arahant Thera Mahinda, who introduced Buddhism to Sri Lanka in the 3rd century BCE, on a full moon day of June (*poson*).

Before we learn more about this saintly figure, let us look back into the island's history and see what the religious background of this country was, before the arrival of Mahā Mahinda, and Saṅghamittā.

Sri Lanka before the Arrival of Mahinda

Although the recorded history of the Sinhalas begins with the landing in Lanka of Vijaya in 543 BCE, the history of Buddhism in

Sri Lanka starts with the arrival of the Arahant Thera Mahinda, the son of Asoka the Great. Nevertheless, one cannot justifiably conclude that before the coming of Mahinda Thera, Buddha and his Teachings were altogether unknown to the people of this island. The Sri Lanka Chronicles, *Mahāvaṃsa* and *Dīpavaṃsa* and the *Samantapāsādikā,* the Vinaya commentary, give vivid descriptions of the Buddha Gotama's three visits to this island, made in the fifth year, and the eighth year after his Enlightenment.

When Mahā Mahinda arrived here in the reign of King Devānampiyatissa, 236 years after the landing of Vijaya, and expounded the Dhamma to the people, they were able to grasp quickly the message of the Master, which spread throughout this island with surprising speed. This indicates that the sowing ground allotted to Mahā Mahinda had already been prepared by reason of earlier contacts with Magadha, where Buddhism flourished. We know that at the request of the ministers of Prince Vijaya, the Pandyan King of Madhura sent his daughter to be the queen of Vijaya. She was accompanied by many maidens from the Pandyan kingdom, craftsmen, and a thousand families of the eighteen guilds. Now these Pandyans were originally a Ksatriya race of the Aryans from the Madhyadesa, the scene of the Buddha's lifelong ministry.

We are also told that Panduvasudeva, the nephew and immediate successor of Vijaya, married Bhaddakaccānā, the beautiful daughter of the Buddha's own first cousin, King Pandu. Further, as we know from the Mahāvaṃsa, the non-Buddhist Indian sects like the *Nigaṇṭhas* and *Paribbājakas* were already in Sri Lanka. We must also infer that the contemporaries and the fellow countrymen of the Nigaṇṭhas also would have been here.

Sri Lanka being very close to the sub-continent of India, there would have been continuous intercourse between the peoples of the two countries. Also, Sri Lanka was often touched by sea-going vessels from India, and we can be sure that Buddhist traders came to this country and spoke of the Buddha and his teachings to the inhabitants whom they met.

From the history of the *Devānampiyatissa* period we can gauge that the institutions which prevailed in India's middle country, Magadha, also prevailed in Sri Lanka. These facts afford abundant evidence that the Buddha and his teaching were known to the people of this island even before the arrival of the great saint Mahā Mahinda and his sister, Therī Saṅghamittā.

The fascinating story of this brother and sister is recorded in our chronicles and in writings dealing with the life and works of King Asoka of India.

The Birth of Mahinda and Saṅghamittā

In the year 326 BCE Alexander the Great of Macedonia invaded the Northern part of India and made Takshasilā (Taxila as the Greeks called it), a great and flourishing city, his capital. His kingdom, however, did not last long, as he passed away at the age of 32, at Babylon in 323 BCE. Following the death of Alexander, Candragupta, known as Sandrocatus among the Greeks, having attacked the officers in command of the Greek garrisons left behind by Alexander, defeated King Nanda, his predecessor, in or about 323 BCE. He became the monarch of Magadha, whose capital was Pataliputra (Patna), and established the Mauryan empire. As Vincent A. Smith writes in the *Oxford History of India*, he is the first strictly historical person who can be properly described as Emperor of India.

Candragupta was succeeded by his son, Bindusāra whose reign came to an end in 273 BCE. Asokavardhana, popularly known as Asoka, one of the sons of Bindusāra, succeeded to the throne. During his father's reign, Asoka had served as Viceroy at Taxila and Ujjain. It is said that while Asoka was proceeding to Ujjain, he tarried for a time at Vedisa, modern Besnager, or Vessanagāra, mentioned in Visuddhimagga, and there fell in love with Devī, a daughter of a banker named Deva. Taking her as wife with her parents' consent, he took her with him toUjjain. There she bore him two children. It was these two who became renowned as Mahinda and Saṅghamittā, two distinguished arahant members of the Order. They worked with undaunted courage to establish the Buddha-sāsana, the Dispensation of the Buddha, in this land of ours.

When King Bindusāra was breathing his last, Asoka was summoned to Patna, and he succeeded his father as the third ruler of the Mauryan Empire. Devī, though she stayed back at Vedisa, her home town, sent her two children to the capital, to their father's court. Asoka was not satisfied with the empire left behind by his father, and being a war-like monarch like his grandfather, Candragupta Maurya, thought of extending his territories. In the eighth year of his coronation he invaded and conquered Kāliṅga. It was a fierce and terrible war in which 100,000 were slain, 150,000 were carried away captive, and many times this number were injured. When Asoka heard of the carnage wrought by his army in Kāliṅga he was deeply worried. Remorse overtook him and he gave expression to his feelings in his longest Rock Edict (No. XIII).

It can be said that the Kāliṅga war was not only the turning point in Asoka's career, but it also became one of the decisive events in the history of the world. He realized the folly of killing and gave up warfare. He is the only military monarch on record who after victory gave up conquest by war (*dig-vijaya*), and initiated conquest by righteousness (*dharma-vijaya*). He sheathed his sword never to unsheath it again, and no longer wished harm to living beings.

According to the Sri Lanka chronicles, it was a little arahant, Sāmaṇera Nigrodha, son of Prince Sumana, a brother of Asoka, who converted Asoka to Buddhism, by a very short but highly illuminating discourse, the theme of which was mindfulness (*appamāda*). Ever after, he who had been called Asoka the Fierce (*Candāsoka*) was known as Asoka the Righteous (*Dhammāsoka*). He became a very generous patron of the Sangha, and a great supporter of the Buddha-sāsana. The spread of the Buddha's creed of compassion throughout the Eastern world was largely due to his enterprise and tireless effort, and Buddhism became the most profound influence that moulded the culture of Asia.

Buddhist principles and ideals coloured the thoughts and feelings of Asoka to such an extent that he became quite a different person altogether, and brought about many changes in his administrative system. He endeavoured to educate the people by popularizing the teaching of the Buddha, especially the ethical aspect of it. He caused those lofty ethical teachings to be engraved on rock, and they became sermons on stones, not metaphorically but actually. Asoka was imbued with that great spirit of tolerance preached by the Buddha, and during his regime all other religions enjoyed absolute freedom.

His devotion to the teachings of the Buddha was so strong that he even permitted his dear son and daughter to be ordained, with their consent. At that time the son was twenty years old and received the *upasampadā*, higher ordination that very same day. The daughter was eighteen.[85]

Asoka's Missionary Zeal

Realizing the immense benefit that humanity would derive from a teaching of compassion and wisdom like that of the Buddha, Asoka made all endeavours to spread the teaching of the Buddha outside India.

When the third Great Council *(Dhamma-saṅgāyana)* was brought to an end (the first was held three months after the passing away of the Buddha, during the reign of Ajātasattu, and the second after hundred years, during the time of Kālāsoka), Asoka with the advice and guidance of the Arahant Moggaliputta Tissa, dispatched the missions to foreign lands. It is stated that each

85 The age of twenty is the minimum for *upasampadā*.

mission consisted of five theras so that it would be possible to perform the *upasampada* ordination in remote districts. The archaeological discoveries made at Sāñchī and Gwalior and so forth, clearly proved that these missions were actual facts.

In those distant days there were disciples of the Buddha who followed their Master's injunction: "Go now and wander for the welfare and happiness of gods and men … Proclaim the Dhamma, the doctrine … Proclaim the life of purity." They were ready to undertake any mission abroad, though contact and communication in those days were most difficult, and travel was full of peril. Aided by Asoka's unceasing missionary zeal, and the effort, determination and courage of those early *Dhammadūtas* (messengers of the Dhamma), Buddhism spread to many countries. Asoka's records speak of missions sent to the Hellenistic kingdoms of Asia, Africa and Europe, to Syria and Egypt, Cyrene, Macedonia and Epirus, to Bactria and Central Asia.

Modern discoveries have proved that Asokan edicts were written not only in an Indian language in Brāhmī characters, but also in Greek and Aramaic (the language which Jesus spoke), indicating that the Greeks and Semitic races, too, had access to the words of the Buddha, which were engraved on rocks by Asoka.

According to the chronicles, King Asoka and Devānam-piyatissa of Sri Lanka, though they had never seen each other were great friends even before the arrival of Mahā Mahinda. It is said that the King of Sri Lanka sent envoys to his friend Dhammāsoka with costly presents, and the latter gratefully sent an embassy of his chosen ministers with gifts and the following message:

"I have taken refuge in the Buddha, his Dhamma, the doctrine, and in the Sangha, the Order. I have declared myself a lay disciple in the religion of the Sakya son; seek then you too, O best of men, converting your mind with believing heart, refuge in these best of gems."

Thus was the ground prepared for the Ven. Mahinda's mission to Sri Lanka.

Now when the Thera Mahā Mahinda was requested by his preceptor, Moggaliputta Tissa Mahā Thera and the Sangha to visit Sri Lanka and establish the Sāsana there, he set out from his monastery, Asokārāma, in Patna, to Vedisagiri, to have a last look at his dear mother and bid farewell to her. With him also went the Arahant Theras Ittiya, Uttiya, Saṃbala and Bhaddasāla, the wonderfully gifted Arahant Sāmaṇera Sumana and the Anāgāmi lay disciple Bhanduka, a grand-nephew of Vedisa Devi.

When they came to Vedisagiri, the mother glad at heart, welcomed her son and his companions, and led them to the lovely Vedisagiri Mahāvihāra, erected by herself, and ministered to them for one month.

Mahinda's Arrival

By this time Tissa's father Mutasiva had passed away and Devānampiyatissa was appointed King of Sri Lanka. After spending one month at Vedisagiri, on the full-moon day of the month of Jeṭṭha, i. e., Poson full-moon, in the year 236 Buddhist Era (i. e., 308 BCE in the eighteenth year of Asoka's reign) Arahant Mahā Mahinda, accompanied by those six others, rose up in the air by supernormal power. Departing from Vedisagiri, they alighted on the Sīlakūṭa of the Missaka hill, the loftiest peak of present Mihintale, eight miles east of Anuradhapura, where, rising suddenly from the plain, the mountain overlooks the city of Anuradhapura.

It was a day of national festival. The king, who was enjoying the pleasure of the chase, suddenly encountered Arahant Mahinda. He was scared by this stranger—the first sight of a monk in saffron-coloured robe—but the Arahant soon put him at ease with these words:

Samaṇā mayhaṃ mahārājā
Dhammarājassa sāvakā
Taveva anukampāya
Jambudīpam idhāgatā.

"Monks are we, O great king,
Disciples of the king of Truth
Out of compassion for thee
Hither have we come from Jambudīpa[86]"

86 India

The story of the arrival of the great mission, their meeting with Tissa, the king of this island, and how he embraced the new faith, with all his forty thousand followers, are graphically described in the ancient chronicles, and it is too long to be detailed here.

The *Cūla Hatthipadopama Sutta,* (No. 27 of the Majjhima Nikāya), was the discourse delivered by Mahā Mahinda to the king. This discourse gives a vivid description of the *tri-ratana,* the Triple Gem, the Buddha, Dhamma and the Sangha, the monastic life of an ideal monk, and emphasizes the value of discriminative examination of facts, and intelligent inquiry.

The news of the arrival of the mission, and the conversion of the king and his followers, were voiced abroad, and people thronged the palace gate. The enthusiastic king made all arrangements for the devotees to hear the teaching. The Venerable Mahā Mahinda's exposition of the Dhamma was so impressive that all who heard him were convinced of the Teachings of the Tathāgata. Before long, the message of the Master quickly spread throughout the length and breadth of this island of Lanka.

On a full-moon day of Poson, 236 years after the landing of Vijaya, the new religion gained official recognition in the island. Later, the Venerable Mahā Mahinda and the arahant theras founded the Order of the Sangha, and the Sāsana was established in this country, now the world's centre of the faith. Relics of the Buddha were obtained from Emperor Asoka and they were enshrined at the Thūpārāma dagaba, the first of its kind to be built in the sacred city of Anuradhapura, where pilgrims and devotees gather in their thousands to celebrate the festival of Poson, in memory of the Saint Mahā Mahinda, the light of Lanka *(dīpapasādaka).* Dagabas, shrines and vihāras were built in the city of Anuradhapura, and in many other holy places. The offering of the Mahā Meghavana park to the Sangha by the king, was an important event, for it was there that the *Mahāvihāra,* the leading monastery and the centre of Buddhist education, was established.

In due course this seat of learning became far-famed and counted amongst its alumni distinguished scholars from many lands. Best known among them was Buddhaghosa of India, the great commentator, who wrote volumes of commentaries on the Buddhist doctrine while residing at the Mahāvihāra. Also from this centre of Buddhist learning were sent *Dhammadutas,* both men and women, to several lands in Asia, to spread the teaching of the Buddha. Even today people of Burma, Thailand, Cambodia and Laos (lands where Theravada Buddhism flourishes) and far away China and Korea acknowledge their indebtedness for the service rendered by the Sri Lanka missions.

When Mahā Mahinda had thus planted the faith in this country and constituted the *Bhikkhu sāsana,* the Order of monks, there came the urge from the women-folk to enter the Order of nuns, the *Bhikkhunī sāsana.* The story behind this strong desire is told in the chronicles, and the Vinaya commentary, *Samantapāsādika.* Mahā Mahinda, an able exponent of the clear-worded exposition of the Buddha, delivered many inspiring discourses. He instructed, enlightened, and gladdened both the king and the commoner. People in large numbers sought refuge in the Buddha, Dhamma and the Sangha. The members of the royalty, too, were there to listen to his illuminating sermons, which were all new to them, for they had not hitherto heard the word of the Buddha.

Queen Anulā, the consort of an *uparāja* (sub-king) named Mahānāga, with 500 of her attendant ladies, having listened to the discourses, gained mental attainments, and implored Arahant Mahinda to grant them ordination. There was, however, no Bhikkhunī Order then in Sri Lanka, and according to Vinaya rules, Mahā Mahinda was not permitted to give ordination to womenfolk. This could be done only by a Buddha or by the members of the Bhikkhunī Order. Hence the Venerable Mahā Mahinda suggested to King Tissa that his sister Saṅghamittā, who was then a Bhikkhunī in India, be invited to Sri Lanka, to bestow ordination on those desirous of it, and thus establish the Bhikkhunī Order in Sri Lanka.

The Arrival of Saṅghamittā

King Devānampiyatissa, glad at heart, made all arrangements to despatch a deputation, headed by Ariṭṭha, one of his ministers, to Emperor Asoka, intimating to him the wish of Mahā Mahinda and himself.

It is reported that when the deputation conveyed this message, Asoka was overcome by grief, over losing also his daughter when his son, too, had left him and the country. Asoka was not an arahant, a perfect one, who had eradicated all personal attachments, and it was in accord with human nature that he tried to dissuade his daughter from leaving him. Saṅghamittā, however, consoled her father by explaining to him that the request had come from her noble brother, and that she would have the rare opportunity, and good fortune, to establish the Bhikkhunī Order in Sri Lanka, thus being of service to the sāsana and the people of Sri Lanka, the womenfolk in particular.

Finally the emperor agreed and, as requested by Mahā Mahinda, suggested that she take with her a sapling of the Sri Mahā-Bodhi tree, under whose shelter the Bodhisatta Gotama gained full enlightenment. A sapling from the southern side of the tree was obtained, and Asoka made all arrangements for Saṅghamittā to take it to Sri Lanka, in the company of eleven arahant bhikkhunīs. Also members of the Kshatriya families, brahmins, ministers and noblemen in Asoka's court, accompanied the Bodhi. As the books mention, it was a solemn ceremony, and Saṅghamittā left the country from the port known as Tamratipti (Tamluk). It is said that Emperor Asoka was at the port, gazing at the departing vessel, with feelings of deep emotions, until it passed out of sight.

The vessel arrived at the port of Jambukola in the north of Sri Lanka, in seven days. King Devanampiya Tissa received the sapling with great honour and full of devout feelings. He caused the sapling to be deposited in a pavilion on the beach. Ceremonies were performed in its honour and on the tenth day the sapling was placed on a chariot and taken, with pomp and pageantry, to Anuradhapura, the capital. There it was planted, with magnificent splendour and ceremony, in the Mahā Megha garden, where it still flourishes, and receives the veneration of millions of devotees. It is also the oldest recorded tree in the world. Saplings from this tree were planted at various places in the island. It is interesting to note that some have been planted in foreign lands, too.

In this connection, it must be borne in mind, that whatever reverence or homage a devotee pays while under the shadow of a Bodhi tree, it is paid not to an inanimate tree, but to what the tree represents. Namely, the supreme Buddha, who attained enlightenment under a Bodhi tree. The tree symbolizes, in a vivid way, the Enlightenment.

The tree is known in Pali as *assattha*, the sacred fig tree, *Ficus religiosa*. Since enlightenment took place under this particular tree it became popularly known as Bodhi (in Sinhala 'Bo'), which means enlightenment. Bodhi tree, therefore, literally means "Tree of Enlightenment" or "Tree of Wisdom."

The Buddha himself refers to the tree at Gaya: "I, now, monks, am an Accomplished One (*arahā*), a Supremely Enlightened One (*samma-sambuddho*). I attained supreme enlightenment under the fig tree (*assatthassa-mūle abhisambuddho*)," (Mahāpadāna Sutta, Dīgha Nikāya).

The Sri Maha Bodhi

The advent of Buddhism to Sri Lanka, and the planting of the sapling of the Sri Mahā Bodhi tree at Anuradhapura, are most sacred moments in Sinhala history, and the accounts of them excite deep feeling.

Writers in Sri Lanka, and historians (most of them foreigners), never forgot to mention these events, and their accounts of them are so lively and fascinating that they are not out of place here.

Dr. Paul E. Peiris (of Sri Lanka) writes: "It is doubtful if any other single incident in the long history of their race has seized upon the imagination of the Sinhalese with such tenacity as this of the planting of the aged tree.

"Like its pliant roots, which find sustenance on the face of the bare rock, and cleave their way through the stoutest fabric, the influence of what it represents has penetrated into the innermost being of the people, till the tree itself has become almost human, and even now on the stillest night, its heart-shaped leaves, on their slender stalks, ceaselessly quiver and sigh, as they have quivered and sighed for twenty three centuries."

H. G. Wells observes: "In Sri Lanka there grows to this day a tree, the oldest historical tree in the world, which we know certainly to have been planted as a cutting from the Bo Tree in the year 245 BCE. From that time to this it has been carefully tended and watered. Its great branches are supported by pillars. It helps us to realize the shortness of all human history to see so many generations spanned by the endurance of one single tree."[87]

Fahien, the Chinese monk and traveller, who visited Sri Lanka in the fifth century after Christ, and spent two years at the Mahā Vihāra, saw the tree in vigorous health and makes mention of it in his records.

Referring to Asoka's mission, Dr. Rhys Davids writes:

"Its central incident is the transplanting to Sri Lanka of a branch of the tree at Bodh Gaya under which the Buddha had achieved enlightenment.

"Now this event is portrayed on two curious bas-reliefs on the Eastern Gateway at Sāñchī, which must be nearly as old as the event itself. In the middle of the lower picture is the Bodhi tree, as it stood at Gaya, with Asoka's chapel rising half-way up the tree. A procession with musicians is on both sides of it. To the right, a royal person, perhaps Asoka, is getting down from his horse by the aid of a dwarf. In the upper picture there is a small Bodhi tree in a pot, and again a great procession, to the left, a city, perhaps Anuradhapura, perhaps Tamralipti, to which the young tree was taken before it went to Sri Lanka. The decorations on either side of the lower bas-relief are peacocks, symbolical of Asoka's family, the Moriyas (the Peacocks), and lions, symbolical of Sri Lanka, or of the royal family of Sri Lanka (that is, of Sinhala, the lion island)…

"It was a great event, an impressive state ceremony, and a fitting climax to that one of the missionary effort of Asoka's reign which was most pregnant of results."

It is also interesting to note what Emerson Tennent has to say with regard to the history of this tree:

"Compared with it, the Oak of Ellersile is but a sapling; and the Conqueror's Oak in Windsor Forest barely numbers half its years.

"The yew-trees of Fountain Abbey are believed to have flourished there twelve hundred years ago; the olives in the Garden of Gethsamane were full grown when the Saracens were expelled from

87 *The Outline of History*, Cassell 1934, p. 392

Jerusalem and the Cypress of Soma in Lombardy is said to have been a tree in the time of Julius Caesar; yet the Bo-tree is older than the oldest of these by a century, and would seem to verify the prophecy pronounced when it was planted that it would 'flourish and be green for ever.'"

Further says Tennent: "Though ages varying from one to five thousand years have been assigned to the baobabs of Senegal, the eucalyptus of Tasmania, the dragon tree of Orotava, the *Wellingtonia* of California, and the chestnut of Mount Etna, all these estimates are matters of conjecture, and such calculations, however ingenious, must be purely inferential. Whereas the age of the Bo-tree is a matter of record, its conservancy has been an object of solicitude to successive dynasties, and the story of its vicissitudes has been preserved in a series of continuous chronicles amongst the most authentic that have been handed down by mankind." *(Sri Lanka)*

Saṅghamittā made the Upāsikā-vihāra, a nunnery within the city, her abode. When the planting of the Bodhi sapling and the ceremonies connected with it were all over, Anulā and her women were ordained, and the Bhikkhunī Order was set up under the able guidance and leadership of the Arahant Therī Saṅghamittā. The Bhikkhunī Order, thus established, flourished in this country for several centuries. History tells us that Sinhala Bhikkhunīs even sailed to far away China and established the Bhikkhunī Order in that country during the time of Yuan Chia (429 CE).

Though some in their enthusiasm venture to say that this Order still exists in China in its pristine purity, it is not so. There are many nuns in China and other Mahāyāna countries. In Taiwan (the Republic of China), for instance, there are more nuns than monks. Some of the large nunneries are well organized and maintained. However, the Bhikkhunī Order established by the Buddha is not found in these countries, nor in any Buddhist country. These nuns do not anymore follow the *Pātimokkha* precepts set forth and laid down by the Buddha. That is why it must be said that no Bhikkhunī Order exists today. They do live a secluded and meditative life, but they are not bhikkhunīs. In Theravada countries like Burma, Siam, etc, there are *upāsikās* who follow the *dasa sīlas,* the ten precepts.

In the absence of a Buddha and the members of the Order of nuns, the Bhikkhunī Order cannot be resuscitated.

Saṅghamittā gave ordination not only to Princess Anulā and members of the royalty and higher strata of society, but to all, irrespective of their standard in society. Women from all walks of life joined the Order. Following in the footsteps of the Buddha, who treated women with consideration and civility, and pointed out to them, too, the path to peace, purity and sanctity, Saṅghamittā did all in her power to raise womankind from lower to higher levels of life. She worked with unflagging devotion and undaunted courage for the moral, intellectual and spiritual uplift of the womenfolk of this country.

Buddhism makes no distinction of sex with regard to doctrinal matters. All follow the same doctrine and discipline set forth by the Buddha. All, irrespective of sex, caste or colour, can reach the highest attainments found in Buddhism provided they follow the path pointed out by the Master, namely the Noble Eightfold Path, which is Buddhism in practice.

The Death of Mahinda and Saṅghamittā

By her saintly character and virtue, her compassion and conscientiousness and service for the religion, Saṅghamittā Therī endeared herself to the people of this country. Like her brother, Mahā Mahinda, she stands a vivid and notable figure. In the annals of history there never was an instance of a brother and sister dedicating themselves to the task of a spiritual ministration abroad with so deep a devotion and such far-reaching results as Mahā Mahinda and Saṅghamittā.

Both Mahā Mahinda and Saṅghamittā survived Devānam-piyatissa who reigned for forty years.

The Venerable Mahā Mahinda, the *Dīpapasādaka,* he who made the island bright—the Light of Lanka—who dedicated his whole life to the weal and happiness of the people of this fair isle, passed away in the eighth year of the reign of Uttiya, younger brother and successor of Devānampiyatissa, at the ripe age of eighty, while he was spending the rainy season (*vassana*) on the Cetiya mountain. King Uttiya carried out the obsequies with great honour and solemnity. A number of stupas were built over the relics which remained after the cremation of the body. One of them was built at Mihintale where Mahā Mahinda spent most of his time.

The passing away of the Venerable Therī Saṅghamittā took place in the following year, at the age of seventy nine, while she dwelt in the peaceful Hatthalhaka nunnery. Her funeral, too was performed by Uttiya, with honour and proper solemnity, at a spot not far from the Bodhi-tree. A monument in her honour was built there.

These great saints are no more, but they still speak to us through the work they did. Their good names will remain ever green in our memory. The people of Sri Lanka are ever grateful to these great beings, and even today, thousands of pilgrims ascend a staircase of 1840 steps, hewn out of rock, to reach the holy spot, Mihintale, where the great brother and sister lived, propagating the Dhamma and setting an example, by their own religious lives, to the people of this country.

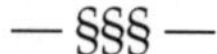

An Actual Religion

Bhikkhu Sīlācāra

Bodhi Leaves No. 58

First published: 1971

An Actual Religion

If one may venture to judge by much that is being said and written and done among thoughtful people today, there has hardly ever been a time when so much interest has been taken in religion—and so little in religions. That is to say: seldom before—in the West at least—has there been such a keen general desire to know what it is that lies behind the superficial appearances of life, and so much indifference toward what current forms of religion officially say lies there. This is a very peculiar state of affairs; but there is a reason for it, as there is for everything.

One might put it roughly by saying that today, in all the more civilised countries of the world, there are fewer infant minds and more grown-up ones than there ever have been before. That is: there are fewer minds that are disposed to accept without question any explanation of life and world offered them upon authority just because it is so offered; and more minds that are simply unable to accept as true whatever is told them on authority only because it is so told them. These grown-up minds possess—for good or ill, according as one chooses to look at it—a keenly developed sense of what is reasonable and probable; and when they encounter anything in the way of offered explanation that offends this sense, that seems at all suspicious, does not fully satisfy their feeling of probability, they incline to pass it by with something like sorrow and disappointment; sometimes, however, according to difference in temperament, with impatience and contempt. And unfortunately, in what is often set before them as explanation of what this puzzling thing life is all about, there is not a little which, if it does not altogether justify, yet goes a long way towards excusing their disappointment and even their scorn. They ask for actuality, and are given what looks to them very like fairy tales. Why this should be so they do not in the least know, and often in a wistful way wonder at it. Yet the answer to the conundrum is simple.

Religions, in their ultimate sense, may not unfairly be defined as metaphysics prepared for the use of the multitude. They are so many explanations of what lies behind the surface appearances of life that are meant to fit the capacity for understanding of the common mass of men. And just because this is so, they do not provide, and do not attempt to provide, strictly and literally accurate explanations of everything about life and the world. The current religions in their current expositions of the metaphysical of what is beyond or behind the physical appearances of things, choose to consider themselves as addressing the infant minds that compose the great majority of mankind, and so confine themselves very largely, almost exclusively, to couching their explanations of man and his place in the universe and what is best for him to do there, in forms suited to the infant mind and give very little heed, if any, to meeting the requirements—and they are the quite legitimate requirements—of the grown up minds of the race. In their various pronouncements, in their formulas and dogmas, they present, not the real truth about things, but a set of ideas well within the infant mind's power of grasp and comprehension which, it may be admitted, are by no means ill-adapted to do all that is evidently required of them, that is, to guard the individual against falling very far into serious error. But it has followed, and could not but follow, that when such pabulum thus concocted for infant understandings, is offered to understandings that have attained to some growth, these cannot do much else but reject it, for they at once perceive that it is not really true. Instead of that actual truth about things, which the acuter minds of the present day so ardently crave to possess, they are offered in the current religions of their day and time merely a sophisticated version of the actual truth. That version is so highly sophisticated in many respects that whatever it was that the original truth was meant to convey is something they find impossible to guess. In their desperate need they are wandering off, many of them, into all sorts of strange byways looking for it, and in their perplexity are much disposed bluntly to dismiss the whole business of religion as nothing but a pack of lies.

Now there is a good deal to be said, and said with respect and reverence, for the original founders of the various religions of the world, in their watering down of metaphysical truth for the consumption of the common man with his but feeble powers of mental digestion, incapable of assimilating and so benefiting from a presentation of pure, undiluted, straight truth. Whether they deliberately pursued this method of dilution and of purpose with forethought, or, as is much more likely, in obedience to an unerring instinct which told them what to do without imparting to them in any clearly conscious fashion the reasons why they should do it, is not known. No Buddhist, at any rate, will wish to condemn offhand the great prophet of Medina for instance, because he offered the uncivilized Arab tribes to whom he came, an eternal heaven of sensual delight after death, in his attempts, entirely successful, to get them to abandon some of their grosser and more savage ways of life. If in the doctrines he put before them in his pronouncements as to what lies beyond the immediately physical, he did not take his followers all the way to the goal, at least he took them a good way in the direction of the goal; and that is much, as human men and human affairs go—and his Arabs were very human. A truly great man, and the performer of a truly great work that has left its mark not only on Arabia but on the world, he did what he did as being the best he could do in his peculiar circumstances, with the material with which he had to deal. One might even risk saying that he did as he did just because he could do no otherwise. In a *saṃsāra* that has no goals to be reached and rested in, but only a direction in which to be ever moving—across toward the other shore—about the most that any man can do for his fellows is just to start them moving in that direction, fast or slow, according as the strength of wave-cleaving hands and feet will take them.

And yet the fact remains that some provision in the way of straight, unsophisticated, undiluted truth ought to be made for those capable of appreciating and appropriating it, and who do not find anything of the kind they want and need in the current dogmas of the current religions, as these are commonly set forth. To such individuals the consequences of not finding what they want, may well be, if not entirely disastrous, yet for a time seriously retarding to their best welfare. Desperate of finding any satisfactory solution of their questionings, many of these acuter minds are strongly tempted to plunge recklessly into courses which in their hearts they despise and loathe. Denied the food they crave, the only kind indeed that their minds will tolerate, they are apt to fling themselves in sheer despair of knowing what else to do, upon mere pig's food, and try, of course vainly, to still their hunger with that. A sad, at any rate, a very disconcerting outcome to what might have been so much better—and quite unnecessary.

For provision does exist for such minds as these. There is in the world a religion that is brave enough, bold enough, daring enough, to offer in its teachings, not sophistications, not diluted versions, not humanised elaborations of the truth about man and the world and life, but the plain, straight truth itself. There is a religion that is not in hidden and recondite manner, dissembled or dissembling, but in perfectly honest and straightforward fashion, true. There is a religion that in its tenets is not dark parable, but clear, daylight fact. There is a religion that is not symbolic but actual. There is an actual religion, a religion that deals with actualities and with nothing but actualities, to the utmost limit that these can be dealt with at all in human speech. Beings there are, even as the Master of actuality himself once said, whose eyes are but a little dimmed with the dust of the world, who, failing to hear this teachings of actuality, only too likely will perish, but coming to hear of that teaching, will be saved from perishing, since it is just what they want and need. In the Dhamma of the Buddha these have all they can ask or want.

Buddhism thus occupies a place by itself among the religions of the world, a position all its own, the position of a religion that presents to men just the truth itself about life, instead of the more or less evasive presentations of it offered elsewhere. So that, from a certain point of view, one might almost be entitled to say that all the other religions of the world are only so many variously modified versions of Buddhism, of the teaching of the Buddha! This idea, however, must not be pushed too far, for more than one of the world's religious systems contain ideas which the Buddha never could have countenanced, and some indeed that are the very opposite of all he taught. And still, to the enquiring, investigating eye that dwells upon them long enough, many of the ideas or dogmas of these other religions, frequently present an interesting appearance of struggling attempts to say, hint at, suggest ideas that are openly and honestly set forth in plain words, in the Buddha-dhamma.

One of the most immediately striking of such ideas is that central doctrine of the Buddha to the effect that man as we know him, is not a fixed, substantial entity, but an expression of an energy, existing literally only from moment to moment—the doctrine called *anattā*. Here the Buddha daringly speaks out the blunt, naked truth which in other religions is only half-spoken, whispered, dimly mooted and, it may not be unpardonable to say, somewhat mutilated, in doctrines of a "reincarnating ego," as in many religions of the East, or of "original sin," as in the Greek Catholic and Roman Catholic churches, and the Calvinistically inclined among other Western religious bodies. In these circles with these dogmas, the obvious concern is to accommodate themselves to the common man's capacity for seizing, understanding the idea of substance, entity, "thing-ness," much more easily than he is able to lay hold of the idea of a perpetually on-flowing force or energy. These other religions take the continuous flow of the *kamma*-force and conform this, in itself unbroken stream, to the mode of comprehension in which the masses are most facile. One set of religions breaks it up into the notion of an actual entity supposed to pass from form to form like a passenger passing from boat to boat in a long line of the same. Others present it as "guilt" or "sin" coming into the present out of the past, something that ought not to have been, that ought not to be.

And one might say that this is good, not bad, so far as it goes; it does give a glimmering of the actual truth. Only it does not go far enough, it does not go nearly far enough; it does not give nearly enough of actual fact to satisfy the acute, critical, grown-up mind. For when, as in this case, the idea of the present moment of any living creature being the heir of a past that stretches far beyond and behind the time during which his present mortal body has been in existence, is put before the man merely as connected with a certain alleged historical occurrence, a particular action said to have been done some six thousand years ago, by a couple of human beings, male and female, assumed to be the progenitors of the whole presently existing human race, in a particular geographical locality, a district of Mesopotamia, the "guilt" or "sin" of which deed lies upon the man of today because that couple are his assumed ancestors—when the man of grown-up mind of today is told this, he can only smile (or perhaps sigh) at such a story being supposed by anybody to be a complete explanation, or any explanation at all, of the questions that are troubling him, and turns away to look elsewhere for some account of his own existence and its inborn tendencies, good and bad, that will seem a little more likely and credible, a little more possible of acceptance.

Such explanations these minds can find in the actual religion, the religion called Buddhism, on this and on every question that troubles them. Here wait for them, not those sophistications of the truth which only weary and repel them, but that of which they are in search, the truth itself. It may be necessary for instance sometimes to tell child-minds that the world was made at a certain point in time out of nothing by the fist of a "creator," just as it is sometimes necessary to tell the child in bodily growth that the doctor brought him his new little brother in a black bag. But the grown-up minds of the race require something more than this sort of "black-baggery" to be given them when they begin to enquire about origins and endings. And on this point also, the Dhamma of the Buddha provides them with that something more; it gives them the plain, unveiled truth of the matter.

It tells them that there is no "world" in the sense in which that word is commonly understood in questions like, "How did the world begin?" and so forth. It tells them that a "world" in the usual sense in which such questions are asked, does not exist. It tells them that there are as many worlds as there are men's heads to carry them, for each man carries a world about with him in his head—the only world he ever knows first-hand from the cradle to the grave—which is distinct from all others existing simultaneously in other heads; and that there, inside these heads the world is being made, has fresh arising, at each succeeding moment of time; as also, at every moment of time, equally is passing away, coming to an end; thus, is rising and falling every instant as long as the brain that bears it is alive and acting. For, "within this six-foot-long body with all its thinkings and imaginings, I declare unto you, O disciples, lies the world, and the arising of the world, and the passing away of the world." So spoke, so speaks, the Buddha. As for the world we infer to exist outside our heads, "without perceivable beginning is this *saṃsāra*."

It may be the opinion of not a few, nay, it certainly will be the opinion of many, upon first hearing it, that the difficulties in the way of accepting this explanation of the "beginning of the world," are quite as great as those attaching to the former. And to a certain extent it may be granted that they have reason on their side—but it is only to a certain extent, only to the extent that this explanation remains uninvestigated.

For there is one difference between it and the other, and it is a very great difference indeed; greater can hardly be imagined. It is this: the more the particular explanations of current religions on this point are looked into and submitted to rigorous examination, the less and less acceptable, the less and less credible, do they become. But the explanation that the Buddha here provides, difficult and disappointing as it may seem at first, the more it is studied and investigated, the more acceptable and credible does it become, until finally, when a man has gone far enough in its study and in the development of his mind which will surely follow thereon, it becomes the only explanation he can ever again, even for a moment, think of accepting.

And this is not the only Buddhist teaching of which the like will be found to hold good. The great difference between all Buddhist teachings and the doctrines or dogmas of other religions, lies precisely in this—that the more the former are studied the more satisfying are they found; whereas the more the latter are looked into and in anywise closely scrutinised, the less are they found satisfactory. And the protagonists of the latter frequently—if unintentionally!—show that they are not unaware of this, in the attitude of discouragement and obstruction which they so often adopt towards any attempt to criticise or analyse their dogmas, admonishing and exhorting their followers instead just to "have faith." Buddhism, in vivid contrast to this, invites, nay, insists that its adherents, to the utmost extent of their capacity to do so, shall test and examine and understand its doctrines, and never accept them on mere trust where testing and trying at all is possible.

To take another point: it may be, doubtless in a way it is, an advantage for the infant mind to be told that "sin is displeasing unto God" and will be "punished" by ages, or in some cases, by an eternity of terrible torment in "hell," since in its practical outcome such a declaration may start the individual travelling in the right direction, so far at least as conduct and behaviour is concerned, even if the soundness of the reason for doing so which he here accepts may be far from readily demonstrable.

But the grown-up mind, by its very constitution, cannot help but question seriously the truth of such a declaration, and will find more credible the statement of the actual religion to the effect that immorality, wrong-doing, at bottom is acute, emphatic self-assertion and because it is this, so long as practised, so long must entail existence in self-assertive, individualised conditions, that is, in a condition of imperfection, and therefore of infelicity; and that if this kind of action is practised continually, then continual also will be existence in conditioned *saṃsāric* existence with all the infelicity this involves, not unfitly in many instances to be called "hell"; and that this is so, not because any hypothesised superior being has passed orders to that effect, but simply because things are so fashioned that it cannot be otherwise.

Here a pertinacious critic may feel inclined to interject that so far as the probable practical results are concerned, there does not seem much to choose between telling a half-truth that is wholly grasped, and telling a whole-truth that is only half grasped, as is likely to be the case with this latter explanation of what wrong-doing is. There is, however, the profound difference between the two cases, that the more the half-truth is examined and analysed, the more does the part of it that is dubious come to light; while the more the whole truth is scrutinised and pondered over, the more is its truth perceived, since truth was all its nature to begin with. The believer in half-truths is always in danger, when he becomes aware of the part of them that is not true, of losing his confidence that there is such a thing as truth at all. No such danger threatens the believer in a whole-truth, even if it does happen to be one that he only half comprehends. Fuller knowledge can only bring him fuller faith therein. But fuller knowledge, in the case of the former kind of believer, runs grave risk of stripping him of all his faith. And so here, in the end, the practical outcome also will be different with a difference all in favour of the believer in whole-truths, that is, the believer in the teaching of the Buddha.

Another burning question that occupies the attention, nay forces itself upon the attention of all but the shallowest and most unthinking of human beings, is the question as to the reason for all the suffering, all the manifold infelicity of one kind and another that abounds in the lives of sentient creatures. And here again current religions only half-say, in their vague phrases about life being a "period of probation," a "time of trial and testing," and the like, what is the actual truth; they only admit that life has suffering, has infelicity. The actual religion, on the other hand, the religion that unflinchingly faces actuality and gives it open expression, without palliation or disguise fearlessly declares: "Life, conditional life, does not have but its limitation, imperfection, therefore infelicity, suffering." By their manner of utterance on this question, current religions suggest, nay, they expressly say, that life of course is infelicitous at the present moment; but at a certain moment in the future, with the supervening of a state called "heaven," it is going to be entirely and unendingly felicitous, happy. Buddhism, however, setting forth the whole, unadulterated truth on this matter as on all others it touches, says that nowhere whatever, in no heaven, in no conditioned state of any kind can life ever be permanently and everlastingly felicitous, that all heaven-states, in the very nature of life, as life is, can only be temporary; however long enduring they may be, at length they must come to an end. As for that final ending of infelicity that all desire and seek, unshrinking it makes known the blunt truth that this may only be sought beyond life, not anywhere within it. Let a man look as long and as diligently as he may, nowhere among all the waves on *saṃsāra's* wide sea will he find one that is not as all the rest, fluid, fleeting, transient; nowhere can he find one that will be solid, that will rest firm beneath his feet. This actual religion, Buddhism, is the religion that refuses to cheat itself or anybody else. It holds fast by actuality, by what is actual fact, that water is—water, fleeting, flowing, and never anything else however much one might wish that it were so. Without blenching it faces the fact, the actuality, that nowhere at all throughout all the realm of the fleeting will ever be found the firm, and tells men honestly and frankly that it is absolutely useless to look for such a thing there. It tells men that only when they are honest enough with themselves to see and admit that this is so, only when they put from them forever all attempt, all desire even to attempt, to cheat themselves into supposed comforting beliefs that somewhere, somewhere, if only one searches long enough, within the transient will be found an intransient, only when thus sternly, starkly honest with themselves, only then is the way open at last for them to come to know that which is not transient; even as is written: "Having known the utter ending of all that is compounded, then is the unmade known." But it is only then, and not till then!

And so with flawless logic the Master of actuality bids men turn their eyes away forever from these shifting, deceitful waters where footing can never be found, and makes the getting beyond life the end and aim of all his teaching. Everything he inculcates in the way of moral precept, all his injunctions as to action. His counsels as to thinking, his instructions as to exercises in super-thought have no other ultimate object but the guiding of mankind from the realm of the fleeting, the unsubstantial, the infelicitous, towards the state of deliverance, utter and complete from all limitation, imperfection, infelicity, suffering, the condition of being freed from all conditions—if such a phrase may be permitted.

But perforce, all phrases, all modes of speech must halt and stumble in the language of the conditioned endeavour to give indication, however remote, of the Unconditioned—of as much of it, that is, as can be dragged through the narrow doorway of a conditioned mind, and given such clothing of speech as such mind is able to give. Here the actual religion, come to the limit of what is possible to say with human tongue, perforce has to stop only because it can go no further. Here at this boundary line of what is possible, confronted by the Unconditioned, it has of necessity to take to the method that other religions adopt by choice in face of the facts of conditioned existence. Here, since it can do nothing else, it gives only hints, inevitably faulty clues to what the ultimate reality is.

There is nothing, however, of the indirect or defective or faulty in the instructions or recommendations it provides as to how that reality may be approached and finally won. This, all of it, is as clear and direct as ever words can make it; and is repeated over and over again in ever so many different ways, so that none can have the least excuse for mistaking what is meant. There is no jealously closed fist here. Nothing is withheld, nothing kept back that can possibly be of use, to any and every kind of mind. The limited mind and the enlarged mind, the infant mind and the grown-up mind, the simple mind and the profound mind, in the practical instruction as to what is to be done to reach the goal, all alike find what they can grasp and appropriate without any difficulty, whatever the stage of understanding to which they have come. It being merely a matter of their power to put into practice what thus they grasp, whether they arrive soon or late at the realisation of the final truth which all along has been presented to them free from distorting, disguise or dissembling mask or concealing sophistication in the one actual religion of the world, the one religion that is brave enough, bold enough, audacious enough to tell the truth, the whole truth and nothing but the truth about life and all connected therewith—the Dhamma of the Buddha.

— §§§ —

Buddhist Lay Ethics

Francis Story

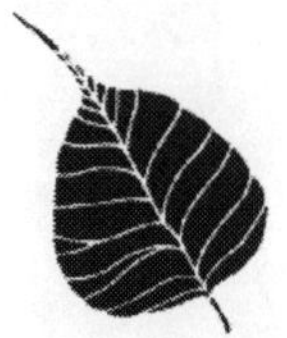

Bodhi Leaves No. 59

First published: 1972

Buddhist Lay Ethics

The life of the Buddhist layman is, or should be, regulated by the five precepts. These constitute the minimal requirements for ethical day-to-day living, to be of benefit both to the individual and to the community. All effort towards higher spiritual achievement must begin with virtue (*sīla*), for without virtue mental concentration (*samādhi*) and wisdom (*paññā*) are not attainable. And without the self-discipline that *sīla* inculcates, civilised life is not possible.

Aside from these obvious truths, the five principles of moral conduct were laid down by the Buddha, the supreme physician, for another reason also. They are to serve as a prophylactic against unwholesome kamma and the misery that results from it; they are the basic rules of mental and spiritual hygiene.

Observance of the precepts is a form of insurance against the risk of rebirth in states of greater suffering, a danger that is always present unless strenuous efforts are made to overcome the taints (*āsava*) and defilements (*kilesa*). Every human being born into this world has in his character an accumulation of unwholesome tendencies from the greed, hatred and delusion (*lobha, dosa, moha*) of the past, mixed with good ones, for if he were free from the craving, antagonisms and ignorance that accompany the illusion of selfhood he would not have been reborn in this or any other sphere. He has to maintain a constant vigilance against these harmful qualities, whose greatest menace is directed towards himself.

Virtue does not develop automatically; it calls for diligent cultivation, sustained by self-analysis and unwavering self-discipline. In the *kāmāvacara-bhūmi*, the realm of sense-desires, there is a natural bias towards self-gratification. It takes many forms, some of them highly deceptive so that we are often victims of the disease to a greater extent than we realise. For this reason it has to be resisted, not spasmodically but all the time, as gravity must be resisted when climbing uphill. Descent is easy and rapid, but ascent is always toilsome and slow.

We do not lack reminders of the inexorable nature of cause and effect, the universal law, for we see evidence of it everywhere.

All around us people are suffering the results of their unwholesome kamma of the past. They expiate it in disease, poverty, deformity, mental deficiency, frustration of their efforts and countless other kinds of misfortunes. There is no truth more obvious than that *dukkha* predominates in life, heavily outweighing man's gleams of momentary and fragile happiness. The happiest man cannot say when misfortune will strike him, or what form it will take; and neither wealth, position nor skill can avail to ward it off. Yet men, even though they have been taught the moral law by a Supreme Buddha, still recklessly pursue their wilful ends, as though intoxicated—which indeed they are. They are intoxicated by craving for sense-pleasures and by the mental defilements which, like the flow of impurity from a suppurating wound (the *āsavas*), work like a poison in the bloodstream, driving them madly on, oblivious of danger.

Just as flies swarm round a jar of honey, crawling to their doom over the bodies of other flies already caught in the alluring trap of death, so men disregard the warning signs given by the suffering of others they see all about them, and are drawn into the same trap by their craving for sense-gratification and the evil courses into which it too often leads them. Like the flies, they see their fellows suffering for their folly, yet they go on to the same end, regardless of the inevitable result. And just as the flies crawl over the struggling bodies of other flies already trapped, so men themselves often go to their doom trampling on the prostrate bodies of their fellow men. This is the grim picture the world presents, a fit subject for compassion. We may look in vain for any evidence of a merciful deity in this amoral wilderness; its creator is ignorance, and its ruler, desire. If it were not for *sīla*, the pitiless jungle law would prevail everywhere.

The Five Precepts of the layman, as distinct from the augmented Eight and Ten Precepts to be observed on Uposatha Days, are meant to be followed by Buddhists at all times, the object being to establish a habit-formation of virtuous and restrained conduct, in opposition to the unwholesome tendencies of greed, hatred and delusion that form a part of human nature and the ego-assertive instinct. Thus they serve a dual purpose, being at once a barrier to unwholesome mental impulses and deeds, protecting one who observes them from generating bad kamma for which he would have to suffer in the future, and a necessary purification to make clear the way for wisdom, insight and ultimate liberation from the round of births and deaths.

From this it naturally follows that the regular observance of the Five Precepts is more beneficial than the occasional observance of the Eight or Ten Uposatha Day vows. The extra precepts added to make up the eight or ten are not ethical rules but vows of a mildly ascetic nature whose purpose is to subdue the senses and strengthen the will. In daily life, it is the moral principles involved in the Five Precepts which, colouring all our associations with other people, go to build up a consistently moral character. More sustained effort is required to keep the Five Precepts all the time than to keep eight or ten on special occasions. It is a mistake to assume, as some people seem to do, that the strict observance of Uposatha Day vows will compensate for a life that is spent, on the whole, in disregard of the five basic precepts. Ideally, both should be observed; but if a choice is to be made it should be in favour of the more difficult task, that of following the rules of disciplined conduct at all times and in all circumstances.

When moral restraint is regarded as psychological treatment, as it is in Buddhism, there is no excuse for allowing it to degenerate into a once-a-week or once-a-fortnight practice—a pious formality carried out as a kind of magic ritual to win the favour of some supposed god, and to ensure good fortune. It is a mental health regimen, and as such must be followed daily, just as one follows the rules of physical hygiene. If human society could develop an ethic that by common consent led people to regard the man who regularly breaks these five basic rules of morality as they regard one who does not bathe, clean his teeth or change his dirty clothes, we should be on the way to evolving a perfect civilisation. Unfortunately, this is far from being the case. In modern society, physical impurities are not tolerated but many impurities of character and conduct are not only tolerated but are actually encouraged. The man who boasts of his conquests with women is not condemned—except by husbands whose marriages he has broken up; and society holds out no particular sanctions against gambling and drunkenness. Lying is accepted as a necessary device from the highest diplomatic circles down to the sphere of the petty shopkeeper who adjusts his prices to the appearance of his customer; while killing is considered a virtue in hunting, fishing and shooting circles; perhaps the only virtue that they recognise. As for theft, if it is done on a large enough scale and successfully, it is considered highly respectable. So, while *sīla* is a necessary part of civilised living, it is interpreted with great elasticity in practice, according to the mores of the particular group in question. While most people subscribe to certain abstract principles, there is no general agreement as to what constitutes the fundamentals of right conduct in specific details. The conventions of society, therefore, offer no reliable guide to one who is seeking universal principles. On the contrary, they have often led to a great deal of confusion.

The English philosopher Hobbes saw man as a being motivated in all his actions by the desire for self-gratification; even the exercise of charity he attributed to this self-regarding urge. Repulsive though this view may appear at first sight, it has never been seriously challenged. All religions tacitly acknowledge it when they hold out hope of rewards for virtue, and the Buddha expressly declared that a man's first duty is towards himself:

> "Let one not neglect one's own good for that of others, however great it may be. One should pursue one's own good, knowing it well."
>
> Dhammapada, v. 166

In Buddhism, one's own good coincides with the good of mankind as a whole, for the Buddha's Teaching was always directed towards the ultimate good of attaining the selfless and therefore desireless state. Those who mistakenly see their own "good" in the gratification of their desires at the expense of others are *bāla*, fools in the realm of morality, and *andhabāla*, mentally blind fools in respect to their own spiritual welfare. In the Buddha's discourses the fool always signifies one who is immoral; that is to say, impure in thought, word and deed. "That man in this very world destroys his own roots" (*yo naro … idhevam eso lokasmiṃ mūlaṃ khanati attano,* Dhp 247). There is no mistaking the powerful emphasis the Buddha laid on the admonition: here, in this very world, the fool destroys himself by his misdeeds.

In view of this, the question whether ethical behaviour is to be considered a means to an end, or the end itself, vanishes. Considered solely as an end, moral activation may be often unsatisfactory in that it fails to produce immediate results in the form of an improvement in worldly conditions or a happier subjective experience; but viewed as a method of attaining supramundane states, it justifies itself both as end and means. In a world that is apparently without moral purpose, the rationalist concept of ethics as a code of conduct to be followed solely for the satisfaction it brings and without any expectation of results, lacks the force that is required to make it universally acceptable. As a way of life unsupported by any solid religious structure or frame of defined principles, it is scarcely even relevant to the human situation, since notions of what constitutes moral conduct have varied widely from age to age and in different parts of the globe. How weak is the simply humanist foundation of ethics in a sceptical and materialistic world is shown clearly by the decline in human standards that we see taking place where religion has lost its hold on the people. There is a weakness also in the fact that in most instances law itself derives its authority from religion, and divine authority has too often been called upon to justify man's acts of selfishness and barbarity. But on the whole, the moral sanctions of religion have provided a sound guide for the development of civilised values. At least, no better has yet been found.

The rules laid down by the Buddha differ from those that characterize the theocratic laws of other religions in that they do not demand any obedience to an unseen, unknown deity, nor do they include any observances of a purely formal, ritualistic and non-ethical type. Whereas other codes lay down prohibitions concerning food, and even in some instances clothing, which may have been useful in certain places at certain periods but cannot be universally adopted and serve no purpose outside the historical context in which they were formulated, the precepts of Buddhism contain only one item dealing with a man's treatment of his own body, and that is a perfectly rational and universal one, the vow to abstain from intoxicants and drugs. The use of intoxicating liquor and stupefying narcotics is the only way in which moral character can be affected by what is taken in by the mouth; so, while elsewhere the Buddha specified for his monks ten kinds of animal flesh (e.g. snakes, elephants, etc) as being unsuitable for consumption, dietary prohibitions form no part of the Five Precepts and are not to be considered in any sense mandatory.

Another fact that renders the Buddhist precepts unique is that they do not make impossible psychological demands. Faith cannot be produced to order, yet many religious commandments literally order the devotee to have faith in what cannot be proved. They also command him to love his fellow-men. Like faith, love cannot be conjured up by command, and Buddhism recognises this truth. *Metta*, or universal benevolence, has to be cultivated systematically; it is no more possible to produce it instantly by willing than it is to grow a new limb. A psychological reorientation away from "self" is necessary before the perfection of loving-kindness, which is one of the *brahma-vihāras*, can be realised.

As exercises in moral restraint, the Five Precepts are necessarily expressed in negative form. The intention is to tell the devotee what he should avoid doing. They are concerned with outward behaviour while the exercises in mental development (*bhāvanā*) are concerned with the development of subjective states tending to the attainment of insight wisdom. While *sīla* (virtue) is essential to the practice of *bhāvanā, bhāvanā* itself fortifies *sīla*; the two are mutually-supporting, and grow side by side. It is as this growth takes place that the positive side of the precepts asserts itself. From the negative vow to refrain from taking life there emerges the positive and active principle of benevolence towards all sentient beings. In time it becomes impossible to break any of the precepts because the will to do so has perished. It fades out from inanition, having no ego-craving on which to subsist.

It is sometimes argued that the first precept to abstain from taking life is a counsel of perfection that cannot be followed in its entirety. Man's existence on earth is subject to the same laws of survival as obtain in the animal realm where it is a question of "kill or be killed." Human beings do not have to fight for existence continually as do the animals, yet if many creatures inimical to man were not destroyed, human life itself would eventually disappear from the planet.

This objection is based on a misunderstanding of the nature and purpose of the Precepts. They are not commandments; they originated as advice on the course of conduct most favourable to the production of good kamma, and are taken voluntarily as vows, with this end in view. The follower of the Buddha is invited to make a choice between the "good" of expediency, which often turns out to be an ethical cul-de-sac, and the highest moral and spiritual good, which is certain and undeviating in its results. The householder who has property and worldly interests to guard, and who owes a duty to society and its laws in return for the protection it affords him, may not always find it possible to observe the first precept. He is in that position because his desire for possessions and family ties has placed him in it. Having made that particular choice he has also chosen to risk whatever consequences may come of it. The dilemmas that confront him at every turn are of his own making. So long as he remains in that position, the only course he can adopt is to minimise as far as possible the need to perform unwholesome actions. There are many ways in which he can do this, the first being to ensure that he engages only in undertakings that do not cause moral confusion (*anākulā ca kammantā*) and supports himself by work of a pure and blameless character (*anavajjāni kammāni*). This comes under Right Livelihood in the Noble Eightfold Path. If this is not sufficient and he aims at the highest moral perfection, he may renounce all worldly responsibilities and connections and enter the Sangha. There he is free to pursue the highest good, unfettered by the demands of mundane life. It was for this purpose that the Buddhist Sangha was established, and so long as it remains there is a refuge for those who wish to shun evil in all its aspects. The standards of perfection in Buddhist ethics do not make them impossible as some have believed. It is an ideal that can be actualized.

The Buddha did not lay down laws for the conduct of human affairs in any but a strictly personal sense. He gave advice to rulers, as he did to ordinary householders, but did not attempt to formulate principles of state policy, as some religious teachers, with varying success, have attempted to do. His Teaching was for those who wish to liberate themselves from *saṃsāra*, not those who desire to improve its conditions. Nevertheless, those teachings, pointing to a goal beyond conditioned existence, have an application in the world of practical affairs. Nibbāna may be an individual, not a collective goal, but the path to it, followed by the individual for his own highest good, has beneficial repercussions on the whole of society. Every man or woman who observes the five precepts and conscientiously tries to follow the Noble Eightfold Path, makes it easier for someone else to do the same. One who works for his own highest good confers blessings on all mankind.

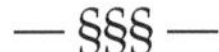

Mindfulness and Awareness

Ñāṇavīra Thera

Bodhi Leaves No. 60

First published: 1973

MINDFULNESS AND AWARENESS

The Pali word for awareness is *sampajañña*. In the suttas it is frequently linked with mindfulness (*sati*) in the compound *sati-sampajañña*, mindfulness and awareness. In the Satipaṭṭhāna Sutta, awareness (of bodily actions) is included in the section on mindfulness of the body, so we can perhaps conclude that, while it is not different from mindfulness, awareness is rather more specialized in meaning. Mindfulness is general recollectedness, not being scatterbrained; whereas awareness is more precisely keeping oneself under constant observation, not letting one's actions (or thoughts, or feelings etc) pass unnoticed.

Here, to begin with, are three sutta passages to indicate the scope of the practice of awareness in the Buddha's Teaching.

1. "And how, monks, is a monk aware? Here, monks, in walking to and fro a monk practises awareness; in looking ahead and looking aside he practises awareness; in bending and stretching ...; in using robes and bowl ...; in eating, drinking, chewing, and tasting ...; in excreting and urinating; in walking, standing, sitting, sleeping, waking, speaking, and being silent, he practises awareness."[88]
2. "And which, monks, is the development of concentration that, when developed and made much of, leads to mindfulness and awareness? Here, monks, feelings are known as they arise, feelings are known as they endure, feelings are known as they vanish; perceptions are known as they arise, perceptions are known as they endure, perceptions are known as they vanish; thoughts are known as they arise, thoughts are known as they endure, thoughts are known as they vanish."[89]
3. "Here, Ānanda, a monk is mindful as he walks to, he is mindful as he walks fro, he is mindful as he stands, he

88 Saṃyutta Nikāya, Vol. IV, p. 211.
89 Aṅguttara Nikāya, Vol. II, p. 45.

> is mindful as he sits, he is mindful as he lies down, he is mindful as he sets to work. This, Ānanda, is a mode of recollection that, when developed and made much of in this way, leads to mindfulness and awareness."[90]

The next thing is to sort out a verbal confusion. When our actions become habitual we tend to do them without thinking about them—they become automatic or instinctive (scratching one's head, for example, or blinking one's eyes). We commonly call these unconscious actions, and this usage is followed by psychology and science generally. But this is a misunderstanding. There is, strictly speaking, no such thing as an unconscious action. The Buddha defines action (*kamma*) as intention (*cetanā*), and there is no intention without consciousness (*viññāṇa*). An unconscious action is no action at all, it is purely and simply movement as when, for example, a tree sways in the wind, or a rock is dislodged by the rain and rolls down a mountainside and derails a train (in this latter case it is quaintly called, in legal circles, "an act of God" but if there is no God, there is no act, only the movement of the rock). In the Buddha's Teaching, all consciousness is action (by mind, voice or body) and every action is conscious. But this does not mean that every action is done in awareness—indeed, what is commonly called an "unconscious action" is merely a conscious act that is done not deliberately, that is done unaware. What we commonly call a "conscious action" is, strictly speaking, a deliberate action, an action that required some thought to perform (as, for example, when we try to do something that we have not done before, or only infrequently). When we do such actions, we have to consider what we are doing (or else we shall make a mistake); and it is this considering what we are doing that constitutes awareness. An action that we do without considering what we are doing is an action that is done without awareness.

So long as we are awake, obviously enough, there is always some degree of awareness present, since new problems, large or small, are always presenting themselves and we are obliged to consider them (even if only for a moment or two) in order to deal with them. When we dream on the other hand, awareness is in abeyance; it is this very fact that distinguishes dreams from waking experience, and why we are unable to look at our dream problems objectively. When we are

90 Aṅguttara Nikāya, Vol. III, p. 325.

awake we are always aware that "I am awake," but when we dream we are not aware that "I am dreaming" and, in fact, when we have a nightmare and struggle to wake up, all we are doing is trying to remember (or become aware) that we are dreaming, and if we succeed we wake up. But though, unlike in sleep, there is always some degree of awareness present in our waking life, it is normally only enough to enable us to deal with unexpected circumstances as they occur, for the rest we are absorbed in what we are doing—whether it be the daily task of earning a livelihood, or our personal affairs with our emotional attitudes towards other people (affection, dislike, fury, lust, boredom and so on). To maintain a detached attitude is difficult when there is much routine work to be done in a hurry, and it robs our personal relationships with others of all emotional satisfaction. We prefer to get through our work as quickly and with as little effect as possible, and then to wallow in our emotions like a buffalo in a mud-hole. We like to keep awareness of what we are doing, which is always an effort, to the absolute minimum. But we cannot avoid awareness altogether, since, as I remarked earlier, it is necessary in order to deal with unexpected problems, however insignificant, when they arise.

But this awareness is practised merely for the purpose of overcoming the obstacles that lie in the path of our daily life—it is practised simply in order to get through the business of living as expeditiously and as efficiently as possible.

Awareness in the Buddha's Teaching, however, has a different purpose: it is practised for the purpose of attaining release from living. These two different purposes, while not directly opposed, do not in fact cooperate—they are, as it were, at right angles to each other; and since the amount of awareness that can be practised at any time is limited, there is competition between these purposes for whatever awareness is available. Thus it happens that in activities requiring much awareness simply for their successful performance (such as writing this letter), there is not much scope for the practice of awareness leading to release (though no doubt if I got into the unlikely habit of writing this same letter twice a day over a number of years I should be able to devote more of the latter to it).

The Buddha tells us (in the Itivuttaka) that three things harm the progress of the *sekha bhikkhu* (one who has reached the Path but who has not yet arrived at arahantship): fondness for work (i.e. building, sewing robes, doing odd jobs, and so on), fondness for talk, and fondness for sleep. In the first two, as we can see, much awareness must be devoted to successful performance of the task in hand (making things, expounding the Dhamma), and in the third no awareness is possible. From the passages I quoted earlier, it is clear that awareness for the purpose of release is best practised on those actions that are habitual and do not require much thought to perform—walking, standing, sitting, lying down, attending to bodily needs of various kinds, and so on. The reference to "sleeping" in passage (1) means that one should go to sleep with awareness, bearing in mind the time to awaken again; it does not mean that we should practise awareness while we are actually asleep. Naturally, a bhikkhu cannot altogether avoid doing jobs of work or occasionally talking but these, too should be done mindfully and with awareness as far as possible: "He is mindful as he sets to work, in speaking and being silent he practises awareness. "The normal person, as I remarked above, does not practise awareness where he does not find it necessary, that is to say, in his habitual actions; but the bhikkhu is instructed not only to do these habitual actions with awareness but also, as far as possible confine himself to these actions. Drive and initiative in new ventures, so highly prized in the world of business and practical affairs, are impediments for one who is seeking release.

And how does one practise this awareness for the purpose of release? It is really very simple. Since, as I have said, all action is conscious, we do not have to undertake any elaborate investigation such as asking other people to find out what it is that we are doing so that we can become aware of it. All that is necessary is a slight change of attitude, a slight effort of attention. Instead of being fully absorbed by, or identified with, our action, we must continue, without ceasing to act, to observe ourselves in action. This is done quite simply by asking ourselves the question, "What am I doing?" It will be found that, since the action is always conscious anyway, we already, in a certain sense, know the answer without having to think about it; and simply by asking ourselves the question we become aware of the answer, i.e. of what we are doing. Thus, if I now ask myself "What am I doing?" I can immediately answer that I am writing, that I am sitting in my bed, that I am scratching my leg and so on almost endlessly.

If I wish to practise awareness, I must go on asking myself this question and answering it, until such time as I find that I am automatically (or habitually) answering the question without having to ask it. When this happens, the practice of awareness is being successful, and it only remains to develop this state and not to fall away from it through neglect. Similar considerations will of course apply to awareness of feelings, perceptions, and thoughts—see passage (2). Here I have to ask myself, "What am I feeling, or perceiving, or thinking?" and the answer once again will immediately present itself.

The objection is sometimes raised that it is not possible to do two things at once and that it is therefore not possible both to act and to be aware of the action at one and the same time. But this opinion is a pure prejudice based upon a certain false notion of the nature of consciousness (or of experience). It is perfectly possible to be doing a number of things at the same time (for example, I am breathing as I write this letter, and I do not interrupt the one in order to do the other). It is not possible to devote equal attention to all of them at the same time, but this is another matter. And this is true also of acting and being aware of the action. This can be verified very simply: all that is necessary is to start walking, and while still walking to ask oneself the question "what am I doing?" It will be found that one can give oneself the answer "I am walking" without ceasing to walk. It is not necessary to come to a halt, or break into a run, or fall down, in order to answer the question.

Why should one practise awareness? I can think of three good reasons immediately, and there are doubtless others besides. In the first place, a person who is constantly aware of what he is doing will find it easier to keep his *sila*. A man who, when chasing his neighbour's wife, knows "I am chasing my neighbour's wife," will not be able to conceal from himself the fact that he is on the point of breaking the Third Precept, and will correct himself sooner than the man who chases his neighbour's wife without considering what he is doing. In brief, awareness leads to self-criticism and thence to self-correction.

In the second place, awareness is cooling and is directly opposed to the passions (either lust or hate), which are heating. This means that the man who constantly practises awareness has a powerful control over his passions; indeed, the constant practice of awareness actually inhibits the passions, and they arise less and less frequently.

In the third place, the practice of awareness is an absolute prerequisite for the understanding of the essence of the Buddha's Teaching. The reason for this is that the Dhamma is concerned not with any one single experience (consciousness, feeling, etc). We do not need a Buddha to tell us how to escape from any one particular experience (whether it is a simple headache or an incurable cancer), but we do need the Buddha to tell us how to escape from all experience. Now in the normal state of being absorbed in what we are doing (that is, of non-awareness), we are concerned only with this or that particular experience or state of affairs ("she loves me; she loves me not …") and we are in no way concerned with experience in general ("what is the nature of the emotion of love?"). But when we become aware of what we are doing (or feeling, etc), the case is different. Though we are still doing (or feeling), we are also observing that doing or feeling with a certain degree of detachment, and at that time the general nature of doing and feeling comes into view (the particular doing and feeling that happen to be present now merely appear as examples of doing and feeling in general); and it is only when this general nature of things comes into view that we are able, with the Buddha's guidance, to grasp the universal characteristics of *anicca, dukkha* and *anattā*.

These three reasons for practising awareness correspond to *sīla, samādhi*, and *paññā* respectively.

ABOUT PARIYATTI

Pariyatti is dedicated to providing affordable access to authentic teachings of the Buddha about the Dhamma theory (*pariyatti*) and practice (*paṭipatti*) of Vipassana meditation. A 501(c)(3) non-profit charitable organization since 2002, Pariyatti is sustained by contributions from individuals who appreciate and want to share the incalculable value of the Dhamma teachings. We invite you to visit www.pariyatti.org to learn about our programs, services, and ways to support publishing and other undertakings.

Pariyatti Publishing Imprints

Vipassana Research Publications (focus on Vipassana as taught by S.N. Goenka in the tradition of Sayagyi U Ba Khin)
BPS Pariyatti Editions (selected titles from the Buddhist Publication Society, co-published by Pariyatti)
MPA Pariyatti Editions (selected titles from the Myanmar Pitaka Association, co-published by Pariyatti)
Pariyatti Digital Editions (audio and video titles, including discourses)
Pariyatti Press (classic titles returned to print and inspirational writing by contemporary authors)

Pariyatti enriches the world by

- disseminating the words of the Buddha,
- providing sustenance for the seeker's journey,
- illuminating the meditator's path.

Made in the USA
Columbia, SC
01 August 2024

e9346a23-a2c1-475b-9ea0-5da820b89b8eR02